IUU Fishing as a Flag State Accountability Paradigm

Queen Mary Studies in International Law

Edited by

Malgosia Fitzmaurice

VOLUME 45

The titles published in this series are listed at *brill.com/qmil*

IUU Fishing as a Flag State Accountability Paradigm

Between Effectiveness and Legitimacy

By

Mercedes Rosello

BRILL
NIJHOFF

LEIDEN | BOSTON

The Library of Congress Cataloging-in-Publication Data is available online at http://catalog.loc.gov
LC record available at http://lccn.loc.gov/

Library of Congress Cataloging-in-Publication Data

Names: Rosello, Mercedes, author.
Title: IUU fishing as a flag state accountability paradigm : between effectiveness and legitimacy / by Mercedes Rosello.
Other titles: Illegal, unreported and unregulated fishing as a flag state accountability paradigm
Description: Leiden ; Boston : Brill Nijhoff, [2021] | Series: Queen Mary studies in international law, 1877-4822 ; volume 45 | Based on author's thesis (doctoral - University of Hull, 2019). | Includes bibliographical references and index. | Summary: "The plight of the ocean calls for our attention with increasing urgency, and illegal, unreported and unregulated or 'IUU' fishing' is a known contributor to its decline. IUU fishing is used as an umbrella term for a wide number of fishing and concomitant activities with the potential of inflicting serious damage to ocean living resources, and to the human communities that depend on them"– Provided by publisher.
Identifiers: LCCN 2021017454 | ISBN 9789004462823 (hardback) | ISBN 9789004463219 (ebook)
Subjects: LCSH: Fishery management, International–Law and legislation. | Fishing–Corrupt practices.
Classification: LCC K3895 .R67 2021 | DDC 343.07/692–dc23
LC record available at https://lccn.loc.gov/2021017454

Typeface for the Latin, Greek, and Cyrillic scripts: "Brill". See and download: brill.com/brill-typeface.

ISSN 1877-4822
ISBN 978-90-04-46282-3 (hardback)
ISBN 978-90-04-46321-9 (e-book)

This book is printed on acid-free paper and produced in a sustainable manner.

Printed by Printforce, United Kingdom

Contents

Acknowledgements

This book is the result of work I carried out as part of my doctoral studies at the University of Hull. Much of it has come to be via myriad revelations and pearls of wisdom by supervisors as well as friends and colleagues. Those to whom I owe a debt of gratitude are too numerous to mention individually, but I would like to thank in particular my first supervisor Prof. Richard Barnes for his guidance, and Drs. Nkiruka Madweke, Eva van der Marel, and Timea Tallodi for their friendship and insight. I also want to specially thank Pierre and the Chenier family for their generosity, and for celebrating with me from the heart the completion of this project. Last, but never least, I thank my parents, Emilio and Mercedes, to whose unwavering support and trust in me I owe everything. This book is dedicated to them, and also to Pi Chenier-Rosello (in memoriam).

Acronyms

AIS	Automatic Identification System
ALC	Automatic Localisation Communicator
ARSIWA	Articles of State Responsibility for Internationally Wrongful Acts
CCAMLR	Commission for the Conservation of Antarctic Marine Living Resources
CCS	Catch Certification Scheme
CCSBT	Commission for the Conservation of Southern Bluefin Tuna
CDS	Catch Documentation Scheme
CMM	Conservation and Management Measures
EC	European Council
EEZ	Exclusive Economic Zone
EU	European Union
FAO	Food and Agriculture Organization
GAIRS	Generally Accepted International Rules and Standards
GT	Gross Tonnage
IATTC	Inter-American Tropical Tuna Commission
ICCAT	International Commission for the Conservation of Atlantic Tunas
ICJ	International Court of Justice
ILC	International Law Commission
IMO	International Maritime Organization
IOTC	Indian Ocean Tuna Commission
IPOA	International Plan of Action
ITLOS	International Tribunal for the Law of the Sea
IUU	Illegal, Unreported and Unregulated
LOA	Length Overall
NEAFC	North East Atlantic Fisheries Commission
NGO	Non-governmental Organisation
PCA	Permanent Court of Arbitration
PCIJ	Permanent Court of International Justice
RFMO	Regional Fishery Management Organisation
SRFC	Subregional Fisheries Commission
TAC	Total Allowable Catch
UN	United Nations
UNCED	United Nations Conference on Environment and Development
UNGA	United Nations General Assembly
UVI	Unique Vessel Identification
VMS	Vessel Monitoring System
WCPFC	Western and Central Pacific Fisheries Commission
WTO	World Trade Organization

International Legislation and Voluntary Instruments

Multilateral Treaties

Charter of the United Nations (1945) *Entry into force October 1945, 1 UNTS XVI*
General Agreement on Tariffs and Trade (1947) *Entry into force January 1948, 55 UNTS 194*
Convention on Fishing and Conservation of the Living Resources of the high Seas (1958) *Entry into force March 1966, 559 UNTS 285*
Convention on the High Seas (1958) *Entry into force September 1962, 450 UNTS 11*
North East Atlantic Fisheries Convention (1959) *Entry into force June 1963, 486 UNTS 157*
International Convention for the Conservation of Atlantic Tunas (1966) *Entry into force March 1969, 673 UNTS 63*
Vienna Convention on the Law of Treaties (1969) *Entry into Force January 1980, 1155 UNTS 331*
Convention on International Trade in Endangered Species of Wild Fauna and Flora (1973) *entry into force July 1975, 993 UNTS 243*
International Convention for the Safety of Life at Sea (1974) *Entry into force May 1980, 1184 UNTS 2*
Convention on the Conservation of Antarctic Marine Living Resources (1980) *Entry into force April 1982, 1329 UNTS 48*
United Nations Convention on the Law of the Sea (1982) *Entry into force November 1994, 1833 UNTS 3*
United Nations Convention on Conditions for Registration of Ships (1986) *Not in force, Unregistered*
Convention for the Prohibition of Fishing with Long Driftnets in the South Pacific (1989) *Entry into force May 1991, IUCN Registration No TRE-001043*
Agreement to Promote Compliance with International Conservation and Management Measures by Fishing Vessels on the High Seas (1993) *Entry into Force April 2003, 2221 UNTS 91*
Convention on Civil Liability for Damage Resulting from Activities Dangerous to the Environment (1993) *Entry into force December 2009, ETS 150*
Convention for the Protection of the Marine Environment of the North-East Atlantic (1993) *Entry into force March 1998, 2354 UNTS 67*
Agreement Establishing the World Trade Organization (1994) *Entry into force January 1995, 1867 UNTS 154*

International Convention on Standards of Training, Certification and Watchkeeping for Fishing Vessel Personnel (1995) *Entry into force September 2012, IMO Register*

United Nations Agreement for the Implementation of the Provisions of the United Nations Convention on the Law of the Sea of 10 December 1982 relating to the Conservation and Management of Straddling Fish Stocks and Highly Migratory Fish Stocks (1995) *Entry into force December 2001, 2167 UNTS 88*

Convention on Access to Information, Public Participation in Decision-Making and Access to Justice in Environmental Matters (1999) *Entry into force October 2001, 2161 UNTS 447*

Convention Concerning Work in the Fishing Sector (2007) *Entry into force November 2017, UN Registration Number 54755*

Agreement on Port State Measures to Prevent, Deter and Eliminate Illegal, Unreported and Unregulated Fishing (2009) *Entry into force June 2016, UN Registration Number 54133*

Cape Town Agreement incorporating the 1977 International Convention for the Safety of Fishing Vessels and its 1993 Torremolinos Protocol (2012) *Not yet in force, IMO Register*

Voluntary Instruments

Paris Memorandum of Understanding on Port State Control (1982)

UNCED, United Nations Conference on Environment & Development: Agenda 21 (1992) *A/CONF.151/26*

FAO Code of Conduct for Responsible Fisheries Doc. 95/20/Rev/1

FAO Technical Guidelines for Responsible Fisheries. Fishing Operations: Vessel Monitoring Systems (1998)

International Plan of Action to Prevent, Deter and Eliminate Illegal, Unreported and Unregulated Fishing (2001)

International Cases

PCIJ and ICJ

The Case of the SS Lotus (*France v Turkey*) [1927] Publications of the Permanent Court of International Justice Publications Series A No 10.

Case Concerning the Factory at Chorzow (*Claim for Indemnity*) [1927] Publications of the Permanent Court of International Justice Series A No 8.

The Corfu Channel Case (*UK v Albania*) [1949] ICJ Reports 4.

Fisheries Case (*United Kingdom v Norway*) [1951] ICJ Reports 116.

Nottebohm (*Lichtenstain v Guatemala*) [1955] ICJ Reports 4.

South West Africa Cases (*Ethiopia v South Africa*) (*Liberia v South Africa*) *Second Phase* [1966] ICJ Reports 6.

North Sea Continental Shelf Cases (*Federal Republic of Germany v Denmark*) (*Federal Republic of Germany v Netherlands*) [1969] ICJ Rep [1969] 3.

Barcelona Traction, Light and Power Co Ltd (*Belgium v Spain*) [1970] ICJ Rep 3.

Nuclear Tests (*Australia v France; New Zealand v France*) [1973] ICJ Reports 99.

Fisheries Jurisdiction Case (*United Kingdom of Great Britain and Northern Ireland v. Iceland*) [1974] ICJ Reports 3.

Fisheries Jurisdiction Case (*Federal Republic of Germany v. Iceland*) [1974] ICJ Reports 175.

Case Concerning Military and Paramilitary Activities in and Against Nicaragua (*Nicaragua v United States of America*) [1986] ICJ Reports 14.

Case Concerning East Timor (*Portugal v Australia*) [1995] ICJ Reports 90.

Grabcikovo-Nagymaros Project (*Hungary v Slovakia*) (1997) ICJ Rep 7.

Fisheries Jurisdiction (*Spain v Canada*) [1998] ICJ Reports 432.

Case concerning Armed Activities on the Territory of the Congo (*Democratic Republic of the Congo v Rwanda*) [2006] ICJ Reports 6.

Case Concerning Pulp Mills on the River Uruguay (*Argentina v Uruguay*) [2010] ICJ Reports 14.

Whaling in the Antarctic (*Australia v Japan: New Zealand intervening*) [2014] ICJ Reports 226.

ITLOS

Southern Bluefin Tuna Cases (*New Zealand v Japan*) (*Australia v Japan*) [1999] ITLOS Reports 280.

The M/V Saiga No 2 (*Saint Vincent and the Grenadines v Guinea*) [1999] ITLOS Reports 335.
MOX Plant (*Ireland v. United Kingdom*) [2001] ITLOS Reports 95.
The Volga Case (*Russian Federation v Australia*) [2002] ITLOS Reports 66.

International Arbitration

Award between the United States and the United Kingdom relating to the Rights of Jurisdiction of United States in the Bering's Sea and the Preservation of Fur Seals [1893] United Nations Reports of International Arbitral Awards XXVIII 263.

Trail Smelter Arbitration (*United States of America v Canada*) [1941] United Nations Reports of International Arbitral Awards Vol III 1903.

Lac Lanoux Arbitration (*France v Spain*) [1957] United Nations Reports of International Arbitral Awards Vol XII 281.

Reparations for Injuries Suffered in the Service of the United Nations [1949] ICJ Reports 174.

In the Matter of the South China Sea Arbitration (*Republic of the Philippines v Peoples' Republic of China*) [2016] PCA Case No. 2013–19.

Advisory Opinions

Reparations for Injuries Suffered in the Service of the United Nations [1949] ICJ Reports 174.

Responsibilities and Obligations of States with Respect to Activities in the Area [2011] ITLOS Reports 10.

Request for an Advisory Opinion submitted by the Sub-Regional Fisheries Commission [2015] ITLOS Reports 4.

European Union Cases

Case C-221/89 *Factortame and Others* [1991] ECR 1991 I-03905.
Case C-62/96 *Commission v. Hellenic Republic* [1997] ECR I-6725 133.
Case C-286/90 *Public Prosecutor v PM Poulsen and Diva Navigation Corp* [1992] ECR I-6019.
Case C-47/02 *Anker and Others v Germany* [2003] ECR I-10447.
Case C-444/08 *Regiao Autonoma dos Azores v Coundil of the European Union* [2008] ECR I-00200.

Domestic Cases

United States of America v Bengis (2013) WL 2922292 [United States].
Expediente Sancionador (2015) 1/2015/SGP [Spain].

Resolutions of International Organisations

UNGA

UNGA *Large-Scale Pelagic Drift-Net Fishing, Unauthorized Fishing in Zones of National Jurisdiction and on the High Seas, fisheries by-Catch and Discards, and other Developments* [2001] A/Res/55/8

UNGA *Official Records of the General Assembly, Fifty-sixth Session, Supplement No 10 and Corrigendum* [2001] A/Res/56/83

UNGA *Report on the Work of the United Nations Open-ended Informal Consultative Process on Oceans and the Law of the Sea* [2014] A/Res/69/90

UNGA *Addis Ababa Action Agenda of the Third International Conference on financing for Development (Addis Ababa Action Agenda)* [2015] A/Res/69/313

UNGA *The Rule of Law at the National and International Levels* [2015] A/Res/70/118

UNGA *Transforming our World: The 2030 Agenda for Sustainable Development* [2015] A/Res/70/1

European Union Decisions

Commission Decision of 15 November 2012 on notifying the third countries that the Commission considers as possible of being identified as non-cooperating third countries pursuant to Council Regulation (EC) No 1005/2008 establishing a Community system to prevent, deter and eliminate illegal, unreported and unregulated fishing (2012) OJEU 55 C 354/13.

Commission Decision of 26 November 2013 on notifying the third countries that the Commission considers as possible of being identified as non-cooperating third countries pursuant to Council Regulation (EC) No 1005/2008 establishing a Community system to prevent, deter and eliminate illegal, unreported and unregulated fishing (2013) OJEU C 346/26.

Commission Decision of 12 December 2014 notifying a third country that the Commission considers as possible of being identified as non-cooperating third country pursuant to Council Regulation (EC) No 1005/2008 establishing a Community system to prevent, deter and eliminate illegal, unreported and unregulated fishing (2014) OJEU C 447/9, C 447/10, C 447/11, C 453/4.

Commission Decision of 10 June 2014 on notifying the Third Countries that the Commission considers as possible of being identified as non-cooperating Third Countries pursuant to Council Regulation (EC) No 1005/2008 establishing a

Community system to prevent, deter and eliminate illegal, unreported and unregulated fishing (2014) OJEU C 185/2, C 185/3.

Commission Decision of 21 April 2015 on notifying a third country of the possibility of being identified as a non-cooperating third country in fighting illegal, unreported and unregulated fishing (2015) C 142/6, C 324/7, C 324/10.

International Maritime Organization

IMO *Resolution A.600(1)* [1987] IMO *Ship Identification Number Scheme*

IMO *Resolution A.1078(28)* [2013] IMO *Ship Identification Number Scheme*

IMO *Circular 1886/Rev.6 Implementation of Resolution A.1078(208)* [2013] IMO *Ship Identification Number Scheme*

RFMOs

Tuna RFMOs

Commission for the Conservation of Southern Bluefin Tuna (CCSBT)
Inter-American Tropical Tuna Commission (IATTC)
Indian Ocean Tuna Commission (IOTC)
International Commission for the Conservation of Atlantic Tunas (ICCAT)
Western and Central Pacific Fisheries Commission (WCPFC)

General RFMOs

Convention on Conservation of Antarctic Marine Living Resources (CCAMLR)
General Fisheries Commission of the Mediterranean (GFCM)
Northwest Atlantic Fisheries Organization (NAFO)
North Atlantic Salmon Conservation Organisation (NASCO)
North-East Atlantic Fisheries Commission (NEAFC)
South-East Atlantic Fisheries Organisation (SEAFO)
South Indian Ocean Fisheries Agreement (SIOFA)
South Pacific Regional Fisheries Management Organisation (SPRFMO)

Introduction

The plight of the ocean calls for our attention with increasing urgency, and illegal, unreported and unregulated or 'IUU' fishing' is a known contributor to its decline. IUU fishing is used as an umbrella term for a wide number of fishing and concomitant activities with the potential of inflicting serious damage to ocean living resources, and to the human communities that depend on them.[1] The United Nations General Assembly has referred to IUU fishing as 'one of the most severe problems currently affecting world fisheries and the sustainability of marine living resources'.[2] As a global phenomenon, the total economic cost of IUU fishing has been estimated to be at least in the region of 10 billion per year.[3] In view of such potential for destruction, it is perhaps unsurprising that the use of the term IUU fishing as a useful approach to categorisation and response has proliferated in international narratives.

Despite its popularity, the IUU fishing idea is not problem-free. For reasons that will be explained in a later chapter, the meaning of IUU fishing in this book is pared back to a narrower concept that is relevant primarily to high seas fisheries. Even when circumscribed to the high seas, the impact of IUU fishing activities is severe. Annually, around 4.3 million metric tonnes of seafood are produced from the high seas, with an aggregate value of US$ 7.6 billion.[4] Although estimating IUU fishing in the high seas presents considerable difficulty, it is believed to have a cost of at least around US$ 1.25 billion.[5] Additionally,

1 R Baird, 'Illegal, Unreported and Unregulated Fishing: an Analysis of the Legal, Economic and Historical Factors Relevant to its Development and Persistence' (2004) 5 *Melbourne Journal of International Law* 299–336, 300. G Pramod et al, 'Sources of Information Supporting Estimates of Unreported Fishery Catches (IUU) for 59 Countries and the High Seas' (Fisheries Centre Research Reports, University of British Columbia, 2008) 5 [accessed on 15 March 2021 via https://open.library.ubc.ca/cIRcle/collections/facultyresearchandpublications/52383/items/1.0058180].

2 United Nations General Assembly (UNGA), Resolution on Large-Scale Pelagic Drift-Net Fishing, Unauthorized Fishing in Zones of National Jurisdiction and on the High Seas, Fisheries By-Catch and Discards, and other Developments' (2001) UN Doc A/Res/55/8, 2.

3 See DJ Agnew et al, 'Estimating the Worldwide Extent of Illegal Fishing' (2009) 4(2) *PloS One* e4570.

4 E Sala et al, 'The Economics of Fishing the High Seas' (2018) 4 *Science Advances* 1–3, 2.

5 L Schiller et al, 'High Seas Fisheries Play a Negligible Role in Addressing Global Food Security' (2018) 4(8) *Environmental Studies* e8351. Organization for Economic Co-operation and Development (OECD), 'Closing the Net: Stopping Illegal Fishing on the High Seas' (2006) 3 [accessed on 15 March 2021 via https://www.oecd.org/sd-roundtable/papersandpublications/39375276.pdf]. The FAO is working on a suite of tools to enable

 | DOI:10.1163/9789004463219_002

although high seas production appears to have plateaued in recent years, IUU fishing continues to increase, and migratory and straddling stocks occurring partially or wholly in the high seas are thought to be overfished at approximately twice the rate of other stocks.[6] The concept of IUU fishing is thought to have emerged as part of arrangements for the management of capacity in such fisheries,[7] and was soon adopted as a fisheries governance instrument by organisations that are generally referred to as 'regional fishery management organisations' (RFMOs).[8]

The idea of IUU fishing was integrated for the first time in a global policy instrument in the International Plan of Action to Prevent, Deter and Eliminate Illegal, Unreported and Unregulated Fishing (IPOA IUU).[9] In this instrument, IUU fishing provides States and RFMOs with an interpretive lens through which to categorise activities that contravene domestic or international legal obligations, or that undermine the rules and measures that are established by RFMOs to regulate the fishing activities concerning stocks under their management. Yet, over time IUU fishing has progressively become a convenient catch-all for undesirable fishing as well as non-fishing activities occurring on board of fishing vessels in any ocean area.[10] Operational synergies between fishing and certain criminal activities have resulted in the term IUU fishing being associated with opportunistic, and often serious, criminality.[11] Commentators have

the production of accurate estimations of IUU fishing activity. See FAO, 'The State of world Fisheries and Aquaculture: Sustainability in Action' (2020) 112.

6 DC Dunn et al, 'Empowering High Seas Governance with Satellite Vessel Tracking Data' (2018) *Fish and Fisheries* 729–740, 730.

7 J Swan, 'IUU Fishing and Measures to Improve Enforcement and Compliance' in *The Future of Ocean Governance and Capacity Development* (Martinus Nijhoff, 2018) 354–360, 354.

8 J Swan, 'Decision-Making in Regional Fishery Bodies or Arrangements: Evolving Role of RFBs and International Agreement on Decision-Making Processes' (2004) FAO Fisheries Circular 995, 1–82, 1.

9 FAO International Plan of Action to Prevent, Deter and Eliminate Illegal, Unreported and Unregulated Fishing (2001) [IPOA IUU].

10 Poseidon Aquatic Resource Management, 'Review of Studies Estimating IUU Fishing and the Methodologies Utilized' (FAO, 2016) 1–103, 3 [accessed 15 March 2021 via http://www.fao.org/3/a-bl765e.pdf].

11 United Nations Organization on Drugs and Crime (UNODC), 'Transnational Organized Crime in the Fishing Industry' (2011) 1–144, 8 [accessed on 15 March 2021 via http://www.unodc.org/documents/human-trafficking/Issue_Paper_-_TOC_in_the_Fishing_Industry.pdf]. United Nations Inter-Agency Project on Human Trafficking (UNIAP), 'Exploitation of Cambodian Men at Sea: Facts about the Trafficking of Cambodian Men onto Thai Fishing Vessels' (2009) 1–8 [accessed on 15 March 2021 via http://apmigration.ilo.org/resources/resource-content/exploitation-of-cambodian-men-at-sea-facts-about-the-trafficking-of-cambodian-men-onto-thai-fishing-boats].

pointed out that its overenthusiastic adoption has to some extent contributed to a loss of meaning, and a blurring of conceptual boundaries.[12]

The original purpose of the IUU fishing idea was to establish an innovative and effective approach to controlling undesirable fishing practices, especially in the areas of the high seas governed by RFMOs.[13] Arguably, the consolidation of RFMOs as authoritative sources of fisheries governance has been instrumental in the development of IUU fishing as a fishery management tool, and the concept has been largely underpinned by the regulatory output of these organisations.[14]

The utilisation of IUU fishing as a type of governance categorisation has risen in the past two decades, alongside the emergence of new international obligations linked to the operation of RFMO s,[15] specially in respect of matters concerning fishing vessel control.[16] Such obligations have been established under the legal framework of the United Nations Convention on the Law of the Sea (LOSC or Convention),[17] and global fishery treaties that add definition and in some cases develop the obligations set out in the Convention.[18] Yet, the popularity and endurance of the IUU fishing idea is also, arguably, a consequence of the historically ineffectual role of States in supressing IUU fishing activities in the high seas.[19] This failure responds to complex factors: Firstly, as many legal commentators have indicated, it may result from inadequacies in the fabric of the international legal framework for the purposes of ensuring appropriate conservation and management of high seas fish stocks,[20] and

12 Baird (2004) at 303, supra at 1. Poseidon (2016) at 3, supra at 10.

13 M Hayashi, 'International Measures to Combat Illegal, Unreported and Unregulated (IUU) Fishing and Japan' (2008) 51 *Japanese Yearbook of International Law* 57–75, 57 and 58.

14 *Ibid.*

15 See D Freestone and Z Makuch, 'The New International Environmental Law of Fisheries: the 1995 United Nations Straddling Stocks Agreement' (1997) 7(1) *Yearbook of International Environmental Law* 3.

16 D Guilfoyle, *Shipping Interdiction and the Law of the Sea* (Cambridge University Press, 2009) 7.

17 United Nations Convention on the Law of the Sea (1982), 1833 UNTS 3 [LOSC].

18 See the Agreement to Promote Compliance with International Conservation and Management measures by fishing Vessels on the High Seas (1993), 2221 UNTS 91 [Compliance Agreement], and in particular the United Nations Agreement for the Implementation of the Provisions of the United Nations Convention on the Law of the Sea of 10 December 1982 relating to the Conservation and Management of Straddling Fish Stocks and Highly Migratory Fish Stocks (1995), 2167 UNTS 88 [UNFSA].

19 R Rayfuse, 'Enforcement of High Seas fisheries Agreements: Observation and Inspection under the Convention on the Conservation of Antarctic Marine Living Resources' (1998) 13 *International Journal of Marine & Coastal Law* 579–605, 579.

20 M Hayashi, 'Global Governance of Deep-Sea Fisheries (2004) 19(3) *International Journal of Marine and Coastal Law* 289–298, 289.

a lack of effective legal mechanisms to ensure appropriate accountability of States in their capacity as high seas fishing activity regulators.[21] This is the case, in particular, when States are not parties to the specialist fishery treaties established under the LOSC.[22] States cannot be bound to treaty obligations to which they have not agreed,[23] and this enables them to avoid the treaty commitments made by others,[24] In addition, poor observance by States of responsibilities emanating from the treaties of which they are a party is unfortunately not uncommon.[25] Overall, States have often perpetuated the subordination of marine conservation objectives to short-term economic interests.[26]

The emergence of the trend to classify certain activities as IUU fishing may be conceived as a pragmatic way to counteract the effect of such failings,[27] and in particular the lack of effectiveness of the flag State primacy principle in matters of high seas fishing regulation and control.[28] Of particular significance for the development and consolidation of the IUU fishing idea has been the irruption of a new governance perspective, and one that is not defined by the LOSC:[29] The 'market' State as regulator of fishing activity, able to develop and apply *ex post* measures not only against persons responsible for foreign fishing vessel operations, but also against the flag States that regulate their

---

21 Baird (2004) at 303, supra at 1.

22 E Franckx, 'Pacta Tertiis and the Agreement for the Implementation of the Straddling and Highly Migratory Fish Stocks provisions of the United Nations Convention on the Law of the Sea' (2000) 8 *Tulane Journal of International and Comparative Law* 49–82, 77–80.

23 J Bodin, *Les Six Livres de La Republique* (Iacques du Puys, 1483) as cited by S Beaulac, 'Emer de Vattel and the Externalization of Sovereignty' (2003) 5 *Journal of the History of International Law* 237–292, 242.

24 See Vienna Convention on the Law of Treaties1969, 1155 UNTS 331 [VCLT], Articles 19–22 regarding reservations, and 34–38 regarding third parties to a treaty.

25 R Churchill, 'The Persisting Problem of Non-Compliance with the Law of the Sea Convention: Disorder in the Oceans' (2013) 27 *International Journal of Marine and Coastal Law* 813–820, 813.

26 See R Bratspies, 'Finessing King Neptune: Fisheries Management and the Limits of International Law' (2001) 25 *Harvard Environmental Law Review* 213–258, 214. T Henriksen, 'Revisiting the Freedom of Fishing and Legal Obligations on States Not Party to Regional Fisheries Management Organizations' (2009) 40(1) *Ocean Development & International Law* 80–96, 81. RA Barnes, 'Entitlement to Marine Living Resources in Areas beyond National Jurisdiction' in Molenaar and Elferink (Eds) *The International Legal Regime of Areas beyond National Jurisdiction: Current and Future Developments* (Martinus Nijhoff, 2010) 87.

27 See D Freestone, 'Modern Principles of High Seas Governance: The Legal Underpinnings' (2009) 39(1) *International Environmental Policy and Law* 44–49, 48.

28 EJ Molenaar, 'Port State Jurisdiction: Toward Comprehensive, Mandatory and Global Coverage' (2007) 38(1–2) *Ocean Development & International Law* 225–257, 226.

29 See paragraphs 9.3, and 65 to 76 of the IPOA IUU.

activities.[30] Building on this conception of the market as source of governance, the European Union (EU) has developed and operationalized what arguably is the highest profile market-based compliance framework in matters of marine fisheries. This EU framework has transformed the notion of IUU fishing into an integral part of a market-based compliance mechanism with considerable global impact.[31] This and other compliance developments have prompted some critiques, and the IUU fishing idea has been described by academics as an illegitimate compliance tool used as a a justification for wielding market power.[32] Arguably, underlying this critique there may be concern over the relative marginalisation of international law by authorities who increasingly rely on managerial tools through which to influence the economic interests that underpin fishing activity.

Acknowledging the validity of these concerns, the study in this book seeks to explore and shed further light into the ways in which the IUU fishing idea (hereinafter just 'IUU fishing') conditions the conduct of States in respect of fishing activity governance. This is then contrasted with the ways in which the international legal obligations of States seek to shape such conduct, so that the respective functional features and strengths and weaknesses of each approach can be more clearly ascertained. This assessment leads to the identification of a number of flaws in some of the mechanisms upon which the IUU fishing idea depends for full effectiveness, arguing that their manifestation may be due to the under-theorisation of the IUU concept as a mechanism of accountability.[33] Accountability, understood through "interactional" theory, emerges as a

30 D Calley, *Market Denial and International Fisheries Regulation: The Targeted and Effective Use of Trade Measures Against the Flag of Convenience Fishing Industry* (Martinus Nijhoff, 2011) 103. M Young, 'International Trade Law Compatibility of Market-Related Measures to Combat Illegal, Unreported and Unregulated (IUU) Fishing' (2016) 69 *Marine Policy* 209–219, 209.

31 M Tsamenyi et al, *Fairer Fishing? Trade and Fisheries Policy Implications for Developing Countries of the European Community Regulation on Illegal Fishing* (Commonwealth Secretariat, 2009) 65. M Tsamenyi et al, 'The European Council Regulation on Illegal, Unreported and Unregulated Fishing: an International Fisheries Law Perspective' (2010) 25(1) *International Journal of Marine and Coastal Law* 5–31, 29.

32 A Serdy, *The New Entrants Problem in International Fisheries Law* (Cambridge University Press, 2016a) 145 and 147. A Serdy, 'Pacta Tertiis and Regional Fisheries Management Mechanisms: The IUU Fishing Concept as an Illegitimate Short-Cut to a Legitimate Goal' (2017) 48(3) *Ocean Development & International Law* 345–364, 354.

33 For an illustration, see P Dann and M von Engelhardt, 'Legal Approaches to Global Governance and Accountability: Informal Lawmaking, International Public Authority, and Global Administrative Law Compared' in Pauwelyn, Wessel and Wouters (Eds) *Informal International Lawmaking* (Oxford University Press, 2012) 116.

blueprint for decision-making capable of transforming the flawed IUU fishing framework in operation today into a 'flag State accountability paradigm'.

By approaching IUU fishing as a State accountability mechanism, this study is also able to highlight problematic areas in the relationship between States and international organisations with regulatory power.[34] The re-conceptualisation of IUU fishing as a State accountability paradigm that is ultimately proposed here reflects upon such debate, and considers factors that are important not only for fostering desirable State governance in the short term, but also more broadly for the effectiveness and long-term development of international law. Underlying this work is the understanding that, despite the existence of well established treaty frameworks, international law can stagnate and wither, and that this is ultimately detrimental to global governance.[35] Through accountability, the IUU fishing idea is re-articulated, and is turned into an instrument that aims to counterbalance that risk.

34 For insight into this general issue, see D Bodansky, 'The Legitimacy of International Governance: a Coming Challenge for International Environmental Law' (1999) 93(3) *American Journal of International Law* 596–624, 597. Also, T Sato, 'Legitimacy of International Organizations and Their Decisions: Challenges that International Organizations Face in the 21st Century' (2009) 37(15) *Hitotsubashi Journal of Law and Politics* 11–30, 15.

35 For general insight in the risks associated to fragmentation, see B Simma and D Pulkowski, 'Of Planets and the Universe: Self-Contained Regimes in International Law' (2006) 17(3) *European Journal of International Law* 483–529, 511.

PART 1

IUU Fishing as Interpretive Lens

CHAPTER 1

Origins and Meaning of IUU Fishing

1.1 How Imperfect Regulatory Frameworks Enable IUU Fishing

In many contemporary narratives, the idea of IUU fishing broadly aims at characterising commercially motivated fishing activity in any part of the ocean, that is destructive or illicit, and globally prolific.[1] Though its causes are multifaceted and complex, there is little disagreement on the importance of fishing activity regulation in preventing and curbing it. International law is important in the design and coordination of regulatory approaches capable of making a difference, because IUU fishing activity often transcends the boundaries of individual States. The powers that States can wield to regulate the activities of persons in their territory and beyond are generally referred to as 'jurisdiction'.[2] State jurisdiction in the utilisation of ocean resources is specified in the LOSC (also referred to here as 'the Convention'). The LOSC is a widely subscribed multilateral treaty that deals with many areas of ocean utilisation, including the conservation and management of marine living resources. The LOSC establishes a 'constitutional' framework,[3] and establishes State rights as well as important obligations. Some of the obligations set out in the LOSC are long-standing norms of customary international law.[4]

States have jurisdiction over vessel activities and/or the living marine resources they impact on, which they must regulate in accordance with LOSC provisions.[5] The obligations imposed on States by the LOSC differ depending on the functional ocean area where the activities take place: The exclusive economic zone (EEZ) is the marine area beyond and adjacent to the 12 nautical mile territorial sea, which lies next to the coast.[6] The EEZ measures up to 200 nautical miles from the coastal baselines established in the Convention.[7] The

---

1 Poseidon Aquatic Resource Management, 'Review of Studies Estimating IUU Fishing and the Methodologies Utilized' (FAO, 2016) 1–103, 3 [accessed 15 March 2021 via http://www.fao.org/3/a-bl765e.pdf].

2 JH Beale, 'The Jurisdiction of a Sovereign State' (1922) 36(3) *Harvard Law Review* 241–262, 241.

3 TB Koh, 'A Constitution for the Oceans' (2012) *Revista de Drept Maritim* 23–26, 23.

4 MA Becker, 'The Shifting Public Order of the Oceans: Freedom of Navigation and the Interdiction of Ships at Sea' (2005) 46(1) *Harvard International Law Journal* 131–230, 133.

5 Y Tanaka, *A Dual Approach to Ocean Governance: The Cases of Zonal and Integrated Management in International Law of the Sea* (Routledge, 2016) 3.

6 LOSC, Article 55.

7 LOSC, Article 57.

 | DOI:10.1163/9789004463219_003

high seas comprises 'all parts of the sea that are not included in the exclusive economic zone, in the territorial sea or in the internal waters of a State, or in the archipelagic waters of an archipelagic State'.[8] This geographic division supports an organisational framework accepted by most States, whereby the activities of fishing vessels can be regulated and governed in a way that facilitates the peaceful utilisation of marine resources by vessels of many nationalities. However, the regulation and governing of fishing activity under this system can be ineffective, resulting in the emergence and proliferation of undesirable activities, including IUU fishing. A number of drivers and enablers are conducive to such outcomes.

1.1.1 *Drivers of IUU Fishing Activity*

Most instances of excessive harvesting or non-compliant activity by fishing operators can be directly linked to economic drivers adverse to conservation.[9] States that can regulate fishing vessels flying their flag in all ocean areas (flag States), can also gain some financial advantages by offering lighter regulation options to vessel owners in what is generally referred to as the 'flag of convenience' model of vessel governance.[10] It implies that States can compete for the custom of vessel owners for registration services and associated regulation options, facilitating opportunities to carry out fishing operations under weaker regulatory controls, including minimal or altogether absent sanctions.[11] This model results in financial benefits to the flag of convenience State, able to attract interested fishing vessel owners, to the detriment of other States who observe more restrictive and costly (and thus less desirable) regulatory standards.[12]

---

8 LOSC Art 86.

9 CC Schmidt, 'Economic Drivers of Illegal, Unreported and Unregulated (IUU) Fishing' 20 *Int'l Journal of Marine and Coastal Law* 3 (2005) 479. B Le Gallic, and A Cox, 'An Economic Analysis of Illegal, Unreported and Unregulated (IUU) Fishing: Key Drivers And Possible Solutions' (2006) 30(6) *Marine Policy* 689–695.

10 FL Wiswall, 'Flags of Convenience' in William Lovett (Ed) *US Shipping Policies and the World Market* (Quorum Books, 1996) 107.

11 Directorate General for Internal Policies of the European Parliament, 'Illegal, Unreported and Unregulated Fishing: Sanctions in the EU' (2014) 25 [accessed on 17 March 2021 via www.europarl.europa.eu/RegData/etudes/STUD/2014/529069/IPOL_STU(2014)529069_EN.pdf].

12 ER De Sombre, 'Globalization, Competition, and Convergence: Shipping and the Race to the Middle' (2008) 14(2) *Global Governance: A Review of Multilateralism and International Organizations* 179–198, 181.

There has been a long-standing association between IUU fishing vessels and flags of convenience.[13] The literature has dedicated considerable attention to them as a consequence of *en-masse* fishing vessel registrations to flags of convenience following the expansion of coastal States' EEZ s, peaking between 1994 and 1997. Then, circa 10% of the merchant fleet had re-registered its vessels to flags of convenience; fishery captures reached exponential levels according to the records of the United Nations Food and Agriculture Organization (FAO),[14] at a time when FAO reporting by flags of convenience was deficient.[15] The General Assembly of the United Nations (UNGA) noted the relationship between flag of convenience registers and vessel owners that sought to evade controls, and issued a call for States to operate fishing vessel registries responsibly.[16] The dynamics that perpetuated the conflation of interests between between vessel owners and open registry flag States continue to this day. As De Coning explains, the provision of vessel registration and regulation services is in many cases considered to be a commercial undertaking, resulting in the protection of fishing vessel owners from regulatory risks. This also results in the flag States involved in the provision of these services being less responsive to the needs of international cooperation for the purposes of IUU fishing control.[17]

Yet, despite the open registry system posing a real and persistent problem for high seas fishery management, IUU activities are not associated exclusively to vessels registered to flag of convenience States. According to a study, around 17.9% of vessels regionally blacklisted for engaging in IUU fishing activities in the high seas are registered to States that have acceded to or ratified the LOSC and its satellite fisheries treaties. States that have only acceded to or ratified some of the relevant treaties have registered 55.6% of blacklisted vessels, and States with no or little uptake of key international legislation register 26.5% of

13 M Gianni and M Simpson, 'The Changing Nature of High Seas Fishing: How Flags of Convenience Provide Cover for Illegal, Unreported and Unregulated Fishing' (Department of Agriculture, Fisheries and Forestry of Australia, International Workers Federation and WWF International, 2005) 12.

14 B Vukas and D Vidas, 'Flags of Convenience and High Seas Fishing: The Emergence of a Legal Framework' in OS Stokke (Ed) *Governing High Seas Fisheries* (Oxford University Press 2001) 55.

15 J Swan, 'Fishing Vessels Operating under Open Registers and the Exercise of Flag State Responsibilities' FAO Fisheries Circular No. 980 (2002) 38, FIPL/C980.

16 General Assembly of the United Nations (UNGA), 'Large-Scale Pelagic Drift-Net Fishing, Unauthorized Fishing in Zones of National Jusridiction and on the High Seas, Fisheries By-Catch and Discards, and other Developments' (2001) paras 11, 16 and 26, A/RES/55/8.

17 E De Coning, 'Why Are Some Flag States Unable or Unwilling to Address IUU Fishing?' (2020) 22 *International Community Law Review* 487–512, 511.

blacklisted vessels.[18] Empirical evidence obtained by NGOs highlights persistent IUU fishing operations by vessels registered to flags of convenience as well as traditional flags,[19] sometimes enabled by the inability or reluctance of coastal States to appropriately address illegal fishing instances.[20] Recent research in West Africa indicates that misreporting by FoC vessels is only 9% of the total, and 30% are Eastern European, 20% West European, 20% Chinese, and the remaining 21% of no known flag affiliation.[21] Noting the overlap between the *modi operandi* of traditional registries and flags of convenience, Calley defines flag of convenience sufficiently widely as to include some powerful traditional registers. Not unlike subsequent reports by NGOs, Calley points out how the latter may have in recent years absorbed IUU fishing capacity that may have previously been registered to the developing States more commonly associated with the operation of convenience registries.[22]

The above suggests that, even if flags of convenience are particularly vulnerable to some economic drivers that may undermine regulatory responsibility, insofar as the conflation of the interests of the registry State and those of vessel owners and captains may result in the relaxation of regulatory rules,[23] they are not the only ones with vulnerabilities. Vessels flagged to all States are susceptible to the economic incentives and behavioural dynamics created by the pressures of competitive harvesting.[24] Further, a number of other economic factors

---

18 DD Miller and UR Sumaila, 'Flag Use Behavior and IUU Activity within the International Fishing Fleet: Refining Definitions and Identifying Areas of Concern' (2014) 44 *Marine Policy* 204–211, 209.

19 See Environmental Justice Foundation (EJF), 'Keeping Illegal Fish Out of Europe: Ensuring Success for the IUU Regulation' (EJF, 2013) 10 [accessed on 15 March 2021 via https://ejfoundation.org/reports/keeping-illegal-fish-out-of-europe-ensuring-success-for-the-iuu-regulation]. EJF, Oceana, Pew Environmental Trusts, and Word Wildlife Fund (WWF), 'Ensuring Better Control of the EU's External Fishing Fleet: One Number, one Boat: The Need for Mandatory IMO Numbers for EU Vessels Fishing Outside of European Union Waters' (EJF, 2016) 1 [accessed on 15 March 2021 via www.whofishesfar.org/files/Case_Studies/Case_Study_FAR_ENG.pdf].

20 EJF (2013) at p. 18, supra at 19.

21 A Doumboya et al, 'Assessing the Effectiveness of Monitoring Control and Surveillance of Illegal Fishing: The Case of West Africa' (2017) 50(4) *Frontiers in Marine Policy* 1–10, 7.

22 D Calley, *Market Denial and International Fisheries Regulation: The Targeted and Effective Use of Trade Measures Against the Flag of Convenience Fishing Industry* (Martinus Nijhoff, 2011) 45.

23 RQ Grafton et al, *Handbook of Marine Fisheries Conservation and Management* (Oxford University Press, 2010) 6.

24 S Barrett, *Why Cooperate? The Incentive to Supply Global Public Goods* (Oxford University Press, 2007) 47. For an economic account of the adverse drivers of common pool resources, see G Hardin, 'The Tragedy of the Commons' (2009) 1(3) *Journal of Natural Resources Policy Research* 243–253.

motivate the predatory fishing activities typically associated with the idea of IUU fishing. Particularly significant is the presence of undiscerning international markets, as seafood products are amongst the most highly traded foods globally.[25] Gains for the persons responsible for the fishing activities and those with whom they interact within the State of destiny are perpetuated through the operation of 'ports of convenience'.[26] Such ports provide to IUU fishers low inspection and control environments that can quickly establish themselves as favoured destinations for unloading and selling IUU fishing products.[27] Such accessibility is often combined with an absence of appropriate State sanctions in cases where infractions are discovered.[28] Thus, IUU fishing actors can function profitably in a low risk environment, in a context of mutually reinforcing benefits that combine to discourage stringent rules, reporting and monitoring, and other compliance controls. Additionally, the subsidisation of excessive fishing activity can increase competitive pressure on vulnerable resources, fostering undesirable and unsustainable outcomes.[29] The cost of harmful subsidies to the global economy has been estimated to be in the region of USD 20 Bn annually.[30]

---

25 Food and Agriculture Organization (FAO), 'The State of World Fisheries and Aquaculture' (2008) 8 [accessed on 15 March 2021 via http://www.fao.org/3/a-i0250e.pdf].

26 UNGA, 'Report of the Review Conference on the Agreement for the Implementation of the Provisions of the United Nations Convention on the Law of the Sea of 10 December 1982 Relating to the Conservation and Management of Straddling Fish Stocks and Highly Migratory Fish Stocks' (2006) para 82, A/CONF.210/2006/15.

GA Petrossian, 'Preventing Illegal, Unreported and Unregulated (IUU) Fishing: A Situational Approach' (2015) 189 *Biological Conservation* 39–48. GA Petrossian et al, 'Where Do "Undocumented" Fish Land? An Empirical Assessment of Port Characteristics for IUU fishing' (2015) 21(3) *European Journal on Criminal Policy and Research* 337–351.

27 J Swan, 'Port State Measures to Combat IUU Fishing: International and Regional Developments' (2006) 7(1) *Ocean & Fisheries Law* 38–43, 38. H Österblom et al, 'Adapting to Regional Enforcement: Fishing Down the Governance Index' (2010) 5(9) *PloS one* e12832.

28 R Cantrell, 'Finding Nemo … and Eating Him: The Failure of the United Nations to Force Internalization of the Negative Social Costs That Result from Overfishing' (2006) 5(2) *Washington Universities Global Studies Law Review* 381–402, 388 and 390.

29 M Milazzo, 'Subsidies in World Fisheries: a Re-Examination' World Bank Technical Paper No 406 (1998) 86. UR Sumaila et al, 'Fuel Subsidies to Global Fisheries: Magnitude and Impacts on Resource Sustainability' Fisheries Centre Research Reports (2006) 38. UR Sumaila et al, 'Subsidies to High Seas Bottom Trawl Fleets and the Sustainability of Deep-Sea Demersal Fish Stocks' (2010) 34(3) *Marine Policy* 495–497.

30 Sumaila et al, 'Global Fisheries Subsidies: An Updated Estimate' (2016) 69 *Marine Policy* 189–193, 189.

1.1.2 *Enablers of IUU Fishing Activity*

The existence of drivers often combines with regulatory frameworks with limitations and flaws that prevent appropriate responses to undesirable fishing practices. For example, laws with weaknesses in the definition of what type of destructive fishing activity may be considered illegal, one with inadequate reporting duties, or no verification mechanisms, could be considered inadequate.[31] It is common for such frameworks to allow vessels to operate without vessel monitoring systems (VMS),[32] or automatic identification systems (AIS).[33] An often seen behaviour is 'flag-hopping', meaning frequent changes across registries, as a method of identification avoidance. Vessel identification, such as the permanent vessel numbers assigned by the International Maritime Organization (IMO), may also be lacking.[34] Other widespread practices that legal frameworks fail to address are unsupervised 'transhipments'.[35] Transhipment has been defined as the fishery support practice of transferring the products of capture activity from one fishing vessel to another, or to a reefer or cargo vessel.[36] This operation, which may take place at sea or in port, can be accompanied by post-harvest product concealment or tampering activities, serving to blur traceability of an IUU product by its mislabelling and/or integration with product consignments of legitimate origin.[37]

IUU fishing activities are often associated to the failure by States in elaborating appropriate legal frameworks and/or exerting sufficient vigilance, and thus failing to secure appropriate governance. This can include any of the drivers and enablers previously discussed, resulting in systems that are

31 Doumboya et al (2017) at 3, supra at 21.

32 E Detsis et al, 'Project Catch: A Space Based Solution to Combat Illegal, Unreported and Unregulated Fishing. Part I: Vessel Monitoring Systems' (2012) 80 *Acta Astronautica* 114–123, 115.

33 MD Robards et al, 'Conservation Science and Policy Applications of the Marine Vessel Automatic Identification System (AIS): A Review' (2016) 92(1) *Bulletin of Marine Science* 75–103, 88.

34 Miller and Sumaila (2014) at 208, supra at 18.

35 National Oceanic and Atmospheric Administration of the United States of America (NOAA), 'Improving International Fisheries Management Report to Congress Pursuant to Section 403(a) of the Magnuson-Stevens Fishery Conservation and Management Reauthorization Act of 2006' (2015) 23–30 [accessed on 17 March 2021 via http://www.cofemersimir.gob.mx/expediente/17096/mir/34790/anexo/951234].

36 FAO, 'Technical guidelines for Responsible Fisheries No. 1: Fishing Operations' (1996) Paragraph 1.2.3(g).

37 M Borit and P Olsen, 'Evaluation Framework for Regulatory Requirements Related to Data Recording and Traceability Designed to Prevent Illegal, Unreported and Unregulated Fishing' (2012) 36(1) *Marine Policy* 96–97, 96 and 98.

not equipped to curb wrongdoing,[38] failing to ensure that infractions can be defined, detected, and addressed through administrative or judicial processes.[39] Judicial responses are particularly important, because fishing operations are vulnerable to certain types of criminality.[40] Operational conditions of anonymity, low regulation, and absence of monitoring in which fishing activity can take place have resulted in opportunities for, and synergies with, crime. This includes tax evasion,[41] and also complex transnational criminal operations, such as the trafficking of drugs and weapons, people smuggling, and grievous abuses of human rights.[42] Additionally, regulatory opacity can also occur, and become a breeding ground for corruption.[43] Nevertheless, it is important to note that IUU fishing is usually a distinct phenomenon from individual acts of criminality, whether they occur on board of fishing vessels, or as part of the corporate operations of fishing companies. A wholesale integration of such crimes into the concept of IUU fishing can lead to confusion.[44]

1.2 Emergence and Function of IUU Fishing as a Governance Tool

Despite contemporary associations of IUU fishing with multiple activities involving capture, trade, and crime in the fishing sector at large, the term IUU

38 JR Nielsen, and C Mathiesen, 'Important Factors influencing Rule Compliance in Fisheries Lessons from Denmark' (2003) 27(5) *Marine Policy* 409–416, 409.

39 WJ Furlong, 'The Deterrent Effect of Regulatory Enforcement in the Fishery' (1991) 67(1) *Land Economics* 116–129, 128.

40 E DeConing, 'Fisheries Crime' in Elliott (Ed) *Handbook of Transnational Environmental Crime* (Elgar, 2016) 158.

41 Organization for Economic Cooperation and Development (OECD), 'Evading the Net: Tax Crime in the Fisheries Sector' (2013) 25 [accessed on 17 March 2021 via http://www.oecd.org/tax/crime/evading-the-net-tax-crime-fisheries-sector.pdf].

42 United Nations Office on Drugs and Crime (UNODC), 'Transnational Organized Crime in the Fishing Industry' (2011) 8 [accessed on 17 March 2021 via http://www.unodc.org/documents/human-trafficking/Issue_Paper_-_TOC_in_the_Fishing_Industry.pdf]. United Nations Inter-Agency Project on Human Trafficking (UNIAP), 'Exploitation of Cambodian Men at Sea: Facts about the Trafficking of Cambodian Men onto Thai Fishing Vessels' (2009) 1–8 [accessed on 17 March 2021 via http://www.ilo.org/wcmsp5/groups/public/---ed_norm/---declaration/documents/publication/wcms_143251.pdf].

43 A Sundström, 'Corruption and Regulatory Compliance: Experimental Findings from South African Small Scale Fisheries' (2012) 36(6) *Marine Policy* 12–55, 12.

44 See KY Page and AJ Ortiz, 'What's in a Name: The Importance of Distinguishing between "Fisheries Crime" and IUU Fishing' in Nordquist, Moore and Long (Eds) Cooperation and Engagement in the Asia-Pacific Region (Brill Nijhoff, 2019) 433.

fishing was originally conceived as a functional tool designed to address furtive or otherwise undesirable fishing activities in internationally shared fisheries.[45] A number of regional bodies generally referred to as 'regional fisheries management organisations' (RFMOs) are dedicated to the management of internationally shared fish stocks.[46] RFMOs were pioneers in the adoption of IUU fishing as a governance idea.[47]

1.2.1 *The Origins of the IUU Fishing Concept*

RFMOs are a product of the need for cooperation in the management of complex transnational fisheries. Early predecessors emerged in the first half of the 20th century, with the establishment of bodies that had an advisory role. Since then, their functions have developed, and their authority has been progressively affirmed through growing international support.[48] RFMOs are typically based on treaty, and are integrated by State parties (here referred to as 'members'). Most are institutionalised to some extent, containing administrative rules for collective decision-making,[49] and processes of participation by members and third parties.[50] RFMOs are sites of recurrent formal and informal processes of consultation and review.[51] A key feature of RFMOs that distinguishes them from purely advisory fishery bodies is their competence to issue rules capable of binding member States regarding access to and allocation of the

45 W Edeson, 'The International Plan Of Action On Illegal Unreported And Unregulated Fishing: The Legal Context Of A Non-Legally Binding Instrument' (2001) 16(4) *International Journal of Marine and Coastal Law* 603–623, 605.

46 See FAO, 'Regional Fishery Bodies (RFBs)' (2008) 1 [accessed on 17 March 2021 via www.fao.org/fishery/rfb/en].

47 MA Palma, M Tsamenyi, and WR Edeson, *Promoting Sustainable Fisheries: The International Legal and Policy Framework to Combat Illegal, Unreported and Unregulated Fishing* (Martinus Nijhoff, 2010) 5.

48 GR Munro, 'The United Nations Fish Stocks Agreement of 1995: History and Problems of Implementation' (2001) 15 *Marine Resource Economics* 265–280, 266.

49 J Swan, 'Decision-Making in Regional Fishery Bodies or Arrangements: The Evolving Role of RFBs and International Agreement on Decision-Making Processes' (2005) FAO Fisheries Circular No 995, 82 [accessed on 17 March 2021 via http://www.fao.org/docrep/006/Y5357E/Y5357E00.HTM].

50 M Ceo et al, 'Performance Reviews by Regional Fishery Bodies: Introduction, Summaries, Synthesis and Best Practices' (2012) FAO Fisheries Circular No 1071, 1 [accessed on 17 March 2021 via www.fao.org/docrep/015/i2637e/i2637e00.htm].

51 See International Institute for Sustainable Development (IISD), 'Summary of the Resumed Review Conference on the Agreement for the Implementation of the Provisions of the UN Convention on the Law of the Sea (UNCLOS) 1982 Relating to the Conservation and Management of Straddling Fish Stocks and Highly Migratory Fish Stocks' (2016) 7(71) *Earth Negotiations Bulletin* 1–14, 2.

managed stock.[52] They regularly establish rules, guidelines, and conservation and management measures (collectively 'rules and measures'), that include capture and operational restrictions, such as quota-setting.[53] RFMO rules and measures are varied in nature, and generally aim at conserving and/or managing the harvested stock.[54] RFMO rules and measures are internalised by States that are members, or otherwise cooperate with those organisations, so that appropriate domestic legislation can be adopted to bind and be enforceable against the persons responsible for the operation of the vessels.[55]

Some RFMOs require access to fishery management data held by States, in conformity with the 1995 Fish Stocks Agreement (also referred to as UNFSA),[56] and with their own internal rules and processes.[57] RFMOs can require States to make available to the RFMO operational and management information, including effort and catch data, in particular formats,[58] and some RFMOs also mandate the reporting of transhipment data.[59] These requirements, which highlight the importance of the implementation of domestic authorisation, and data recording and verification procedures by States, can extend into matters of vessel monitoring and compliance verification.[60] These and other

52 UNGA, 'Sustainable Fisheries, Including Through the 1995 Agreement for the Implementation of the Provisions of the United Nations Convention on the Law of the Sea of 10 December 1982 relating to the Conservation and Mangement of Straddling Fish Stocks and Highly Migratory Fish Stocks, and Related Instruments' (2004) Resolution 59/25, para 57.

53 MW Lodge et al, 'Recommended Best Practices for Regional Fisheries Management Organizations: Report of an Independent Panel to Develop a Model for Improved Governance by Regional Fisheries Management Organizations' (Chatham House, 2007) 27 and 28 [accessed on 21 March 2021 via https://www.oecd.org/sd-roundtable/papersandpublications/39374297.pdf].

54 *Fisheries Jurisdiction (Spain v Canada)* Judgment [1998] *ICJ Reports* 461, 69.

55 R Rayfuse, 'Regional Fishery Management Organizations' in Rothwell et al (Eds) *The Oxford Handbook* of the Law of the Sea (Cambridge University Press, 2015) 439.

56 United Nations Agreement for the Implementation of the Provisions of the United Nations Convention on the Law of the Sea of 10 December 1982 relating to the Conservation and Management of Straddling Fish Stocks and Highly Migratory Fish Stocks (1995) 2167 UNTS 88 [UNFSA].

57 See UNFSA Articles 20.3, 20.5 and 21.12.

58 For an overview of RFMO reporting requirements, see Y Tanaka, *A Dual Approach to Ocean Governance: The Cases of Zonal and Integrated management in International Law of the Sea* (Routledge, 2016) 102.

59 C Ewell et al, 'Potential Ecological and social Benefits of a Moratorium on Transhhipment on the High Seas' (2017) 81 *Marine Policy* 293–300, 297.

60 See DM Dzidzornu, 'Marine Environment Protection under Regional Conventions: Limits to the Contribution of Procedural Norms' (2002) *Ocean Development and International Law* 291–298, 291.

measures underpin the very function of RFMOs as centres for transnational fishery governance. Being based to a great extent on information reporting and sharing, the performance of RFMOs largely depends on the epistemic quality of information disclosures made by States.[61] As Tanaka has pointed out, it is self-evident that accurate fishery activity and stock data is essential to successfully designing and implementing rule frameworks for fishery conservation and management, and RFMOs are no exception in this regard. State reporting rules afford these organisations an official source of knowledge, enabling them to not only manage stock allocation, but also to identify IUU fishing activities and to oversee member State compliance with applicable rules and measures.[62]

It is believed that the origin of IUU fishing as a fisheries management concept is traceable to a fishery body that, through broader in remit, also performs functions equivalent to those of an RFMO.[63] The terms 'illegal' and 'unreported' are generally attributed to the 16th conference of the Commission for the Conservation of Antarctic Marine Living Resources (CCAMLR).[64] 'Unregulated' fishing appears to have emerged initially in association to the absence of fishery data made available to CCAMLR by the States responsible for the vessels flagged to non-member States of that organisation, which were not regulating their vessels' activities in accordance with its regulations.[65] A year later, another RFMO, the International Commission for the Conservation of Atlantic Tunas (ICCAT) went on to adopt the IUU fishing idea.[66] The General Assembly of the United Nations promptly followed, with the incorporation of the term IUU fishing in its declarations.[67] It first appeared formally in 1999 in

61 Tanaka (2016), at 100, supra at 58.

62 Tanaka (2016), at 209 and 210, supra at 58.

63 With the exception of the exclusive economic zones of the French islands of Kerguelen and Crozet, where France has privileged rights to exclude conservation and management decisions taken by CCAMLR. See in particular Statement by the Chairman of the Conference on the Conservation of Antarctic marine Living Resources, paras 2 and 3 [accessed on 17 March 2021 via https://www.ccamlr.org/en/organisation/camlr-convention-text].

64 Convention for the Conservation of Antarctic Marine Living Resources (1980) 1329 UNTS 48. See in particular CCAMLR, 'Communication Policy with Non-Contracting Parties Relating to Illegal, Unreported and Unregulated Fishing in the CCAMLR Convention Area' *Report of the Sixteenth Meeting of the Scientific Committee* (1997) Annex 6 Paras 4.55 and 2.13 SC-CCAMLR-XVI.

65 *Ibid.*

66 ICCAT, 'Resolution by ICCAT Concerning the Unreported and Unregulated Catches of Tuna by Large-Scale Longline Vessels in the Convention Area' (1998) Resolution 98/18.

67 UNGA, 'Report on the Work of the United Nations Open-ended Informal Consultative Process on Oceans and the Law of the Sea at its fifteenth meeting' (2014) para 75(a), A/69/90.

the 23rd session of the FAO Committee on Fisheries,[68] and was soon replicated in numerous FAO declarations and reports.[69]

1.2.2 *Integration of the IUU Concept in the International Legal Framework*

IUU fishing has subsequently been incorporated into treaty law by virtue of the adoption of the 2009 Agreement on Port State Measures to Prevent, Deter and Eliminate Illegal, Unreported and Unregulated Fishing (PSMA).[70] Article 1(e) of the PSMA indicates:

> 1(e) illegal, unreported and unregulated fishing refers to the activities set out in paragraph 3 of the 2001 FAO International Plan of Action to Prevent, Deter and Eliminate Illegal, Unreported and Unregulated Fishing, hereinafter referred to as 'IUU fishing'.

The 2001 International Plan of Action to Prevent, Deter and Eliminate Illegal, Unreported and Unregulated Fishing (IPOA IUU),[71] is a voluntary instrument adopted by consensus under the auspices of the FAO to assist States seeking to adopt measures against IUU fishing.[72] The IPOA IUU was the first global instrument to attempt a definition of IUU fishing, which is set out in its paragraph 3, as follows (emphasis added):

3.1 *Illegal fishing* refers to activities:

- 3.1.1 Conducted by national or foreign vessels in waters under the jurisdiction of a State, without the permission of that State, or in contravention of its laws an regulations;
- 3.1.2 Conducted by vessels flying the flag of States that are parties to a relevant regional fisheries management organisation but operate in contravention of the conservation and management measures adopted by that organization and by which the States are bound, or relevant provisions of the applicable international law; or

---

68 FAO, 'Report of the 23rd Session of the Committee on Fisheries' (1999) para 72, CL-116/7 [accessed on 21 March 2021 via http://www.fao.org/docrep/meeting/X1647e.htm].

69 See E Hey, 'Global Fisheries Regulations in the First Half of the 1990s' (1996) 11(4) *International Journal of Marine and Coastal Law*, 459–491, 459.

70 Agreement on Port State Measures to Prevent, Deter and Eliminate Illegal, Unreported and Unregulated Fishing (2009), UN Registration Number 54133 [PSMA].

71 FAO International Plan of Action to Prevent, Deter and Eliminate Illegal, Unreported and Unregulated Fishing (2001) [IPOA IUU].

72 IPOA IUU, Introduction, para 2.

3.1.3 In violation of national laws or international obligations, including those undertaken by cooperating States to a relevant regional fisheries management organization.

3.2 *Unreported fishing* refers to fishing activities:

3.2.1 Which have not been reported, or have been misreported, to the relevant national authority, in contravention of national laws and regulations; or

3.2.2 Undertaken in the area of competence of a relevant regional fisheries management organization which have not been reported or have been misreported, in contravention of the reporting procedures of that organization.

3.3 *Unregulated fishing* refers to fishing activities;

3.3.1 In the area of application of a relevant regional fisheries management organization that are conducted by vessels without nationality, or by those flying the flag of a State not party to that organization, or by a fishing entity, in a manner that is not consistent with or contravenes the conservation and management measures of that organization; or

3.3.2 In areas or for fish stocks in relation to which there are no applicable conservation or management measures and where such fishing activities are conducted in a manner inconsistent with State responsibilities for the conservation of living marine resources under international law.

The lack of parsimony is an evident feature of the approach taken to the definition of IUU fishing in paragraph 3. Edeson expressed concern about its inaccurate nature, particularly as he foresaw the likelihood that the definition would migrate onto other instruments,[73] as indeed has been the case. One of the few things that can be established with confidence is that the definition concerns vessel activities, or State conducts that are related to the oversight of fishing activities. It is evident that the text of the IPOA does not extend to the non-fishing operations that are often associated to IUU fishing, such as tax avoidance by a fishing company, or trafficking of drugs or persons occurring on board of a fishing vessel.[74] The differentiation of these activities has been noted by authors concerned with fisheries crime, and calls have been made for a re-conceptualisation in order to more clearly and effectively accommodate

73 Edeson (2001) at 619, supra at 45.

74 See section 1.1 above.

instances of criminality that are often associated to IUU fishing.[75] Beyond this, paragraph 3 of the IPOA does not establish any substantive parameters as to what specific activities IUU fishing refers to. It is unclear whether the reference to *fishing activities* in paragraphs 3.2 and 3.3 includes the broad spectrum of acts that may be implied in *activities conducted by vessels*, as stated in paragraph 3.1, which could be interpreted to include supporting activities such as transhipment. A narrow interpretation would carry the implication that fishing activities in the IPOA IUU incorporate only capture activities. The 2009 Port State Measures Agreement refers to *fishing* as well as *fishing related activities*, which includes transhipment, shedding some interpretive light into this issue.[76]

The lack of clarity and parsimony in paragraph 3 of the IPOA has prompted commentators to suggest that IPOA IUU paragraph 3 is not a definition as such. According to Theilen, paragraph 3 is a description or explanation,[77] and according to Molenaar, a definition of three separate elements.[78] Yet, Edeson suggests that paragraph 3 appears to have been intended to operate as a unitary concept by the participants in the elaboration of the IPOA, even if some openly recognised its less than perfect nature.[79] As Serdy further points out, the unitary character of IUU fishing is reinforced by the fact that the text of the IPOA after paragraph 3 is steadfast in referring to the expression IUU fishing as a single issue.[80] In the Port State Measures Agreement, IUU fishing 'refers to the activities set out in paragraph 3' of the IPOA, yet paragraph 3 of the IPOA contains a series of categories, rather than listing fishing activities as such. Despite these heterogeneous takes on IPOA paragraph 3, it can in principle be concluded that the provision contains neither a definition nor a description, but a system designed for pragmatic categorisation and interpretation. In other words, IUU fishing as envisaged in IPOA paragraph 3 is an *interpretive framework or 'lens'*. Despite its characteristic three elements, the IUU lens is in fact integrated by

75 See N Oral, 'Reflections on the Past, Present, and Future of IUU Fishing under International Law' (2020) 22 *International Community Law Review* 368–376, 374. See also E de Coning and E Witbooi, 'Towards a New 'Fisheries Crime' Paradigm: Africa as an Illustrative Example' (2015) 60 *Marine Policy*, 208–215, 209.

76 PSMA, Articles 1(c) and 1(d).

77 JT Theilen, 'What's in a Name? The Illegality of Illegal, Unreported and Unregulated Fishing' (2013) 28 *International Journal of Marine and Coastal Law* 533–550, 534.

78 EJ Molenaar, 'CCAMLR and Southern Ocean Fisheries' (2001) 16(3) *International Journal of Marine and Coastal Law* 465–500, 483.

79 Edeson (2001) at 619, supra at 45.

80 See A Serdy, *The New Entrants Problem in International Fisheries Law* (Cambridge University Press, 2016) 143.

two distinct *lens filters*, each with different interpretive parameters: one legal, and one hybrid filter containing legal and non-legal features.

1.2.2.1 Legal Interpretive Filter: Illegal Fishing

Firstly, it is self-evident from the text that the first and second paragraphs, concerning illegal and unreported fishing, are respectively a category and subcategory of fishing activities that take place in contravention of law: indeed, both subsections concern *contraventions*. Palma, Tsameny and Edeson consider this sub-categorisation to be unsatisfactory, given that from a management perspective it may be useful to know what unreported fishing is taking place, even in cases when reporting duties may not have been established in law.[81] Indeed this eventuality may include cases of legal but nevertheless unquantified fishing, or be residually captured in the notion of unregulated fishing under paragraph 3.3. The potential for confusion latent in this classification is evident, and exemplary of the lack of parsimony that characterises paragraph 3.

As Theilen has noted, the illegal fishing category and its unreported subcategory in paragraphs 3.1 and 3.2 of the IPOA IUU concern two types of scenarios:[82] firstly, violations of the domestic laws established by the State by the persons responsible for the vessel. Under this scenario, illegal activities will be determined by the domestic law of each State, and may vary from one State to the next. This is an important category for the governance of fisheries activities in waters under State jurisdiction, as well as the high seas. There are a range of domestic legal tools at the disposal of States, which enable the exercise of preemptive as well as reactive controls over fishing activities categorised in national law as infractions, alongside corresponding enforcement responses and sanctions.[83] A second scenario of 'illegal' fishing concerns the violation by States of their international obligations. Contraventions of international treaties including those underpinning the RFMOs are, as indicated in IPOA IUU paragraphs 3.1.2 and 3.2.2, categorised as illegal fishing, even if vessels are operating within the legal parameters established by the States with oversight over their operations (and therefore not breaching domestic law as it applies to them). This integration of the international and domestic planes could be seen as functionally valuable from a pragmatic perspective, as it results in domestically legal activities being associated with the 'IUU fishing' lens, and thus identified as undesirable, and susceptible in theory at least to triggering questions

81 Palma, Tsameny and Edeson (2010) at 44, supra at 47.
82 Theilen (2013) at 536 and 538, supra at 77.
83 See M Yusuf, AR Muhadar, and MS Karim, 'Legal Effectiveness in Combating Illegal Fishing' (2018) 72 *Journal of Law, Policy and Globalization* 66–79, 68.

of State responsibility. Nevertheless, as Serdy has pointed out, the integration of the domestic and international planes in a single 'illegal fishing' category is likely to cause confusion as to the meaning of 'illegal', and the appropriate site of responsibility.[84]

1.2.2.2 Hybrid Interpretive Filter: Unregulated Fishing

In accordance with paragraphs 3.3 and 3.4 of the IPOA, unregulated fishing constitutes a separate category. Its principal characteristic is that it refers to fishing activities that may either contravene international obligations, or merely be inconsistent with them. This means that this is a hybrid interpretive filter, with the potential for incorporating legal and non-legal elements of analysis, and for causing significant confusion.[85] Theilen has proposed that under paragraph 3.4 of the IPOA unregulated fishing should be constructed as being a subcategory of illegal fishing.[86] The mentioned paragraph reads as follows:

> 3.4- Notwithstanding paragraph 3.3, certain unregulated fishing may take place in a manner which is not in violation of applicable international law, and may not require the application of measures envisaged under the International Plan of Action.

The narrow reading that Theilen gives to this paragraph does not appear to be shared by other commentators, who directly or indirectly have acknowledged that IUU fishing incorporates elements of a non-legal nature.[87] Practice by States and international organisations also supports a broader reading of the unregulated fishing interpretive filter. Unregulated fishing is a heterogeneous package, which appears to have been adopted as a tool with which to address a number of diverse cases where assessments of legality may not

---

84 Serdy (2016) at 158, supra at 80.

85 See ER Van Der Marel, 'Problems and Progress in Combating IUU Fishing', in Caddell and Molenaar (Eds) Strengthening International Fisheries Law in an Era of Changing Oceans (Hart, 2019) 297.

86 Theilen (2013) at 543, supra at 77.

87 R Baird, 'Illegal, Unreported and Unregulated Fishing: an Analysis of the Legal, Economic and Historical Factors Relevant to its Development and Persistence' (2004) 5 *Melbourne Journal of International Law* 299–336, 300. DM Sodik, 'Non-Legally Binding International Fisheries Instruments and Measures to Combat illegal, Unreported and Unregulated Fishing' (2008) 15(1) *Australian International Law Journal* 129–164, 133. V Ventura, 'Tackling Illegal, Unregulated and Unreported Fishing: The ITLOS Advisory Opinion on Flag State Responsibility for IUU Fishing and the Principle of Due Diligence' (2015) 12(1) *Brazilian Journal of International Law* 50–67, 57. Serdy (2016) at 147, supra at 80.

be straightforward, or perhaps even desirable, depending on the interpreter. Three different scenarios can be identified, as follows:

Paragraph 3.3.1 specifically refers to two cases where legal assessment may be problematic. Firstly, fishing vessels flagged to fishing entities, a concept that is useful to address the problematic nature of Taiwan's status, in order to support its by cooperation and integration in the activities of the RFMOs relevant to its fishing interests.[88] Secondly, the case of vessels without nationality is also mentioned in paragraph 3.3.1 of the IPOA. Comparable cases are referred to in Articles 92(1) and 92(2) of the LOSC, whereby vessels may not fly more than one flag simultaneously, and may be assimilated to vessels without nationality when they do. Under Article 110.1(d) of the LOSC, vessels without nationality may be subjected to interdiction by any other State. Genuine statelessness cases are uncommon, and should be distinguished from another rather more regular occurrence: that of vessels that are actually registered with a flag State, but that are seen operating without an apparent flag affiliation, having successfully concealed all external vessel markings in order to evade links to a source of regulation.[89] These eventualities should be addressed by the domestic legal frameworks of flag States to ensure that the genuine link between them and their vessel is maintained at all times,[90] and that these actions constitute infractions of the domestic legal framework (and can therefore be dealt with as illegal fishing).

Secondly, paragraph 3.3.1 also refers to a category of cases where enforcement is problematic. This is the concerning issue of fishing in RFMO regulated areas by vessels flagged to States that are not members, and that operate in a manner that is not consistent with, or contravenes the measures established by those organisations. The drafting of the paragraph contains a juxtaposition of *contravention* on the one hand, suggesting a legal obligation exists, with *inconsistency* on the other, suggesting that it does not. As Theilen, points out, this reflects the reality that certain States, even if not members of an RFMO, would nevertheless be legally bound to observe applicable measures, if they are parties to the UNFSA, under the operation of Article 8 of this agreement.[91] For

88 H Djalal, 'The Emergence of the Concept of Fishing Entities: A Note' (2006) 37(2) *Ocean Development and International Law* 117–122, 119.

89 See UNGA, United Nations Conference on Straddling Fish Stocks and Highly Migratory Fish Stocks (1993) paras v(d) and v(e), A/CONF.164/10. See also DD Miller and UR Sumaila, 'Flag Use Behavior and IUU Activity within the International Fishing Fleet: Refining Definitions and Identifying Areas of Concern' (2014) 44 *Marine Policy* 204–211, 204.

90 See AN Honniball, 'Unilateral Trade measures and the Importance of Defining IUU Fishing' (2020) 7(2) *The Journal of Territorial and Maritime Studies* 7–26, 18.

91 Theilen (2013) at 543, supra at 77.

those States, such eventualities would therefore become subsumed into the 'illegal' fishing category of IPOA paragraph 3.1 operating on the international plane. In respect of fishing activities of vessels flagged to States that are neither RFMO members or cooperating non-members, nor parties of the UNFSA, the unregulated fishing category applies residually. As will be discussed more fully in the next chapter, international legal obligations stemming from the UNFSA and RFMO treaties are only binding on States that have formally consented to be bound by them. This is a result of the operation of the *pacta tertiis nec procent nec prosunt* (*pacta tertiis*) principle, as specified in the 1969 Vienna Convention on the Law of Treaties.[92] *Pacta tertiis* is a principle of general international law, and is opposable to all States in respect of the effects and application of international treaties.[93]

Lastly, paragraph 3.3.2 again returns to cases where legal assessment might be problematic, this time concerning ocean areas where no RFMO or equivalent measures have been established, but where the fishing activities are inconsistent with State obligations under international law. In order to fully explore the meaning of unregulated fishing under IPOA paragraph 3.3.2 it is first necessary to embark upon a brief excursus into the international legal regime, as established in the LOSC. The LOSC sets out a number of obligations for States in respect of high seas fisheries, primarily by reference to Articles 91 to 94, and 117 to 119, and also through the obligations established in Articles 192 and 194 of the Convention in respect of all ocean areas. Nevertheless, these provisions are characterised by considerable imprecision,[94] as well as a margin of flag State autonomy,[95] as has been pointed out in a recent international arbitration award.[96] Addressing uncertainties in this regard often requires recourse to other more specific rules and standards. Although existing fisheries treaties and the rules and measures of RFMOs may at least in some cases perform that function, they are not universally ratified. The protections they offer only have legal force against States that have formally agreed to be bound by

92 See Vienna Convention on the Law of Treaties (1969) 1155 UNTS 331. See Articles 19–22 on the subject of Reservations, and 34–38 on the subject of third parties to a treaty.

93 E Franckx, 'Pacta Tertiis and the Agreement for the Implementation of the Straddling and Highly Migratory Fish Stocks provisions of the United Nations Convention on the Law of the Sea' (2000) 8 *Tulane Journal of International and Comparative Law* 49–82, 78.

94 Theilen (2013) at 547, supra at 77.

95 Y Takei, 'Assessing Flag State Performance in Legal Terms: Clarifications of the Margin of Discretion' (2013) 28(1) *International Journal of Marine and Coastal Law* 97–133.

96 *In the Matter of the South China Sea Arbitration (Republic of the Philippines v Peoples' Republic of China)* Award [2016] PCA Case No. 2013–19, para 754.

the respective treaties.[97] The limited reach of these treaties has also left voids in high seas fishing when it comes to applicable conduct rules that are also specific and precise. Thus, determining what a State's responsibility may be in a particular context (or for the purposes of the IPOA IUU, ascertaining what constitutes a case of 'illegal fishing' on the international plane) can be marred with difficulties. Accordingly, governance actors may feel that it can be more practical to residually categorise those cases through the hybrid 'unregulated fishing' filter.[98]

The situation is quite different in the EEZ, where the notion of unregulated fishing appears superfluous.[99] A number of commentators in their respective treatment of IUU fishing in the EEZ have simply used the term 'illegal fishing', albeit without further elaboration.[100] In a recent advisory opinion concerning the obligations of States in respect of IUU fishing occurring in the EEZ, ITLOS considered the notion of 'unregulated fishing', and its applicability to address the actions of States as fishery regulators in the context of EEZ fisheries. In paragraph 96 of the advisory opinion, ITLOS delivers the following statement (emphasis added):

> With respect to *unregulated fishing* (...) the Tribunal wishes to point out that, in accordance with the Convention, the adoption by the coastal State of conservation and management measures for all living resources within its exclusive economic zone is mandatory. Article 61, paragraph 2, of the Convention requires that the coastal State *shall ensure through proper conservation and management measures that the maintenance of the living resources in the exclusive economic zone is not endangered by over-exploitation.*[101]

Thus, in this paragraph, ITLOS appears to indicate that in the EEZ, significant legal voids in the domestic legal framework for the regulation of fishing

97 K Gjerde, 'High Seas Fisheries Governance: Prospects and Challenges in the 21st Century' in Vidas and Schei (Eds) *The World Ocean in Globalisation: Challenges and Responses* (Martinus Nijhoff, 2011) 221.

98 This is discussed in detail in Chapter 4.

99 But see G Handl, 'State Responsibility for Illegal, Unreported and Unregulated Fishing in Foreign EEZs' (2014) 44(1–2) *Environmental Policy and Law* 158–167, 163.

100 Theilen (2013) at 544, supra at 77. Serdy (2016) at 145, supra at 80. VJ Schatz, 'Combating Illegal Fishing in the Exclusive Economic Zone – Flag State Obligations in the Context of the Primary Responsibility in the Coastal State' (2016) 7(2) *Goettingen Journal of International Law* 383–414, 384 and 387.

101 *Request for an Advisory Opinion submitted by the Sub-Regional Fisheries Commission* [2015] Advisory Opinion, ITLOS Reports 2015 4, para 96 [SRFC].

resources may imply an infringement by the coastal State of its international obligations. RFMOs rely on the provision of fishery information by States in respect of regulated stocks that straddle or migrate through the EEZ in order to fulfil their management function.[102] Flag States retain jurisdiction over their vessels in the EEZ of a coastal State, although they defer to the primary prescriptive and enforcement jurisdiction of the coastal State in this area.[103] Coastal State obligations in the EEZ include duties of cooperation over the regulation of straddling and highly migratory species,[104] and are subjected to a high threshold of due diligence, as the ITLOS has confirmed in its advisory opinion.[105] Hence, although it may at first appear that a failure by the coastal State to regulate fishing activity in respect of RFMO managed fish stocks occurring in its EEZ might give rise to a void in regulation apt for capture by the *unregulated fishing* lens filter of paragraph 3.3.2, this is arguably not the case. All fishing activities by vessels of any nationality in areas under the jurisdiction of the coastal State must be authorised and regulated by that State. This must be done in a manner that satisfies LOSC Articles 61 to 64, as well as the general obligation contained in LOSC Article 192, and duties in respect of fragile ecosystems and vulnerable species as per LOSC Article 194 where applicable. Hence, coastal States have to set adequate conditions for the protection and management of fish stocks as part of their international legal obligations. A lack of appropriate regulation is therefore more appropriately captured by the 'illegal' fishing filter, as set out in paragraph 3.1.3. Pursuant to this analysis, it is arguable that the IUU fishing lens, when considered holistically as a unitary interpretive framework that includes both the illegal and the unregulated fishing lens 'filters', is only really appropriate for high seas fisheries.

1.3 Conclusion

Shortfalls in domestic legal frameworks provide opportunities for IUU fishing activities. The absence or insufficiency of reporting duties and capture limits, poor monitoring and evaluation mechanisms, an absence of appropriate sanctions, and the presence of undesirable incentives, all play a role in the

102 Y Tanaka, 'Reflections on Reporting Systems in Treaties Concerning the Protection of the Marine Environment' (2009) 40(2) *Ocean Development and International Law* 146–170, 156.

103 SRFC para 124, supra at 101.

104 LOSC Articles 63 and 64.

105 SRFC para 207, supra at 101.

perpetuation of IUU fishing activity. The effects of such flaws are exacerbated in the high seas, where successful management depends on coordination across States, which cannot be achieved without substantial and ongoing international cooperation. Such cooperation has over time been consolidated through the work of RFMOs and other similar fishery bodies. International law has not always been capable of ensuring sufficient cooperation and fishery conservation and management. IUU fishing emerged as a governance innovation with the potential to address some of those limitations, and aid RFMO management, especially in respect of species occurring partly or wholly in the high seas. Yet, despite its pragmatic aims, IUU fishing is a complex idea, lacking in parsimony and capable of causing confusion.

The analysis contained in this chapter results in the proposition that IUU fishing should be interpreted broadly, to include transhipment operations. Also, it maintains that is not a description or a definition, but an interpretive lens. It contains two distinct interpretive filters: firstly, *illegal fishing*, which incorporates unreported fishing. It operates as an interpretive mechanism through which activities are assessed by reference to domestic legal frameworks, or international responsibility parameters. Secondly, the hybrid interpretive filter of *unregulated fishing* contains a combination of assessment criteria, which only narrowly refer to international legal responsibility. The analysis carried out in this chapter supports an argument that unregulated fishing is not an appropriate interpretive device for fishing activities that take place in waters under the jurisdiction of coastal States. Consequently, IUU fishing as a unitary interpretive lens that comprises both illegal and unregulated fishing, arguably has comprehensive functional application only in respect of high seas fisheries.

CHAPTER 2

Rationale for an IUU Fishing Interpretive Lens

Introduction

The previous chapter has explored the features of IUU fishing as an interpretive lens, and has delimited its functional characteristics and scope of application. It has been clarified that IUU fishing is a hybrid interpretive lens through which it is possible to identify not only breaches of domestic law, but also responsibility under international law, and activities that undermine the measures taken by RFMOs. These last two interpretive parameters frame the enquiry undertaken in this Chapter 2, whereby the effectiveness of the IUU fishing idea in its international dimension is explored. The aim of this enquiry is to evaluate whether, and to what extent, the IUU fishing interpretive lens is superior in effectiveness to a broad international legal perspective, commencing with a functional analysis of the relevant global fishery treaties. A similar enquiry is then undertaken by reference to the additional types of rules and measures to which the IUU fishing lens refers. Findings are contrasted in order to ascertain the extent to which the IUU fishing lens may be contributing to improving the effectiveness of the international legal instruments under review. This enquiry into effectiveness is concerned only with the comprehensiveness and functionality of legal and non-legal rules, in the context of the empirical realities of the undesirable fishing practices that take place in the high seas, and which the IUU fishing interpretive lens attempts to conceptualise and categorise.

2.1 International Law and the IUU Fishing Interpretive Lens

The IUU fishing interpretive lens, as already discussed, implies the convergence of a legal and non-legal perspective, which the lens combines in its functional scope over high seas fisheries regulation. For the purposes of ascertaining the value that such a hybrid approach may deliver, it is first necessary to evaluate the performance of a solely legal approach, and its ability to ensure that States address IUU fishing adequately. The legal blueprint that grounds the legal order of the oceans is set out in the LOSC. It sets out a comprehensive framework of rights and obligations, reflecting broad compromises made

 | DOI:10.1163/9789004463219_004

during the decades of negotiation that preceded its adoption.[1] The legal framework of the LOSC establishes certain principles for ocean utilisation,[2] on the basis of a zonal approach upon which the principle of sovereign State equality is combined with a recognition of the need to assume duties of conservation and cooperation.

Except for certain 'general' obligations that are binding on all States by virtue of their customary status,[3] the obligations established in the LOSC have legally binding force only on State parties to the treaty.[4] Obligations derived from treaty bind States through their explicit consent.[5] This results from the operation of the general international legal principle known as *pacta tertiis*, already discussed in the previous chapter.[6] The *pacta tertiis* principle operates so that obligations in treaties cannot bind or erode the rights of States who have not formally agreed to be bound by them.[7] This ensures the protection of the State's autonomy, and enables States to prioritise their own interests, whilst maintaining a horizontal system of interaction with other States, preserving the State supremacy upon which the traditional international legal order has been established.[8] State sovereignty also underpins the requirements of general practice and acceptance upon which the emergence of a customary norm depends.[9] Due to these principles, the importance of the number of State parties to treaties dealing with issues of utilisation of internationally shared resources cannot be overstated. Although the LOSC does not have universal adherence, the very high number of ratifications, accessions, and successions

1 H Caminos and MR Molitor, 'Progressive Development of International Law and the Package Deal' (1985) 79(4) *American Journal of International Law* 871–890, 873.

2 HS Schiffman, 'The Dispute Settlement Mechanism of UNCLOS: A Potentially Important Framework for Marine Wildlife Management' (1998) 1(2) *Journal of International Wildlife Law & Policy* 293–306, 294.

3 J Crawford, *Brownlie's Principles of Public International Law* (Oxford University Press, 2012) 384.

4 See Statute of the International Court of Justice (1945) 3 Bevans 1179. Treaties are a source of legal obligation for the State parties to the agreement, according to Article 38 of the Statute.

5 1969 Vienna Convention on the Law of Treaties, 1155 UNTS 331, Article 12 [VCLT].

6 JA Pastor Ridruejo, 'Los Efectos de los Acuerdos Internacionales Respecto a los Terceros' (1960) 13(3) *Revista Espanola de Derecho Internacional* 387–412, 388.

7 See VCLT Article 34. The principles operates as an obstacle to the obligation of third States through treaty, but it may be removed where the treaty obligation is superseded by a general obligation brought about by custom, as per Article 38 of the VCLT.

8 B Kingsbury and M Donaldson, 'From Bilateralism to Publicness in International Law' (2011) New York University Public Law and Legal Theory Working Paper 256, 81.

9 H Bull, *The Anarchical Society: A Study of Order in World Politics* (Palgrave Macmillan, 2012) 147.

by maritime States means that its importance is indisputable.[10] The LOSC does not mention IUU fishing explicitly,[11] but sets out the jurisdictional parameters within which States may prescribe and enforce laws on legal and natural persons under their jurisdiction in respect of marine fisheries.[12]

2.1.1 *Jurisdiction*

Prior to exploring the features of the LOSC in respect of the regulation of high seas fisheries, it is necessary to explore the meaning and implications of jurisdiction. On this topic, Barnes points out:

> International law generally allocates authority to States in a number of ways, but there are two core principles: the territorial principle and the nationality principle. The territorial principle provides that States enjoy exclusive power to regulated activities occurring within their territories. This covers both criminal and civil matters. (…) As States are aggregates of individuals, it follows that the nationality principle allows them to regulate their nationals. An extension of the nationality principle permits States to regulate the activities of vessels flying their flag.[13]

Contemporary flag State jurisdiction law and practice for the purposes of high seas fisheries originates from the XIXth century, when the nationality of a vessel became distinct from the nationality of its owner.[14] The nationality of the vessel became independently established, upon registration with a flag State.[15] Initially, the requirement for a 'genuine link' between the vessel and its flag State had been associated to requirements that such assignation ought to be sufficient for its recognition by other States,[16] and later to the

10 The number of ratifications, accessions, and successions to the LOSC currently stands at 168. See DOALOS, Chronological lists of ratifications of, accessions and successions to the Convention and the related Agreements [accessed on 20 March 2021 via http://www.un.org/depts/los/reference_files/chronological_lists_of_ratifications.htm].

11 *Request for an Advisory Opinion submitted by the Sub-Regional Fisheries Commission* [2015] Separate Opinion of Judge Paik, ITLOS Reports 2015 102, para 5 [SRFC].

12 Y Tanaka, *A Dual Approach to Ocean Governance: the Cases of Zonal and Integrated Management in International Law of the Sea* (Routledge, 2016) 4–5.

13 RA Barnes, 'The Law of the Sea 1850–2010' in Starkey and Heidbrink (Eds) *A History of the North Atlantic Fisheries, Volume 2* (German Maritime Museum, 2012) 179.

14 BA Boczek, *Flags of Convenience* (Harvard University Press, 1962) 94.

15 I Brownlie, 'The Relations of Nationality in Public International Law' (1963) 39 *British Year Book of International Law* 284–364, 284.

16 *Nottebohm* (*Lichtenstain v Guatemala*), Judgment [1955] ICJ Reports 1955 4, para 83. For the evolution of the term, see ML Mc Connell, 'Darkening Confusion Mounted Upon

requirement of an economic link between the operation of the vessel and its flag State.[17] However, the development of the genuine link as something other than an effective jurisdictional link between a vessel and its flag State was criticised,[18] and those initial requirements did not survive into contemporary law.[19] In the *Saiga* case, for example, ITLOS denied that that the genuine link could operate as a basis for third party recognition of vessel nationality.[20] It is now broadly accepted that the genuine link implies a domestic jurisdictional nexus that is established by the municipal law of the flag State, and that it must be of sufficient quality to enable the flag State to exert prescriptive and enforcement control over the vessels flying its flag.[21] Under LOSC Article 91 States that register vessels are obliged to fix the conditions for the assignation of their nationality to the ship, and issue appropriate documentation to that effect.[22]

In the high seas, the flag State has 'exclusive' prescriptive and enforcement authority over the fishing vessel, its activities, and all persons on board,[23] in accordance with LOSC Article 92.1. However, as the flag State must observe conditions established by the LOSC, and the rights of other States,[24] its jurisdiction may more appropriately be understood as 'primary', rather than truly

Darkening Confusion: The Search for the Elusive Genuine Link' (1985) 16 *Journal of Maritime Law and Commerce* 365–395. VP Coglianti-Bantz, 'Disentangling the Genuine Link: Enquiries in Sea, Air and Space Law' (2010) 79(3) *Nordic Journal of International Law* 383–432.

17 United Nations Conference on Trade and Development (UNCTAD), 'Action on the Question of Open Registries' (1981) iii, TD/B/C.4/220. This was reflected in the collapsed United Nations Convention on Conditions for Registration of Ships (1986) (not in force), Articles 7 to 10.

18 See MS McDougal, WT Burke, and IA Vlasic, 'The Maintenance of Public Order at Sea and the Nationality of Ships' (1960) 54(1) *American Journal of International Law* 25–116.

19 Convention on the High Seas (1958) 450 UNTS 11, Articles 5 and 6.

20 *The M/V Saiga No 2 (Saint Vincent and the Grenadines v Guinea)* Judgment [1999] ITLOS Reports 335, para 80.

21 AG Oude Elferink, 'The Genuine Link Concept: Time for a Post Mortem?' in Dekker and Post (Eds) *On the Foundations and Sources of International Law* (TCM Asser, 2003) 47. EJ Molenaar, 'Participation, Allocation and Unregulated Fishing: The Practice of Regional Fisheries Management Organisations' (2003) 18(4) *International Journal of Marine and Coastal Law* 457–480, 460.

22 PW Birnie, and AE Boyle, *International Law and the Environment* (Oxford University Press, 1994) 707.

23 Y Tanaka, *The International Law of the Sea* (Cambridge University Press, 2012) 153. E De Sombre, 'Flags of Convenience and Property Rights in the High Seas' in Allen, Joseph and Squires (Eds) *Conservation and Management of Transnational Tuna Fisheries* (Wiley-Blackwell, 2010) 270.

24 LOSC Articles 109 to 111.

exclusive.[25] Despite this qualification, the freedom of fishing combined with the primary jurisdiction of the flag State in the high seas have been understood to be a persistent obstacle to fisheries conservation. This perception is illustrated by the depositions made in not too distant international case law.[26] The primary jurisdiction of the flag State in the context of the legal regime of the high seas is considered a norm of customary international law.[27] The customary and conventional obligations contained in the text of the LOSC to which the flag State is subjected have been developed by additional global, regional, and bilateral agreements.[28] These have clarified the prescriptive and enforcement competences and obligations of flag States in the specific context of IUU fishing control to a considerable extent.[29]

2.2 The Due Diligence Nature of Flag State Obligations

Most State obligations associated with high seas fisheries are of a 'due diligence' nature. This type of obligation appears eminently suitable to the IUU fishing context: Firstly, it implies the assumption by the State of a 'responsibility to ensure' that appropriate laws and regulations are adopted.[30] Secondly, it requires the application of effort and vigilance in their implementation, which implies a need to monitor the activity, and identify and respond to infractions.[31] In principle, this seems appropriate to ensure State control over fishing activities, as vessels are normally operated and owned by private persons, and not directly by States or their agencies.[32] However, the nature and extent of the vigilance and effort that are required depends on the specific content of the

25 D Guilfoyle, *Shipping Interdiction and the Law of the Sea* (Cambridge University Press, 2009) 210.

26 *Fisheries Jurisdiction (Spain v Canada)* Judgment [1998] ICJ Reports 432, para 12.

27 RR Churchill, and AV Lowe, *The Law of the Sea* (Manchester University Press, 1988) 204 and 208.

28 See JE Carroz and MJ Savini, 'The New International Law Of Fisheries Emerging From Bilateral Agreements' (1979) 3(2) *Marine Policy* 79–98, 79. Y Takei, *Filling Regulatory Gaps in High Seas Fisheries* (Martinus Nijhoff, 2013) 253.

29 See JG Xue, 'China's Distant Water Fisheries and its Response to Flag State Responsibilities' (2006) 30(6) *Marine Policy* 651–658, 652.

30 *Responsibilities and Obligations of States with Respect to Activities in the Area*, Advisory Opinion [2011] ITLOS Reports 10, paras 110–112.

31 See *Request for an Advisory Opinion Submitted by the Sub-Regional Fisheries Commission*, Advisory Opinion [2015] ITLOS Reports 4, paras 129, 137 and 138 [SRFC].

32 *The Volga Case (Russian Federation v Australia)* Dissenting Opinion of Judge Ad-Hoc Shearer [2002] ITLOS Reports 66, para 19.

flag State duties that may be applicable under treaty or general international law to specific cases.[33] As a result, the mere existence of activities that can be interpreted as IUU fishing through the lens of IPOA paragraph 3 *may not necessarily always imply a breach* of a due diligence obligation. Each case has to be considered in its own light, in the circumstances in which the actions or inactions of the State took place, and against the specific obligations that were applicable to it in that context. The substantive and procedural content of theobligations that are more directly relevant to the control by flag States of fishing activities in the high seas is explored in the following three sections.

2.3 Conservation and Management

Fishing activity necessarily implies human interaction with the marine environment and its living resources in a way that impacts on target and non-target species, and on marine trophic chains and habitats. Certain fishing activities such as deep trawling can potentially have substantial and detrimental effects on physical structures of the marine environment that sustain animal and plant life. Hence, the framework of international obligations created for the protection of the marine environment, and for conservation and management of marine species, are an essential part of high seas governance. They shape and condition the regulatory action of flag States, in order to balance the protection of the natural resources and human dependency on their exploitation. Amongst those obligations, the most directly relevant to high seas fishing are set out in the LOSC and its satellite fisheries treaties. The following sections examine the main instruments and rules.

2.3.1 *The LOSC*

Two sections of the LOSC, namely Part VII on the high seas, and Part XII on the protection and preservation of the marine environment, are relevant to flag State control of IUU fishing. In matters of high seas fisheries, due diligence is underpinned by the principle of the freedom of fishing, established in LOSC Article 87.1(e). Subject to the duties established by the Convention, the freedom of fishing in the high seas is enjoyed by all States.[34] This provision reflects

33 *In the Matter of the South China Sea (Republic of the Philippines v the Peoples' Republic of China)* Award [2016] PCA Case No 2013–19, para 754 [South China Sea].

34 RR Churchill and AV Lowe, *The Law of the Sea* (1999) at 204, cited in JA Roach, 'Today's Customary International Law of the Sea' (2014) 45(3) *Ocean Development & International Law* 239–259, 247.

a regime whereby high seas living resources may be concurrently harvested by vessels regulated by any State,[35] and is residually an open access regime.[36] The freedom principle predates the LOSC, having been set out previously in Article 2 of the 1958 Convention on the High Seas.[37] However, the freedom of the high seas is not absolute. There is an underlying principle of State responsibility that also predates the adoption of the LOSC. It featured in the 1893 *Behring Sea Fur Seals* arbitration case,[38] and was subsequently reflected in the 1958 Geneva Convention on Fishing and Conservation of the Living Resources of the High Seas.[39] The balancing of rights and duties that is characteristic of the freedom of fishing is highlighted in Article 116, where it is established that States have the right for their nationals to fish the high seas, albeit subject to the relevant obligations of the Convention and any other applicable treaty obligations. The obligations of the flag State in respect of the conservation and management of high seas fisheries are established in articles 117 and 119 of the LOSC. LOSC Article 117, establishes a duty on each State to take, or to cooperate with other States in taking, measures for their respective nationals 'as may be necessary for the conservation of the living resources of the high seas'.

But as Rayfuse indicates, the key conservation and management obligations in the legal text of the LOSC are characterised by a considerable degree of uncertainty.[40] Baird has further stated that the extent of the responsibilities established in the Convention, combined with the principle of the primacy of flag State jurisdiction, results in the obligations being excessively diluted in practice.[41] Henriksen, on the other hand, emphasises that the freedom of fishing is conditional, and that some duties do emanate from the LOSC with practical implications for States, such as duties derived from Article 119.2 regarding data exchange. Yet, he nevertheless acknowledges that any duties may be weak for the purposes of conservation, and better associated to matters

35 Tanaka (2012) at 16, supra at 23. PW and AE Boyle, *International Law and the Environment* (Oxford Press, 1994) 707.

36 See *Fisheries Case* (*United Kingdom v Norway*) Judgment [1951] ICJ Reports 116, page 131.

37 Convention on the High Seas 1958, 450 UNTS 11.

38 *Award between the United States and the United Kingdom relating to the Rights of Jurisdiction of United States in the Bering's Sea and the Preservation of Fur Seals*, Decision [1893] United Nations Reports International Arbitral Awards XXVIII 263, page 269.

39 1958 Convention on Fishing and Conservation of the Living Resources of the High Seas Article 2, 559 UNTS 285.

40 R Rayfuse, 'International Fisheries and Sustainability: Dealing with Uncertainty' (2000) 14 *Ocean Yearbook* 114–137, 120.

41 R Baird, 'CCAMLR Initiatives to Counter Flag State Non-Enforcement in Southern Ocean Fisheries' (2005) *Victoria University Wellington Law Review* 733–756, 734.

of cooperation.[42] Article 119 of the Convention contains a series of provisions of both a substantive and a procedural character. Firstly, under Article 119.1 States must determine the total allowable catch (TAC), and establish conservation measures for high seas stock, relying in matters of substance on the best scientific evidence available to them. Under subparagraph (a), States must take measures on the basis of the best scientific evidence available to them to achieve certain substantive outcomes. The provision specifically refers to maximum sustainable yield, considering empirical information, such as existing fishing patterns, and stock interdependence. Subparagraph (b) contains a soft provision whereby States should 'take into account' the effects of fishing on associated or dependent non-target species so that they are not seriously threatened. Measures taken must not discriminate against the fishermen of any State, according to Article 119.3.

Takei has argued that these conservation and management duties fail to establish identifiable conservation and management parameters, with the exception of establishing a TAC.[43] Far from providing a suitable standard of conservation upon which States can rely to determine the TAC, the maximum sustainable yield provision established in Article 119.1(a) has proven an insufficiently sophisticated tool. It has failed to take into consideration the complex relationships that influence the dynamics of stock erosion and replenishment, and their intrinsic instability and relationship with their environment and other stocks.[44] Thus, the very nature of the maximum sustainable yield as presented in the LOSC appears to contradict the objectives of Article 119.1(b), whereby such interrelationships should be taken into account. As De Yturriaga has pointed out, the text of Article 119 leaves much to be desired in terms of certainty as to what measures State would have to adopt in accordance with the objectives of the provision.[45] Takei similarly considers that the subjective considerations set out in Article 119, whereby States may qualify conservation and management measures by economic and development factors, are insufficiently precise. They enable considerable discretion to prioritise immediate

---

42 T Henriksen, 'Revisiting the Freedom of Fishing and Legal Obligations on States Not Party to Regional Fisheries Management Organizations' (2009) 40(1) *Ocean Development & International Law* 80–96, 91.

43 Y Takei, 'Assessing Flag State Performance in Legal Terms: Clarifications of the Margin of Discretion' (2013) 28 *International Journal of Marine and Coastal Law* 97–133, 108.

44 Rayfuse (2000) at 122, supra at 40.

45 JA de Yturriaga, 'Fishing in the High Seas: From the 1982 UN Convention on the Law of the Sea to the 1995 Agreement on Straddling and Highly Migratory Fish Stocks' (1995) 3 *African Yearbook of International Law* 151–182, 153.

domestic interests over long-term conservation and management objectives.[46] Yet, although neither Article 117 nor 119 appear to shed light into what the duties of States are in ensuring optimum management, certain red lines do exist. The utilisation of science, the need to consider existing fishing activities and their impacts on stocks and tropic chains, and the requirement to act in accordance with existing standards, are clearly set out. Further, the need for conservation arguably draws a red line before extinction events.

According to Article 192 in Part XII of the LOSC, which concerns all ocean areas, States must protect the marine environment as a whole, including the preservation of marine living resources.[47] The duty, which predates the LOSC,[48] has been referred to as being a customary norm of international law.[49] This general obligation has been judicially interpreted to include a requirement on States to ensure that fishing vessels under their jurisdiction do not engage in IUU fishing.[50] What this interpretation, which was offered by ITLOS as part of an advisory opinion, means in practice is not entirely clear. The Tribunal referred to the obligation as implying the deployment of effort by States in establishing both prescriptive and enforcement measures with regard to conservation and management measures.[51] According to Tanaka, Article 192 possesses an 'ecosystems' dimension. This means that the prescriptive and enforcement actions of States need to ensure that the fishing activities do not undermine the ecosystem in which the fishery is located. Tanaka refers to those instances as 'environmentally harmful fishing', and recognises that IUU

46 See Takei (2013) at 99, supra at 43, in reference to JP Cot, 'The Law of the Sea and the Margin of Appreciation' in Ndiaye and Wolfrum (Eds) *Law of the Sea, Environmental Law and Settlement of disputes: Liber Amicorum Judge Thomas A Mensah* (Martinus Nijhoff, 2007) 396.

47 *Southern Bluefin Tuna Cases* (*New Zealand v Japan*) (*Australia v Japan*) Provisional Measures [1999] ITLOS Reports 280, para 70 [Bluefin Tuna]. Similarly, the PCA has referred to the general nature of Article 194.2. 194.5 and its application to depleted fisheries: see South China Sea at para 960. On a possible defence regarding lack of awareness, see para 963. See also SRFC at para 120.

48 Convention on the High Seas (1958) 450 UNTS 11. Convention on Fishing and Conservation of the Living Resources of the High Seas (1958) 559 UNTS 285.

49 JA Roach, 'Today's Customary International Law of the Sea' (2014) 45(3) Ocean Development & International Law 239–259, 250, citing Pulp Mills on the River Uruguay (Argentina v. Uruguay), Judgment, [2010] ICJ Rep. 14, 193. L Guruswamy, 'The Promise of the United Nations Convention on the Law of the Sea (UNCLOS): Justice in Trade and Environment Disputes' (1998) 25 *Ecology Law Quarterly* 189–228, 209. On the general character of the duty, see SRFC, paragraphs 111, 120, 124 and 216. See also Southern Bluefin Tuna, para 70.

50 SRFC, paras 96 and 124. South China Sea, paras 950–966, 956.

51 SRFC, paragraph 136–138.

fishing may in some cases pertain to this category. The degree to which the fishing activity is likely to be environmentally harmful is, according to Tanaka, to be determined by scientific parameters established by appropriately qualified experts.[52] In the context of vulnerable species and habitats, the degree of effort invested by States may need to be greater. Under LOSC Article 194.5 special care must be taken to protect and preserve rare or fragile ecosystems, and the habitats of depleted, threatened or endangered species. However, the precise measures whereby such effort must be applied are, again, not specified.

The conditional freedom established under the Convention has been delimited by subsequent agreements, which have influenced the manner in which States approach the conservation and management of high seas stocks. According to Oral, the systemic interpretation of these and other environmental protection agreements may further serve to strengthen the LOSC, particularly in providing additional substance to the general duty to protect the marine environment established in Article 192. This duty has the potential of being informed by other agreements to which a State may also be a party.[53] Similarly, Article 194(5) concerning the protection of fragile ecosystems, was also referred to in the award. In particular, egregious acts of destruction *of which the flag State had knowledge* but refused to address through the elaboration of laws and regulations and their enforcement, could be considered breaches of these obligations.[54] It is noteworthy that the need to compile data emerges under the award as also essential for flag States to be able to meet their conservation and management obligations. In addition, in paragraph 956 of the award, the tribunal clarifies the role that specific treaty provisions can have in the clarification of obligations. In its discussion concerning the meaning and reach of the general obligation contained in LOSC Article 192, the tribunal mentions another treaty, the Convention on International Trade in Endangered Species (CITES).[55] This treaty contains important provisions for the identification of at-risk species, which the tribunal considered important in clarifying the substance of the mentioned LOSC obligation.

---

52 Y Tanaka, 'Reflections on the Implications of Environmental Norms for Fishing: The Link between the Regulation of Fishing and the Protection of Marine Biological Diversity' (2020) 22 International Community Law Review 389–409, 398 & 400.

53 See N Oral, 'The south China Sea Arbitral Award: A Triumph for Part XII of UNCLOS and the Protection and Preservation of the Marine Environment' in Jayakumar, Koh, Beckman, Davenport and Phan (Eds) *The South China Sea Arbitration: The Legal Dimension* (Elgar, 2018) 223.

54 *Ibid.*

55 Convention on International Trade in Endangered Species of Wild Fauna and Flora (1973) 993 UNTS 243 [CITES].

2.3.2 *The UNFSA*

Over a decade after the LOSC, another treaty came to be adopted under the auspices of the FAO: the 1995 UN Fish Stocks Agreement. As the title and preamble of this important fisheries instrument explicitly state, the scope of the treaty concerns exclusively straddling and highly migratory stock. Despite specifically referring to the conservation and management of such stock, the UNFSA establishes an extensive and detailed legal framework that transcends issues of stock conservation and management, and includes important normative principles, as well as an innovative cooperative framework for the conduct of fishing activities in respect of the mentioned stocks.

The UNFSA supports a cooperation framework for straddling and highly migratory fisheries that seeks to transcend the zonal jurisdictional partitions of the LOSC, and harmonise conservation and management provisions across the high seas and the EEZs of coastal States.[56] Through the UNFSA regime, States can operationalize the regulation of target and non-target stock following a regional approach that has better compatibility with the transnational habitats and migratory patterns of the target stocks.[57] The UNFSA fosters a level of coordination that is absent from the LOSC,[58] consolidating the roles of RFMOs and their competences as central to transnational fishery management.[59] Under the UNFSA, RFMOs are indispensable fora for the cooperative conservation and management of straddling and highly migratory fish stocks.[60] This 'institutional' approach to decision-making is, without doubt, an important development.[61]

The overriding objective of the UNFSA is set out in its Article 2, whereby the agreement states the aim to ensure a long-term approach to conservation, and

---

56 DA Balton, 'Strengthening the Law of the Sea: The New Agreement on Straddling Fish Stocks and Highly Migratory Fish Stocks' (1996) 27 *Ocean Development & International Law* 125–151, 138.

57 See D Freestone and Z Makuch, 'The New International Environmental Law of Fisheries: the 1995 United Nations Straddling Stocks Agreement' (1997) 7(1) *Yearbook of International Environmental Law* 3–51, 20.

58 P Orebech, K Sigurjonsson, TL McDorman, 'The 1995 United Nations Straddling and Highly Migratory Fish Stocks Agreement: Management, Enforcement and Dispute Settlement' (1998) 13(2) *International Journal of Marine and Coastal Law* 119–142, 120.

59 M Ceo et al, 'Performance Reviews by Regional Fishery Bodies: Introduction, Summaries, Synthesis and Best Practices' (2012) FAO Fisheries and Aquaculture Circular No 1071, 1 [Accessed on 20 March 2021 via www.fao.org/docrep/015/i2637e/i2637e00.htm].

60 See OECD, Fishing for Development, Background Paper for Session 5: The Role of Regional Fisheries Management Organisations (2014) TAD/FI(2014)11, 4.

61 GR Munro, 'The United Nations Fish Stocks Agreement of 1995: History and Problems of Implementation' (2001) 15 *Marine Resource Economics* 265–280, 266.

highlights the need for the 'sustainable management' of straddling and highly migratory stock, a term which is not defined in the LOSC. This was addressed by ITLOS in its SRFC advisory opinion, by reference to how the LOSC might be developed.[62] ITLOS understood sustainable management to mean to conserve and develop the straddling and highly migratory stocks.[63] By development the ITLOS meant as follows:

> (...) that these stocks should be used as fishery resources within the framework of a sustainable fisheries management regime. This may include the exploitation of non-exploited stocks or an increase in the exploitation of under-exploited stocks through the development of responsible fisheries, as well as more effective fisheries management schemes to ensure the long-term sustainability of exploited stocks. This may also include stock restoration, guided by the requirement under article 61 of the Convention that a given stock is not endangered by over-exploitation, thus preserving it as a long-term viable resource.

It should be noted that the Tribunal made no explicit reference to the UNFSA in its elaboration of the term sustainable management, despite language parallelisms. The use of innovative language in the UNFSA when contrasted to the LOSC is consistent with the trend that characterised the early 1990s, which was dominated by the United Nations Conference on Environment and Development (UNCED),[64] and the proliferation of innovative multilateral approaches to the most pressing environmental problems perceived at the time, of which the UNFSA was a part.[65] The progressive ethos of this period resulted in the UNFSA embracing concepts and principles of the era.[66] The general principles are established in Article 5 on the UNFSA, and take into consideration the social and biological dimensions of the fishery, incorporating the principles of precaution, and the ecosystems approach. Article 6 expands on the parameters whereby a precautionary approach is to be applied to stock management, with detailed guidelines for the application of precautionary

62 SRFC, paras 202 to 204.
63 SRFC, para 190.
64 See The Rio Declaration on Environment and Development (1992) A/CONF.151/26.
65 D Freestone, 'Modern Principles of High Seas Governance: The Legal Underpinnings' (2009) 39(1) *International Environmental Policy and Law* 44–49, 48.
66 EJ Molenaar, 'Participation, Allocation and Unregulated Fishing: The Practice of Regional Fisheries Management Organisations' (2003)18(4) *International Journal of Marine and Coastal Law* 457–480, 458.

reference points. The UNFSA in addition has established a reference point system in its Annex II and, although it has been indicated that the diversity in availability of reference points in any one fishery may generate selection difficulties in practice, the approach is nevertheless considered to be a substantial improvement over the MSY approach to conservation and management established LOSC.[67] In addition, several provisions of Article 5 of the treaty reflect important procedural duties that were also consolidated during the UNCED process, particularly the duty to impact assessment, outlining State duties of data collection and appropriate monitoring of the fishing activity.

Article 7 of the UNFSA is important for fleshing out LOSC provisions in respect of the management of straddling and highly migratory species, and achieving compatibility between stock conservation and management in the high seas and in/across the EEZs of coastal States.[68] Article 7.1 of the UNFSA establishes provisions to ensure the compatibility of said conservation and management measures. According to subparagraphs (a) and (b), coastal States and the flag States whose nationals operate in adjacent waters to the relevant EEZs shall seek mechanisms of cooperation. Article 7.2 indicates that conservation and management measures agreed upon by States must take into account *previously agreed measures* established for the relevant stock in both the high seas and the EEZ, including conservation and management measures taken by RFMOs. As noted by Hayashi, the importance of this article lies in the fact that it elaborates upon the cooperation principle established by the LOSC with regard to the conservation and management of straddling and highly migratory species, for which the Convention does not establish clear parameters in Articles 63 and 64.[69] In general, the compatibility measures established in the UNFSA have been well received by scholars, and have been considered adequate to ensure a coherent approach to conservation across flag and coastal States.[70]

---

67 L Juda, 'The 1995 United Nations Agreement on Straddling Fish Stocks and Highly Migratory Fish Stocks: A Critique' (1997) 28(2) *Ocean Development and International Law* 147–166, 153.

68 AE Boyle, 'Problems of Compulsory Jurisdiction and the Settlement of Disputes Relating to Straddling Fish Stocks' (1999) 14(1) *International Journal of Marine and Coastal Law* 14–25, 20.

69 M Hayashi, 'The 1995 Agreement on the Conservation and Management of Straddling and Highly Migratory Fish Stocks: Significance for the Law of the Sea Convention' (1996) 29(1–3) *Ocean and Coastal Management* 51–69, 57.

70 See MW Lodge, and SN Nandan, 'Some Suggestions towards Better Implementation of the United Nations Agreement on Straddling Fish Stocks and Highly Migratory Fish Stocks of 1995 (2005) 20(3) *International Journal of Marine and Coastal Law* 345–379, 350. DM

2.3.3 *Effectiveness Limitations*

As discrete high seas and the specially vulnerable deep sea species generally remain outside the spectrum of the UNFSA, the high seas and general conservation provisions of the LOSC remain the residual legal fabric of application to those species.[71] This is problematic, given the comparative lack of specificity in the relevant obligations the LOSC.[72] The consolidation of RFMOs under the UNFSA framework has not served to eliminate such voids: with the exception of the RFMOs concerned with the regulation of tuna,[73] the high seas coverage area of the remaining RFMOs is uneven substantively as well as geographically, with significant integration shortfalls.[74] Hence, the regulatory landscape developed under the UNFSA has established a regime that represents advancement upon the LOSC in many respects, but the system it has created is ultimately incomplete.[75] Finally, the Fish Stocks Agreement is of course only applicable to States that have consented to be bound by it. This is a consequence of the operation of the *pacta tertiis* principle, as previously discussed. The UNFSA does not enjoy the same level of ratifications as the LOSC, with globally significant fishing flag States not having yet ratified the agreement.

2.4 Flag State Control over Fishing Vessels' High Seas Activities

As already explained, the flag State has primary jurisdiction over vessels in the high seas, which it is obliged to maintain in accordance with LOSC Articles 91, 92, and 94. In this context, it should be recalled that IUU fishing activities

---

Sodik, 'Post-LOSC Legal Instruments and Measures to Address IUU Fishing' (2009) 15 *Asian Yearbook of International Law* 71–124, 93.

71 M Hayashi, 'Global Governance of Deep-Sea Fisheries' (2004) 19(3) International Journal of Marine and Coastal Law 289–299, 295.

72 D Freestone, 'International Governance, Responsibility and Management of Areas Beyond National Jurisdiction' (2012) 27 *International Journal of Marine and Coastal Law* 191–204, 195.

73 YH Song, 'The Efforts of ICCAT to Combat IUU Fishing: The Roles of Japan and Taiwan in C Conserving and Managing Tuna Resources' (2009) 24(1) *International Journal of Marine and Coastal Law* 101–140, 115.

74 R Rayfuse and R Warner, 'Securing a Sustainable Future for the Oceans Beyond National Jurisdiction: The Legal Basis for an Integrated Cross-Sectoral Regime for High Seas Governance for the 21st Century' (2008) *International Journal of Marine and Coastal Law* 399–422, 402.

75 K Gjerde, 'High Seas Fisheries Governance: Prospects and Challenges in the 21st Century' in Vidas and Schei (Eds) *The World Ocean in Globalisation: Challenges and Responses* (Martinus Nijhoff, 2011) 221.

can typically unfold by taking advantage of inadequate domestic regulation parameters that are established by flag States, and that present certain common features. These include flawed processes of vessel registration, weak laws regarding authorisation, monitoring and control, inadequate enforcement, and weak or nonexistent sanctions. This section surveys the provisions of the LOSC and subsequent global fisheries treaties, setting out the manner in which they have covered these shortcomings, so as to fully explore the effectiveness of the relevant treaty provisions.

2.4.1 *The LOSC*

Jurisdiction over fishing vessels in the high seas has been previously discussed, but has not been contextualised into the broader freedom regime established by the LOSC for high seas activities. Under Article 87.1(e) and 117, flag States have the right to provide for their nationals' access to high seas living resources, subject to the conservation provisions of the LOSC, and any others assumed under a treaty by the State. In addition, under Article 94.1 of the Convention, flag States must exercise their jurisdiction and control in administrative, technical and social matters over ships flying their flag. Article 94.2 establishes a duty to ensure that flag States have administrative control over vessels operating in the high seas. The provision states:

> 2. In particular every State shall:
>
> (a) maintain a register of ships containing the names and particulars of ships flying its flag, except those which are excluded from generally accepted international regulations on account of their small size; and
> (b) assume jurisdiction under its internal law over each ship flying its flag and its master, officers and crew in respect of administrative, technical and social matters concerning the ship.

Judicial interpretation by ITLOS in its SRFC advisory opinion has clarified that the list of flag State obligations is not exhaustive, and may be understood in some contexts at least to imply a duty to ensure that the vessels are prevented from engaging in IUU fishing.[76] The act of vessel registration and recording of the vessel name and particulars is explicitly referred to in LOSC Article 94.2(a). Nevertheless, the precise standards that may be expected from flag States

76 SRFC, paras 116 to 119. SRFC, Separate Opinion of Judge Paik, paras 6 to 10, and para 16.

concerning fishing vessel registration are not specified, and thus the provision does little to ensure that registration procedures facilitate vessel identification. It is also the case that, as explained in the previous chapter, IUU fishing vessels can hide or change their names with ease, and the absence of more specific standards for fishing activity supervision under Article 94 LOSC, despite their expansive interpretation by ITLOS, means that the provision remains weak.[77] The South China Sea award has highlighted the importance as well as the difficulty of ascertaining the specific standards that may be expected of a flag State when it comes to supervising fishing vessels.[78] The arbitral tribunal stated as follows (emphasis added):

> In many cases, the precise scope and application of the obligation on a flag State to exercise due diligence in respect of fishing by vessels flying its flag (…) may be difficult to determine. *Often, unlawful fishing will be carried out covertly, far from any official presence, and it will be far from obvious what the flag State could realistically have done to prevent it.*[79]

As previously mentioned, a key step for establishing a breach of a LOSC obligation in matters of fishery conservation implies the need for the specific vessel activity to have been identified and documented. However, the manner in which such identification is to take place is unclear. As Ventura points out, the jurisdiction of the flag State over vessels entitled to fly its flag in the high seas is supervisory in nature.[80] Enforcement of conservation duties under the LOSC has been interpreted by the ITLOS in its SRFC advisory opinion as being part of the scope of jurisdiction over the vessel covered by Article 94, with Article 94.6 specifically referring to the issue of enforcement.[81] Enforcement mechanisms include investigation and the imposition of sanctions of sufficient severity to deprive perpetrators of their illicit gains.[82] These are intrinsic to the duties of the flag State under Article 94. Nevertheless, there is also broad discretion by

---

77 With the exception of vessel registration, which is a previous regulatory stage to the supervision of fishing operations. See V Ventura, 'Tackling Illegal, Unregulated and Unreported Fishing: The ITLOS Advisory Opinion on Flag State Responsibility for IUU Fishing and the Principle of Due Diligence' (2015) 12(1) *Brazilian Journal of International Law* 50–67, 14 and 15.

78 South China Sea, paras 972 and 974.

79 South China Sea, para 754.

80 Ventura (2015) at 57, supra at 77.

81 SRFC, paras 137 to 139.

82 SRFC, para 140.

the flag State in how to define those standards.[83] This results in a grey area of discretion in the regime of flag State due diligence for the purposes of carrying out appropriate oversight over the activities of fishing vessels in the high seas. This grey area has been addressed by subsequent international agreements, as will be discussed in the next section.

Oversight over vessels without a flag is a particularly difficult issue under the LOSC. As previously discussed, some IUU fishing vessels purport to operate without a flag, or are temporarily flagless between registrations.[84] Cases of technical statelessness may also occur, as vessels are considered to have lost their nationality when they are operating simultaneously under two or more flags.[85] Problematically, vessels without nationality, although referred to in Articles 92(1) and 92(2) of the LOSC, are not clearly dealt with by the Convention. Given that the flag State jurisdiction principle governs high seas activities, and that LOSC Article 116 indicates that it is States that have the right for their nationals to fish the high seas, authentically stateless vessels may be lacking a link to such right.[86] Such vessels may be subject to the jurisdiction of any State.[87] Article 110.1(d) of the Convention establishes a right of visit, so that the vessel may be inspected and, if found to be in breach of the obligations established for the vessels of the inspecting States, may be assimilated to its jurisdiction. This means that, in the event that the vessel was found engaging in unauthorised fishing, this could be addressed under the domestic law of the enforcing State, once the vessel has been assimilated to its domestic jurisdiction.[88] However, a legal link may also be determined via the nationality of the persons responsible for the operations of the vessel.[89] This is supported by the reference to nationals in LOSC Article 116 if it is understood as persons, as the provision does not differentiate between the nationality of ships or persons.[90]

83 SRFC, para 138.

84 TL McDorman, 'Stateless Fishing Vessels, International Law and the UN High Seas Fisheries Conference' (1994) 25(4) *Journal of Maritime Law and Commerce* 531–558, 531 and 533–34.

85 LOSC Article 92(2). The provision was also contained in the 1958 High Seas Convention, Article 6(2).

86 See DM Warner-Kramer, and K Canty, 'Stateless Fishing Vessels: the Current International Regime and New Approach' (2000) 5(2) *Ocean and Coastal Law Journal* 227–244, 230.

87 EM Kornblau, 'United States v. Marino-Garcia: Criminal Jurisdiction over Stateless Vessels on the High Seas' (1983) 9(1) *Brooklyn Journal of International Law* 141–156, 149.

88 RE Fife, 'Elements of Nordic Practice 2006: Norwegian Measures Taken against Stateless Vessel Conducting Unauthorized Fishing on the High Seas' (2007) 76(2–3) *Nordic Journal of International Law* 301–304, 302.

89 D O'Connell, *The International Law of the Sea* (Oxford University Press, 1984) 757.

90 LOSC Article 116.

This suggests that access to high seas resources depends on the existence of a jurisdictional link, whereby it is possible to establish an applicable law, but not necessarily on the presence of a flag.[91] The functionality of ex-post enforcement approaches aimed at persons in respect of irregular fishing operations has been illustrated by recent State practice.[92] Despite the powers assigned to States under the LOSC for the exercise of jurisdiction in these circumstances, no due diligence obligations are established by the Convention in respect of vessels that become stateless and continue operating without nationality. According to the provisions of Article 91 of the LOSC, flying the flag of a State is considered a right, rather than a duty. Logically, States are obligated to establish the conditions whereby they are prepared to grant that right, and to facilitate the documentary evidence that may be necessary to prove it. Once granted, the maintenance of such right is governed by the provisions of Articles 92 in respect of the exercise of exclusive jurisdiction, and Article 94 in respect of State oversight of fishing activities in the high seas.

2.4.2 *The Compliance Agreement*

The void left by the LOSC concerning oversight over fishing vessels in the high seas was acknowledged as part of the UNCED Agenda 21 work stream, in the context of which States were exhorted to prioritise policies of improved regulation of high seas fisheries. These included a number of aspects of flag State supervision, namely vessel registration processes to address re-flagging,[93] as well as other types of vessel activity management and control.[94] The first of the fisheries treaties to emanate from the momentum created by Agenda 21 was the 1993 Agreement to Promote Compliance with International Conservation and Management Measures by Fishing Vessels on the High Seas (the Compliance

91 McDorman reaches this conclusion without reference to Article 116. See McDorman (1994) at 538, supra at 84.

92 See in particular *United States of America v Bengis* (2013) WL 2922292 [accessed on 1 March 2018 via http://law.justia.com/cases/federal/appellate-courts/ca2/13-2543/13-2543-2015-04-16.html]. The case involved criminal fines to American nationals by a US court of circa US$ 22.5 Million, in restitution to South Africa for the harvesting of seafood in contravention of domestic South African laws, and subsequent illicit importation of the product into the US. See also for a recent Spanish case in which operators were fined in excess of Euro 17 Million in respect of IUU fishing activities in the Southern Ocean MAGRAMA, *Expediente Sancionador* 1/2015/SGP, [accessed on 20 March 2021 via http://www.magrama.gob.es/es/prensa/160317resolucionexpedienteoperacionsparrow_tcm7-415228_noticia.pdf].

93 Agenda 21: Programme of Action for Sustainable Development (1992) Chapter 17, paragraphs 17.45 and 17.52, A/Conf.151/26 [Agenda 21].

94 Agenda 21, Chapter 17, paragraphs 17.51, 17.46(d) and 17.86(c).

Agreement).[95] This agreement specifically sought to strengthen flag State obligations of vessel control in the high seas.[96] Its Preamble sets out the specific objective of addressing 'the failure of flag States to fulfil their responsibilities with respect to fishing vessels entitled to fly their flag'.[97] Despite the re-flagging issues that have historically characterised many cases of IUU fishing, it is important to point out that the operation of open registries is not forbidden by the treaty.[98] Instead, the aim of the Compliance Agreement is to strengthen the jurisdiction of the flag State through the further specification of its responsibilities.[99] The flag of convenience approach to vessel regulation is, despite known weaknesses, strongly endorsed by contemporary State practice.[100] Arguably, the operation of open registries is a permanent feature in the context of international State practice. As Sodik says, the emphasis of the Compliance Agreement is placed on the need for all States to operate open vessel registries *responsibly*.[101]

The Compliance Agreement has had the effect of adding definition to the administrative jurisdiction and national control provisions of LOSC Articles 94.2 and 117. Article III.1(a) establishes an obligation on flag States to ensure that fishing vessels do not engage in activities that undermine international conservation and management measures. This provision might be acknowledged as a prelude to paragraph 3.3 of the IPOA IUU, whereby activities that undermine the conservation and management measures of RFMOs are categorised as *unregulated fishing*. Hence, as a conservation provision, Article III.1(a) lacks teeth of its own, in the absence of well-defined and binding conservation and management measures. Beyond this provision, the thrust of the Compliance Agreement gravitates around the establishment of procedures for the registration of fishing vessels, and particularly for linking registration with the authorisation of fishing operations, the establishment of regulatory duties alongside the granting of authorisation, and information-recording with regard to both the registration and the authorisation of fishing vessels.

---

95 Agreement to Promote Compliance with International Conservation and Management Measures by Fishing Vessels on the High Seas, (1993) 2221 UNTS 91 [Compliance Agreement].

96 Compliance Agreement Preamble, and Articles II to IV.

97 Compliance Agreement, Preamble, paragraph 9.

98 This is implied in the Preamble of the Compliance Agreement.

99 Compliance Agreement, Preamble, paragraph 10.

100 For practice in the EU, see Case C-221/89 *Factortame and Others* [1991] ECR 1991 I-03905; Case C-62/96 *Commission v. Hellenic Republic* [1997] ECR 1-6725 133; Case C-47/02 *Anker and Others v Germany* [2003] ECR-I 10447.

101 Sodik (2009) at 81, supra at 73.

With regard to registration, in a clear attempt to address abusive vessel reflagging, Article III.7 of the Compliance Agreement requires flag States to compile and record relevant fishing vessel information for the act of registration. Article IV requires flag States to give effect to the assignation of the link to the domestic jurisdiction of the flag State to the vessel upon registration.[102] Swan has interpreted this provision as a reinforcement of the genuine link,[103] which had been diluted, as discussed previously. Further, under Article III.2 of the Compliance Agreement, no State party is to allow fishing vessels entitled to fly their flag to operate in the high seas without authorisation. Article III also requires diligence by the flag State prior to the granting of authorisation, which it should refuse if the vessel has a history of infractions or outstanding sanctions. It also establishes the need for flag States to condition to the continuity of the registration any fishing authorisation that they grant, so that the registration and the right to fish are extinguished together. As Balton has indicated, this has the effect of linking both processes, reinforcing the jurisdiction of the flag State over fishing activities.[104] The article also requires flag States to take enforcement action in case of infraction, including the imposition of sanctions of sufficient severity to ensure that perpetrators do not benefit from their wrongdoing.

2.4.3 *The UNFSA*

In respect of procedures of vessel registration and authorisation, the UNFSA adds clarity to the provisions of the Compliance Agreement. It clarifies the rationale for the need for authorisation and licensing, establishing in Article 5(h) that States must take measures to prevent or eliminate overfishing, and to ensure that fishing activity does not exceed the limits of the fishery with regard to its sustainability. The need for the individual authorisation measures established for fishing vessels to reflect the rules and measures of RFMOs is established in UNFSA 18.1, and to be mindful of its own implementation capacity in UNFSA 18.2. UNFSA Article 18.3(b)ii requires flag States to prohibit high seas fishing by vessels that are not authorised or licensed, or that operate outside the limits of such licence or authorisation, thus making the authorisation provisions under Article III.2 of the Compliance Agreement watertight. Specific reference to fishing licences, authorisation and permits and their

102 Compliance Agreement Article VI.

103 J Swan, 'Fishing Vessels Operating under Open Registers and the Exercise of Flag State Responsibilities: Information and Options' (2002) *FAO Fisheries Circular No 980* 11.

104 DA Balton, 'The Compliance Agreement' in Hey (Ed) *Developments in International Fisheries Law* (Kluwer, 1999) 50.

conditions in the exercise of fishing vessel control is made in UNFSA Article 18.3. Lastly, flag States are to include transhipment in their authorisation and licensing regime is established in UNFSA 18.3(h). Despite the instrumental role of transhipment in IUU fishing activities, the Compliance Agreement did not include it in its remit of application: albeit in respect of highly migratory and straddling stock only, this omission is now addressed by this and other provisions of the UNFSA.[105]

The UNFSA also contains a number of specific obligations whereby States must ensure that fishing vessels operate under reporting duties. Article 14.1 of the UNFSA establishes a duty to ensure that fishing vessels report the fishing catch data required to to facilitate stock assessment, that it is submitted in a timely manner, and that it is subject to verification. Article 14.2 establishes an obligation to agree upon the specification and format of the data and related analytical approaches to stock assessment, either directly, or through RFMOs where relevant. Related obligations are also referred to in Article 18.3(e) to record and report fishery data in respect of target and non-target species, and fishing effort. Under Article 18.3(f) this is to be complemented with verification of fishing and fishery support operations data, including transhipment, such as reports by inspectors, observers, and loading or unloading reports. Monitoring, control and surveillance of vessels and their fishing activities incorporate traditional monitoring methods, such as inspections schemes, and national and international observer programmes, and the development and implementation of electronic VMS systems, including as appropriate automated information systems via satellite (AIS).[106]

The UNFSA also develops the granularity of obligations under the LOSC in certain matters involving compliance and enforcement. UNFSA Article 19.1 indicates that States must ensure compliance by vessels flying their flag with the conservation and management measures of RFMOs, and must investigate violations, and where appropriate subject the vessels to physical investigation. Where violations of applicable RFMO conservation and management measures are ascertained, it must enforce the appropriate measures irrespective of where the violations occurred, and must inform the competent RFMO of the outcome of the investigation. The UNFSA further specifies what constitutes the legal basis for an infraction. Whilst not referring openly to IUU fishing, Article 20 of the agreement covers enforcement operations for the purposes of identifying and investigating the activities of what the UNFSA calls 'unauthorised'

105 See also UNFSA Article 18(f), Article 23(3), and Article 6 of Annex I.

106 UNFSA Article 18.3(g).

fishing vessels.[107] The nature of such activities is clarified in Article 21.11 of the UNFSA, which sets out for the first time a typology of conducts to which it refers as 'serious violations'.

Article 21.11 covers a significant proportion of the IUU practices, and in effect has the effect of providing substantive content to the IUU fishing interpretive lens for the purposes of domestic regulation by State parties to the UNFSA. The following conducts are specified in the article:

(a) fishing without a valid licence, authorization or permit issued by the flag State in accordance with article 18, paragraph 3 (a);
(b) failing to maintain accurate records of catch and catch-related data, as required by the relevant subregional or regional fisheries management organization or arrangement, or serious misreporting of catch, contrary to the catch reporting requirements of such organization or arrangement;
(c) fishing in a closed area, fishing during a closed season or fishing without, or after attainment of, a quota established by the relevant subregional or regional fisheries management organization or arrangement;
(d) directed fishing for a stock which is subject to a moratorium or for which fishing is prohibited;
(e) using prohibited fishing gear;
(f) falsifying or concealing the markings, identity or registration of a fishing vessel;
(g) concealing, tampering with or disposing of evidence relating to an investigation;
(h) multiple violations which together constitute a serious disregard of conservation and management measures; or
(i) such other violations as may be specified in procedures established by the relevant subregional or regional fisheries management organization or arrangement.

The position of Article 21 in Part VI of the UNFSA, and its title of 'subregional and regional cooperation in enforcement' is evidence of the intended role of these provisions in enabling RFMO clarification and coordination for enforcement purposes. Thus, the list performs a catalyst function for State prescription and enforcement, aiming to harmonise responses across States participating

107 UNFSA Article 20(4) and 20(6).

in the different RFMO frameworks.[108] However, a *modus operandi* frequently linked to IUU fishing, unauthorised transhipment, is omitted from the scope of article 21.11: Unauthorised transhipment, which has been amply documented as a frequent activity in IUU fishing operations, and should have merited inclusion in this provision.[109]

The UNFSA also directly covers sanctions in a much greater degree of detail than the Compliance Agreement: UNFSA Article 19.1 develops the contents of Article III.8 of the Compliance Agreement, albeit within the remit of the UNFSA, which is limited to highly migratory and straddling stock. Of particular importance is the provision in 19.1(c), which requires the flag State to ensure that reporting duties exist so that the vessel gives information to investigating authorities regarding vessel position, catches, fishing gear, fishing operations, and related activities in the area where the alleged violation took place. The article further establishes a duty of flag State compliance with RFMO measures, which includes obligations of enforcement in any ocean area, prompt and comprehensive investigation, commencement of proceedings, and a prohibition to operate in the high seas until outstanding sanctions have been met. UNFSA 19.2 indicates that where sufficient evidence is available, the case must be referred to the appropriate authorities in order to institute proceedings. Similarly to the Compliance Agreement, sanctions are required to be adequate in severity in order to ensure compliance and discourage further violations, depriving offenders of the benefits accruing from their infractions.

The standard requirements that States must take into account in adopting domestic laws and regulations whereby vessels must record and report fishery data are set out in considerable details in Annex I of the agreement. Article 1 of the Annex indicates:

> The timely collection, compilation and analysis of data are fundamental to the effective conservation and management of straddling fish stocks and highly migratory fish stocks. To this end, data from fisheries for these

108 See M George, 'Fisheries Protections in the Context of the Geo-Political Tensions in the South China Sea' (2012) 43(1) *Journal of Maritime Law and Commerce* 85–128, 112, in respect of implementation across regional organisations.

109 Transhipment would later be referenced in another treaty, the 2009 Port State Measures Agreement, and is a focal point of other legislation, such as European Union (2008), Council Regulation (EC) No. 1005/2008 of 29 September 2008 establishing a Community system to prevent, deter and eliminate illegal, unreported and unregulated fishing, amending Regulations (EEC) No 2847/93, (EC) No 1936/2001 and (EC) No 601/2004 and repealing Regulations (EC) No 1093/94 and (EC) No 1447/1999, Official Journal of the European Union, L 286/1, Article 3.

> stocks on the high seas and those in areas under national jurisdiction are required and should be collected and complied in such a way as to enable statistically meaningful analysis for the purpose of fishery resource conservation and management. These data include catch and fishing effort statistics and other fishery-related information, such as vessel-related and other data for standardizing fishing effort. Data collected should also include information on non-target and associated or dependent species. All data should be verified to ensure accuracy.

Article 3 of Annex I establishes a duty to compile basic fishery data, which includes information on catch and effort by fishery and fleet, total catch by species, discard statistics, effort statistics, and fishing location, date, and time. These are to be collected in accordance with agreed procedures. Article 4.2 requires flag States to collect navigation and position fixing aids, and communication equipment and international radio call sign. The duty to record crew size, whilst not directly relevant to IUU fishing as a fishery management paradigm, is nevertheless important in respect of crew control mechanisms that may be required to prevent the opportunistic labour infractions and people trafficking crimes that sometimes accompany fishing activity.[110] The State is to verify the data provided by the vessel operator in accordance with Article 6 of the annex, via VMS, in respect of vessel position verification, observer programmes, vessel trip, landing and transhipment reports, and port sampling. The list in the article is cumulative, meaning all those elements are required.

Thus, the UNFSA introduces a considerable level of definition to the vessel control provisions of the LOSC, also covering much wider operational parameters than the Compliance Agreement, to which is also adds specificity with regard to the authorisation and licensing of vessels.

2.4.4 *Effectiveness Limitations*

Although LOSC Article 94.2(a) establishes a duty of vessel registration and recording of the vessel name and particulars, there is otherwise a lack of specificity that has resulted in lax and variable practices of vessel control across flag States. Article 117.2 makes clear that in the high seas the jurisdiction of the flag State is supervisory in nature, but there is little in the LOSC to clarify what those supervision parameters may be. Broad discretion is enabled by the Convention in respect of the regulation of vessels and their operations.

110 See DeConing E, 'Fisheries Crime' in Elliott and Schaedla (Eds) *Handbook of Transnational Environmental Crime* (Elgar, 2016) 158.

Despite its important contributions, the Compliance Agreement has limitations. The agreement lacks reach when it comes to the type of vessel in its remit. It defines 'fishing vessel' so as to specifically target fishing vessels of 24 metres or more, and does not include vessels engaged in the transhipment of fish.[111] A related problem of the Compliance Agreement is the broad autonomy it grants to State parties in taking some important decisions. For example, in respect of flag State regulatory obligations concerning fishing vessel marking,[112] requirements are to be adopted by reference to international standards, but the flag State has autonomy in respect of smaller vessels.[113] Similarly, in Article III.3, the Compliance Agreement encourages the flag State to consider whether it is able to exercise jurisdiction effectively over a vessel prior to granting it the benefit and protection of its register. This provision, however, is hortatory in tone, leaving the ultimately decision to the flag State alone. Lastly, the Compliance Agreement does not possess a high number of State parties.[114] As already explained, the operation of the *pacta tertiis* principle means the agreement cannot bind any States that have not explicitly agreed to be bound by it.

The UNFSA adds further scope and clarity to the provisions of the Compliance Agreement, complementing it in some important respects, particularly in respect of the prohibition of high seas operations without authorisation and the regulation of transhipment, albeit only in respect of straddling and highly migratory stocks. The UNFSA contains an important provision to substantiate the IUU fishing paradigm with a list of actual activities that States are required to treat as serious infractions. However, this list does not include transhipment. The main failure of the UNFSA in this context is that its critically important obligations on the flag State to establish regulations of licensing, data recording, disclosure and submission to verification obligations and to surveillance, do not extend beyond straddling and highly migratory stock.

111 F Orrego Vicuña, *The Changing International Law of High Seas Fisheries* (Cambridge University Press, 1999) 133.

112 Compliance Agreement Article III.6.

113 Compliance Agreement Articles I(a) and II(b). The agreement's definition of fishing vessels includes only directly engaged in fishing operations, casting doubt as to whether transhipment to and from reefers would be covered by the definition. Further, flag States may exempt vessels of less than 24 meters from its application in some circumstances.

114 State parties are 42 at the time of writing. See 2221 UNTS 91 registration page [accessed on 20 March 2021 via https://treaties.un.org/pages/showDetails.aspx?objid=080000028007be1a].

2.5 The Duty to Cooperate

The duty to cooperate is dynamic in nature, meaning that it transcends simple due regard to existing rights and duties,[115] implying in addition a duty of effort to engage in consultation with a view to reaching agreement.[116] It is a general obligation that, being essentially procedural, requires a context in order to acquire substance and specificity.[117] In the context of internationally shared fisheries, Burke suggests that the duty implies a requirement of taking joint decisions by reference to available science and other relevant data, in order to adopt appropriate regulatory measures.[118] The manner in which the LOSC, the Compliance Agreement and the UNFSA deal with the duty to cooperate is explained in the following paragraphs.

2.5.1 *The LOSC*

Part XII of the LOSC, which deals with matters of marine environment protection in all ocean areas, refers to the duty to cooperate in its broad, procedural sense of working towards regulation in common. Article 197 of the LOSC, which unlike many of the provisions contained in Section XII, is not specifically drafted to be applied in the context of marine pollution, indicates as follows:

> States shall cooperate on a global basis and, as appropriate, on a regional basis, directly or through competent international organizations, in formulating and elaborating international rules, standards and recommended practices and procedures consistent with this Convention, for the protection and preservation of the marine environment, taking into account characteristic regional features.

---

115 J Harrison, 'Safeguards Against Excessive Enforcement Measures in the Exclusive Economic Zone – Law and Practice' in Ringbom (Ed) *Jurisdiction over Ships: Post UNCLOs Developments in the Law of the Sea* (Martinus Nijhoff, 2015) 217.

116 SRFC, para 212 and 216. The Tribunal similarly highlighted the obligations of due regard that States have inter-se under LOSC Articles 56.2 and 58.3.

117 Y Tanaka, 'The South China Sea Arbitration: Environmental Obligations Under the Law of the Sea Convention' (2018) *Review of European, Comparative & International Environmental Law* 1–7, 6.

118 WT Burke, *The New International Law of Fisheries: UNCLOS 1982 and Beyond* (Clarendon Press, 1994) 99. See also *Fisheries Jurisdiction Case (United Kingdom of Great Britain and Northern Ireland v. Iceland)* Judgment [1974] I.C.J. Reports 3, para 72. *Fisheries Jurisdiction Case (Federal Republic of Germany v. Iceland)* Judgment [1974] I.C.J. Reports 175, para 200.

In the high seas, where no claims of sovereignty may be made,[119] effective flag State cooperation is essential for successful management of internationally shared stocks. A corresponding duty of cooperation is established in LOSC Article 118, whereby States whose nationals exploit the same fisheries, or different stocks in the same areas, are obliged to enter negotiations, with a view to taking conservation and management measures, and to establish regional organisations (such as RFMOs) for such purposes. Quoting Oda, who argued that the duty to cooperate under Article 118 appears abstract in nature,[120] Hayashi indicates that in accordance with the jurisprudence of the International Court of Justice (ICJ) in the North Sea Continental Shelf cases,[121] the duty to cooperate involves a dual commitment to enter processes of negotiation, and to conduct oneself in a manner that makes the negotiation meaningful.[122] Hayashi continues to argue, by reference to the ICJ's jurisprudence in *Lac Lanoux*,[123] that it is not necessary to reach a particular outcome, given the due diligence nature of the duty. Nevertheless, unjustified refusals to take part in the negotiation, disregard of the agreed procedures, or systematic refusals to consider proposals being presented by other parties would be considered contrary to the obligation.[124]

The importance of the provision of relevant information by all States that participate in a high seas fishery conservation and management regime is highlighted in Article 119.2 of the Convention, whereby:

> Available scientific information, catch and fishing effort statistics, and other data relevant to the conservation of fish stocks shall be contributed and exchanged on a regular basis through competent international organizations, whether subregional, regional or global, where appropriate and with participation by all States concerned.

It is noteworthy that the exchange of fishery catch and effort and other conservation-relevant data, a provision that is essential to cooperation, is

119 LOSC Article 89.

120 S Oda, 'Fisheries Under the United Nations Convention on the Law of the Sea' (1983) 77 *American Journal of International Law* 739–755, 751.

121 *North Sea Continental Shelf Cases (Federal Republic of Germany v Denmark) (Federal Republic of Germany v Netherlands)* Judgement [1969] ICJ Rep [1969] 3, page 47.

122 M Hayashi, 'The Management of Transboundary Fish Stocks under the LOS Convention' (1993) 8(2) *International Journal of Marine and Coastal Law* 245–262, 252.

123 *Lac Lanoux Arbitration (France v Spain)*, Award [1957] United Nations Reports of International Arbitral Awards Vol XII 281.

124 Hayashi (1993) at 252, supra at 122.

referred to by the LOSC in its main high seas conservation provision, Article 119.2, rather than Article 118. If nothing else, this is an indicator of the intimate connection between these two obligations. If read narrowly, the inclusion of these provisions in Article 119 could imply some limitations in the high seas conservation regime of the LOSC in the context of IUU fishing control. Firstly, if the duty is concerned directly with the conservation and management of the resource, it may not extend to concerns not directly involving capture activity, such as those involving, for example, the identification of fishing vessels or their location. Nevertheless, it can at least be assumed that the duty incorporates cooperation in matters involving catch data, seeing as it is necessary if jointly taken conservation and management measures are to have a basis in material reality.[125] To be meaningful, data driven cooperative decisions would need to be taken by reference to scientific, environmental, and physical fishery operation criteria, as specified in Article 119.

2.5.2 *The Compliance Agreement*

The Compliance Agreement develops and refines the duty to cooperate under the LOSC, and clarifies its remit in one narrow but important aspect for IUU fishing control: Article V.1 requires State parties to cooperate for the purposes of exchanging information, including evidence-relevant material, regarding fishing vessel activities. The objective is to ensure assistance in the identification of vessels that have undermined international conservation and management measures, so that the obligations referred to in Article III of the agreement can be met. These are, essentially, duties to ensure vessels keep their activities to the limits of their authorisation and licensing. Further, article V.3 includes a sweeping provision in more or less hortatory terms requesting that States cooperate in the promotion of the agreement and the achievement of its objectives. Additionally, Article VI establishes a cooperation framework through communications with the FAO. Notifications include the vessel name, registration number, port of registry and previous names and flags if known, radio call sign, name and address of owners, where and when built, type of vessel and length.[126] The flag State must also register the name and address of the vessel operators, the type of fishing methods used, the depth, beam,

125 DA Balton, and HR Koehler, 'Reviewing the United Nations Fish Stocks Treaty' (2006) 7(1) *Sustainable Development Law & Policy* 4–10, 8. W Edeson, 'The Role of Soft International Instruments to Control Fishing' (1999) 20 *Australian Yearbook of International Law* 83–104, 96.

126 Compliance Agreement Article VI.1.

gross tonnage and engine power of the vessel, and furnish them to the FAO,[127] reporting any subsequent changes.[128]

2.5.3 *The UNFSA*

The fundamental principle of cooperation is established in Article 5.1 of the UNFSA, whereby State parties are required to adopt conservation and management regulations and to ensure compliance through adequate monitoring and enforcement. The principle is complemented with a requirement for compatibility with pre-existing regulations, as per Article 7.[129] Other key cooperation provisions of the UNFSA are contained in Article 8 of the agreement. Article 8.1 establishes the duty to pursue cooperation either directly or through RFMOs. Article 8.2 develops the provision by conferring onto cooperation an urgent character in new fisheries or in respect of depleted stock. Article 8.3 sets down parameters of cooperation, addressing the substance void that is apparent in the LOSC, and substituting the uncertainty left by lack of agreement with ready made content in the shape of decisions already taken by RFMOs. In particular, Article 8.3 indicates that where a competent RFMO exists, States shall give effect to their duty to cooperate by either becoming members or participants, or by agreeing to apply the conservation and management measures adopted by the competent RFMO. As LOSC Article 118 does not contain references to participation in existing agreements or any requirement to give effect to existing provisions therein, this UNFSA provision constitutes a significant development in the understanding of the duty to cooperate. Article 8.3 also stipulates that RFMOs should be open to the participation of all States 'with a real interest'.

Molenaar explains that Article 8 establishes a duty to participate in competent RFMOs that is applicable to all UNFSA State parties in respect of fisheries in which they have a real interest, including those that are flags of convenience.[130] Critically, the meaning of real interest is not defined. Molenaar argues that the structure of the agreement implies that States whose vessels have a history of fishing in an RFMO regulated area may, through such activity, possess

127 Compliance Agreement Article VI.2.

128 Compliance Agreement Article VI.3.

129 A Tahindro, 'Conservation and Management of Transboundary Fish Stocks: Comments in Light of the Adoption of the 1995 Agreement for the Conservation and Management of Straddling Fish Stocks and Highly Migratory Fish Stocks' (1997) 28(1) *Ocean Development and International Law* 1–58, 16.

130 EJ Molenaar, 'The Concept of Real Interest and Other Aspects of Co-Operation through Regional Fisheries Management Mechanisms' (2000) 15(4) *International Journal of Marine and Coastal Law* 475–532, 490.

a real interest.[131] As he also explains, the practice of States in RFMOs is heterogeneous and does not produce additional clarity on this point. Some RFMOs have closed access to States without a history of fishing, at least in respect of substantive allocations, which most RFMOs separate from procedural issues of participation.[132] This has denied them the opportunity to engage in dynamic cooperation, and to access resources that they may well wish to exploit. In this regard, UNFSA Article 8.4 carries an implication of *de facto* substantive fishery closure for some UNFSA State parties, as it signals that access to RFMO regulated stock is contingent upon RFMO participation. Juda warned that this provision has the potential to challenge the high seas freedom established in the LOSC.[133] But Franckx has correctly countered such argument, as the agreement does not apply to non-parties,[134] and it can therefore only condition the rights of access protected by high seas freedom via their consent. This is a point with which other scholars have concurred.[135] Thus, Article 8.4 enables the exclusion of State parties to the UNFSA by RFMOs of which they are not members. It can be said that the net effect of the UNFSA is a rather top-down approach to high seas cooperation, with RFMOs acquiring a key management role with significant potential impact on non-members.[136] Finally, UNFSA 8.5 requires that, in the absence of RFMOs, States cooperate for their establishment, and also contemplates the option of entering into other forms of cooperative arrangement, and some States have in discrete circumstances opted for direct arrangements.[137]

As stated earlier in this chapter, Article 21.11 of the UNFSA gives content to the IUU fishing interpretive lens by specifying the actual activities that States and RFMOs must regulate as serious infractions. The substantive content of this provision is important not only for individual State regulation purposes, but also for cooperation. Indeed, it addresses an important area of opacity: the

131 Molenaar (2000) at 495, supra at 130.

132 Molenaar (2000) at 499, 507 to 522, and 530 supra at 130.

133 Juda (1997) at 155, supra at 67.

134 Franckx (2000) at 81, supra at 93.

135 R Rayfuse, 'The United Nations Agreement On Straddling And Highly Migratory Fish Stocks As An Objective Regime: A Case Of Wishful Thinking' (1999) 20 *Australian Yearbook of International Law* 253–278, 276. For an appraisal of the requirements of objective regimes, see RA Barnes, 'Objective Regimes Revisited' (2000) 9 *Asian Yearbook of International Law* 97–146.

136 See Orebech, Sigurjonsson and McDorman (1998) at 119, supra at 58.

137 See RR Churchill, 'The Barents Sea Loophole Agreement: a "Coastal State" Solution to a Straddling Stock Problem' (1999) 14(4) *International Journal of Marine and Coastal Law* 467–490, 467.

problematic nature of discontinuities in regulation across different States, which enable operators to move across the more permissive regulatory options under the open registry system. The UNFSA also contains extensive provisions on cooperation in enforcement, and sets out procedures ensuring that RFMO measures are underpinned by shared mechanisms of investigation, mutual assistance, and shared boarding and inspection under Articles 20 to 22. Articles 20.1 and 10(h) require States to cooperate with each other and with RFMOs, in the establishment of mechanisms of monitoring, control and surveillance (MCS), a critical duty for the successful identification of activities captured under the IUU fishing interpretive lens at any one time.

In addition to these provisions, the UNFSA also establishes a series of cooperation procedures based on information-sharing. Article 18.3 in the main body of the UNFSA obliges States to provide access to the information in their vessel record to States with an interest, subject only to applicable domestic confidentiality laws. In respect of the establishment of MCS and other data-sharing cooperation processes, the UNFSA contains extensive and detailed provisions in Annex I, setting out protocols in respect of the verification, protection, and sharing of management and compliance data. Under Article 7 of Annex I, data must be shared with other States, and with RFMOs, for the RFMOs to make it available to all interested States under the terms established by the organisation. Like Article VI of the Compliance Agreement, Article 7 of Annex I of the UNFSA has also established a role for the UN FAO for the collection and dissemination of data at the global level. Article 2 of Annex I calls for fishery data recorded and reported by vessel operators to be verified by States, and reiterates the need for agreed data frameworks for cooperation as established in Article 14 in the main body of the agreement. Article 4.1 of Annex I is important for facilitating intelligible communication across States, and across States and RFMOs. The article indicates that certain types of data should be collected for standardisation purposes, such as data frameworks on how to identify vessels, flags and ports of registry, vessel types, and specifications.

2.5.4 *Effectiveness Limitations*

The duty to cooperate that the LOSC establishes for the high seas is a due diligence obligation of a procedural nature, with no indication as to outcome. Commentators have noted that the parameters of the obligation imply the need for a State to participate in negotiations aimed at the establishment of management obligations in good faith. It is not clear whether specific information beyond data that is directly relevant to the conservation of the target stocks, and already available to the flag State, is included in the obligation. This uncertainty extends to important information for IUU fishing control purposes, such as vessel identity and other documentation details that may not be directly linked to capture activity and the conservation and management of the stock.

The Compliance Agreement has contributed to the definition of the duty cooperate by establishing an obligation that is critically important for IUU fishing control, whereby States must contribute to the FAO key information about the vessel and the persons responsible for its operation, as well as any changes. Indisputably, the UNFSA has also established a comprehensive system of cooperation that has been praised for its overall ambition, and which is underpinned by the regulatory output of RFMO s. This includes wide-ranging cooperation mechanisms that ensure all UNFSA parties observe RFMO measures, and that substantial information is obtained and shared across fishery participants. A number of treaty provisions ensure that data is standardised, and that monitoring and enforcement mechanisms are developed and implemented cooperatively. Beyond its key limitation in scope regarding the lack of protections for discrete high seas species, other limitations do nevertheless exist. Among the most important is the lack of definition of the UNFSA to the concept of real interest. A lack of synergy between the text of the UNFSA and that of the LOSC has meant that the issue cannot be resolved through the interpretation of the legal texts alone. This has given rise to confusion, and the evolution of disparate practices across RFMO s. New entrants to the regulatory frameworks have not often been excluded from the full spectrum of action of the RFMO s, however. Often, they have been allowed participation in the procedural mechanisms of the organisation, but excluded from access to significant quota. The net effect of this is the crystallisation of a dominant position for RFMO member States in matters of cooperation. Indeed, it could be argued that UNFSA furnishes the duty to cooperate with substance, but at the expense of the careful procedural balance established in the LOSC.

2.6 IUU Fishing Issues Not Covered in the Fisheries Treaties

One important feature that has been associated to the emergence and perpetuation of IUU fishing activities is the provision by flag States of subsidies that may encourage IUU fishing. Yet, none of the treaties discussed above deals with subsidies. Discussion on appropriate international approaches to eradicate harmful subsidies are currently on-going at the World Trade Organization (WTO), with progress having been unsatisfactory to date, being mired in complex difficulties of a socio-economic nature.[138] The matter of subsidies has also been referred to in paragraphs 23 and 88 of the IPOA IUU, and has been discussed within and among RFMO s.[139] However, no RFMO has taken a substantive position on the subsidisation of the fishing vessels operating under their regulatory areas.[140] Currently, over-subsidized fishing is not considered to fall within the interpretive spectrum of the IUU fishing lens.

2.7 General Conduct Standards

Articles 94.5, and 119.1(a) of the LOSC refer to the implementation of obligations in accordance with generally accepted international rules and standards (GAIRS).[141] The value of such standards is based on their ability to support through practice-elaborated mechanisms the implementation of open textured obligations with a normativity that flows from LOSC itself.[142] Caution must be had, however, in appropriately contextualising GAIRS to generally accepted practices, and to the relevant legal obligations, which they may assist in defining, but not expanding or replacing.[143] LOSC Article 217 has established an operative framework for marine pollution, which has been greatly developed by treaty under the auspices of the IMO.[144] Uniform international

138 See Y Cho, 'The Concept of "Developing Countries" in the Context of the WTO Fisheries Subsidies Negotiation' (2018) 9(2) *Beijing Law Review* 137–152.

139 ICCAT, Report of the Second Joint Meeting of Tuna Regional Fisheries Management Organizations (RFMO s), San Sebastian (2009) Attachment 1 of Appendix 6 [accessed on 20 March 2021 via https://www.iccat.int/Documents/Meetings/Docs/2009_TRFMOs_REP_ENG.pdf]. CCAMLR, Performance Review Panel Report (2008) [accessed on 20 March 2021 via https://www.ccamlr.org/en/system/files/e-Prfrm%20Review%20Report%20Jun09_0.pdf].

140 The subject is absent from the performance reviews of the world's major RFMO s, according to the reports published by CCAMLR (*ibid*) and the tuna RFMO s in their joint website [accessed on 20 March 2021 via http://www.tuna-org.org/index.htm].

141 J Barrett, 'The UN Convention on the Law of the Sea: A "Living" Treaty?' in Barrett and Barnes (Eds) *Law of the Sea: UNCLOS as a Living Treaty* (British Institute of International and Comparative Law, 2016) 21.

142 C Redgwell, 'The Never Ending Story: The Role of GAIRS in UNCLOS Implementation in the Offshore Energy Sector' in Barrett and Barnes (Eds) *Law of the Sea: UNCLOS as a Living Treaty* (British Institute of International and Comparative Law, 2016) 174.

143 C Redgwell, 'Mind the Gap in the GAIRS: The Role of other instruments in UNCLOS Regime Implementation in the Offshore Energy Sector' (2014) 29 *International Journal of Marine and Coastal Law* 600–621, 604.

144 J Harrison, *Making the Law of the Sea: A Study in the Development of International Law* (Cambridge University Press, 2013) 171. Takei (2013), at 120, supra at 43.

standards have been developed in the context of shipping due to the practical requirements of safety in navigation.[145] Goodman has argued that no equivalent effort is discernible in the context of fisheries conservation and management, as a consequence of a lack of uniform practice among flag States.[146] Nevertheless, a number of practices have over recent years been established regionally, and some degree of convergence may have been attained across regions as a consequence of the homogenising effect of the UNFSA, and other global environmental agreements. Other practices that may have contributed are RFMO interactions with other RFMOs, discrete regional initiatives such as some adopted in respect of IUU fishing control by the EU, and the ongoing implementation by States of global FAO voluntary instruments, such as the IPOAs developed as part of the Code of Conduct for Responsible Fisheries.

It will be recalled from the Introduction that a common method often relied on by IUU fishing operators is to shun unique vessel identification numbers (UVI).[147] The most widespread iteration of the UVI is the one issued by the IMO, or 'IMO number'.[148] The IMO number is permanently applied to the hull of the vessel, which permits verification of its identification by any inspecting authority.[149] The IMO number is required under the Safety of Life at Sea Convention (SOLAS),[150] has been made mandatory for cargo vessels of at least 300 gross tonnes (GT) and passenger vessels of at least 100 gross tonnes.[151] By contrast, the IMO number had been recommended for fishing vessels of 100 GT and above,[152] though this recommendation was subsequently expanded to include vessels operating outside the waters under the national jurisdiction

145 Churchill and Lowe (1999) at 265, supra at 34.

146 C Goodman, 'The Regime for Flag State Responsibility in International Fisheries Law – Effective Fact, Creative Fiction, or Further Work Required' (2009) 23(2) *Australian and New Zealand Maritime Law Journal* 157–169, 161.

147 See FAO, 'The Marking and Identification of Fishing Vessels' (2016) 1 [accessed on 20 March 2021 via www.fao.org/3/a-i7783e.pdf].

148 The IMO number scheme was adopted by IMO Resolution A.600(1) on 19 November 1987. The scheme was applicable to all vessels of 100 gross tonnes or more, but the resolution originally exempted fishing vessels. This exemption was removed, and the application of the scheme extended to fishing vessels of 12 metres or over able to operate outside waters under national jurisdiction through IMO Circular 1886/Rev 6 of 2016.

149 See IHS Global Limited, 'IMO Identification Numbers for Ships, Companies and Registered Owners' (2017) 1 [accessed on 20 March 2021 via www.imonumbers.lrfairplay.com].

150 International Convention for the Safety of Life at Sea (1974) 1184 UNTS 2 [SOLAS].

151 SOLAS, Regulation 3.

152 IMO Resolution A.1078(28) IMO Ship Identification. See also FAO, 'Global Record of Fishing Vessels, Refrigerated Transport Vessels and Supply Vessels' (2016) [accessed on 20 March 2021 via http://www.fao.org/global-record/en/].

of the flag State and measuring over 12 meters in overall hull length (LOA).[153] Currently, the IMO number is mandatory for all fishing vessels of 12 metres and over fishing inside the waters of the EU, and vessels of a length of 24 metres and above 100 GT operating beyond, as well as all foreign fishing vessels operating in EU waters.[154] In addition, it is obligatory for fishing vessels of 100 GT or more operating under the conservation rules of all the major RFMO s.[155] Such extended practice suggests that the assignation of an IMO number to fishing vessels reaching or exceeding 100 GT and operating in the high seas. This requirement might be developing into a trend that approximates the status of GAIRS, and which may assist in the interpretation of the flag State obligation to ensure administrative control over vessels established by Article 94 of the LOSC in certain contexts. Similarly, a trend has been emerging for some time in respect of the installation of vessel monitoring systems (VMS) on fishing vessels operating in the high seas, which report the location of the fishing vessel to the monitoring authorities of the flag State. Despite some inconsistencies across RFMO s, the installation of VMS is increasingly considered a necessary element in the regulation of distant water fishing vessel activity.[156]

Additionally, the FAO has launched a programme for the adoption of a Global Record of Fishing Vessels, Refrigerated Transport Vessels and Supply vessels (Global Record).[157] The Global Record will require certain vessel details to be held in the public domain:[158] the IMO number; flag flown by the vessel;

153 See IMO Resolution A.1117(30).

154 Commission Implementing Regulation (EU) No. 2015/1962 of 28 October 2015 amending Implementing Regulation (EU) No. 404/2011 laying down detailed rules for the implementation of Council Regulation (EC) No. 1224/2009 establishing a Community control system for ensuring compliance with the rules of the common fisheries policy.

155 Generally, the requirement is limited to vessels of 100 GT or more, or a minimum length that varies between 15 and 24 metres. See CCAMLR Resolution 10–2 (2013). CCSBT Resolution on a CCSBT Record of Vessels Authorised to Fish for Southern Bluefin Tuna. GFCM Resolution 33/2009/6. IATTC Resolution C-14-01. ICCAT Recommendation 13–13. IOTC Resolution 15/05.

156 See HR Koehler, 'Promoting Compliance in Tuna RFMOS: A Comprehensive Baseline Survey of the Current Mechanics of Reviewing, Assessing and Addressing Compliance with RFMO Obligations and Measures' (ISSF, 2013) 35.

157 See FAO, 'The Global Record of fishing Vessels, Refrigerated Transport Vessels and Supply Vessels: Providing a Single Access Point for Information on Vessels Used for Fishing and Fishing Related Activities to Combat Illegal, Unreported and Unregulated Fishing' (2016) [accessed on 20 March 2021 via www.fao.org/fishery/global-record/en].

158 FAO, 'The Global Record of Fishing Vessels, Refrigerated Transport Vessels and Supply Vessels: Providing a Single Access Point for Information on Vessels Used for Fishing and Fishing Related Activities to Combat Illegal, Unreported and Unregulated Fishing' (2016) 2 and 7 [accessed on 20 March 2021 via http://www.fao.org/3/a-mr484e.pdf] [GRWG].

name of the vessel as registered; overall vessel length; and GT of the vessel.[159] The Global Record expands on the duties to grant access to the information in the vessel registry and fishing vessel and operational records established in Article 18.3 of the UNFSA and the FAO notifications contained in Article VI of the Compliance Agreement. The Global Record contains a broad definition of fishing that includes transhipment,[160] and is likely to reinforce compatible standards established by the FAO, particularly the FAO Standard Specifications for the Marking and Identification of Fishing Vessels.[161] Further, it might also foster harmonisation across certain data recording and publication practices of RFMOs. In particular, the adoption and publication of vessel black and white lists, whereby the identities of vessels are publicised.[162] The white lists permit the compilation and publication of key data concerning the name and characteristics of fishing vessels, as well as their authorisation and permits. Unfortunately, it is not clear to what extent the characteristics of such lists have been harmonised across the different RFMOs at present.[163]

Chapter 1 discussed that *modi operandi* aiming at maintaining the identity and nationality of a vessel hidden from possible detection by authorities is a characteristic of IUU fishing operations. Hence, the establishment of domestic regulation that addresses anonymity loopholes is critical for IUU fishing control. Despite inconsistencies in the practices of RFMOs, the adoption of the Global Record might finally consolidate the assignation of an IMO number as GAIRS. It may also propel the establishment of minimum standards of information recording and publication that may be required in the implementation of LOSC Article 119.1 concerning the exchange of information, and Article 94 regarding the exercise of jurisdiction over fishing vessels. Once established,

159 GRWG, page 2.

160 References to fishing vessels include fishing and fish carrier vessels, excluding recreational vessels and container ships that only carry fish if it has been previously landed. See FAO Technical Consultation to Identify a Structure and Strategy for the Development and Implementation of the Global Record of Fishing Vessels, Refrigerated Transport Vessels and Supply Vessels (2010) 3 FIRO/R956.

161 The specifications contain essential harmonization compliance rules for domestic agencies to be able to identify fishing vessels and establish compatible observer programmes. See T Aqorau and A Bergin, 'The Federated States of Micronesia Arrangement for Regional Fisheries Access' (1997) 12(1) *International Journal of Marine and Coastal Law* 37–80, 54.

162 T Lobach, *Law, Technology and Science for Oceans in Globalisation* (Martinus Nijhoff, 2010) 111.

163 ISSF, 'Tuna RFMO Authorised Vessel Lists: A Comparative Analysis to Identify Best Practices' ISSF Technical Report (2018) 6 [accessed on 20 March 2021 via https://iss-foundation.org/download-monitor-demo/download-info/issf-2019-05-tuna-rfmo-authorised-vessel-lists-a-comparative-analysis-to-identify-best-practices/].

such standards would confer considerable additional effectiveness to the critically important FAO notification obligations contained in Article VI.2 and VI.3 of the Compliance Agreement. However, until States and RFMOs effectively populate the Global Record with the required data, the existence of GAIRS in respect of vessel detail publication remains speculative.

A related phenomenon should be highlighted with regard to standards that appear consistently across treaties and voluntary instruments. Sanctioning provisions in Articles III.8 of the Compliance Agreement and 19.2 of the UNFSA establish that sanctions should be of sufficient gravity as to deprive offenders of the benefit of their infractions. References to sanctions along identical lines have also been established in paragraph 7.7.2 of the Code of Conduct for Responsible Fisheries, and paragraph 21 of the IPOA IUU. ITLOS has interpreted the duties of the flag State to impose sanctions that are sufficient to deprive perpetrators of illicit gains from the general wording in Article 94.6 of the LOSC obliging the flag State to 'take any action necessary to remedy the situation'.[164] Arguably, under the broad terminology of LOSC Article 94.5, the Tribunal has considered the persistent incorporation of a sanctioning standard across all global fisheries instruments sufficient to its establishment as a standard of general application.

Lastly, the utilisation of destructive fishing gears is another factor commonly associated with IUU fishing practices. Particularly high profile in this regard has been the high seas deployment of damaging large-scale pelagic drift-nets. The use of large-scale driftnets has been addressed by UNGA Resolutions 46/215 and 45/197, two instruments that, although nonbinding in nature, might arguably have become part of the corpus of international law through extensive State practice.[165] The practice has also been addressed to varying degrees in bilateral and multilateral frameworks, including those of some RFMOs,[166] and in the legislative output of the European Union.[167] To the extent that preventing the deployment of large-scale driftnets might be considered to have

---

164 SRFC, para 140.

165 See R Caddell, 'Caught in the Net: Driftnet Fishing Restrictions and the European Court of Justice' (2010) 22(2) *Journal of Environmental Law* 301-314.

166 R Rayfuse, 'Regulation and Enforcement in the Law of the Sea: Emerging Assertions of a Right to Non-flag State Enforcement in the High Seas Fisheries and Disarmament Contexts' (2005) 24 *Australian Year Book of International Law* 181–200, 250.

167 See Council Regulation (EC) No. 1239/98 of 8 June 1998 amending Regulation (EC) No 894/97 laying down certain technical measures for the conservation of fishery resources, and Council Regulation Council Regulation (EC) No 809/2007 of 28 June 2007 amending Regulations (EC) No 894/97, (EC) No 812/2004 and (EC) No 2187/2005 as concerns drift nets.

become general State practice, then this activity could be understood as illegal fishing under the IUU fishing lens. Characterising it in this manner assumes that the practice implies either a breach of domestic law, or a breach of a specific aspect of the general duty to protect and preserve the marine environment, in relation to which it could be considered to perform the role of a general conduct standard.

2.8 Contribution to Effectiveness of the IUU Fishing Interpretive Lens

Chapter 1 discussed that the IUU fishing lens is a hybrid interpretive mechanism incorporating two possible perspectives for the identification of fishing activities and the degree to which they may be considered to be 'IUU' fishing: one legal (illegal fishing, which includes unreported fishing), and one which is also hybrid, containing some legal and predominantly non-legal elements (unregulated fishing). It is of course the case that the two elements of the IUU fishing interpretive lens are not static: the more legal duties are expanded and clarified, and the more they are assumed by States, the less relevant the unregulated fishing aspect of the lens will become, given that activities cannot be illegal and unregulated at the same time. It may thus be assumed from the above paragraphs that the effect of the Compliance Agreement, the UNFSA, and any rules accepted as GAIRS in clarifying and adding granularity to the obligations contained in the LOSC will result in a further effect: to define what may be considered to be illegal fishing, and progressively diminish the scope and functionality of the unregulated fishing part of the IUU fishing lens. At the same time, RFMO rules and measures are similarly useful in progressively closing in on certain areas where the legal framework lacks definition, in the context of the regions and/or species that are RFMO managed. The ability of RFMO rules and measures to add substance to open textured obligations is dependent on them being binding, rather than issued as guidance. However, compulsory measures have to be implemented by member States, and also by State parties to the Fish Stocks Agreement if their vessels operate in the regulated area, whether they are RFMO members or not. This naturally follows from the application of the *lex specialis* principle in the operation of legal obligations,[168] in the absence of conflict with general obligations.[169]

168 J Crawford, 'The ILC's Articles on Responsibility of States for Internationally Wrongful Acts: A Retrospect' (2002) 96(4) *American Journal of International Law* 874–890, 879.

169 A Lindroos, 'Addressing Norm Conflicts in a Fragmented Legal System: The Doctrine of Lex Specialis' (2005) 74(1) *Nordic Journal of International Law* 27–66, 27.

It may be concluded from the previous sections in this chapter that despite the progress made by the UNFSA, the Compliance Agreement, and the regulatory activity of the RFMOs, a number of grey areas remain in existence. The lack of granularity of general obligations, combined with the very limited availability of GAIRS in the fisheries context, treaty fragmentation, and the fact that neither the LOSC nor the global fisheries agreements are universally ratified results in a legal landscape with important effectiveness weaknesses in respect of high seas fisheries. Yet, RFMO rules can be considered through the IUU fishing lens, rather than from the perspective of the binding force that derives from the status of States as parties to RFMO foundational treaties, or to the UNFSA. From the perspective of unregulated fishing in particular, and in the context of an analysis denuded of any legal considerations, States can be accused of undermining RFMO measures, and thus be associated with the undesirable IUU label. In this regard at least, the IUU fishing lens can validly be said to be potentially enhancing the effectiveness, or at least the visibility, of RFMOs and their governance output.

2.8.1 *Effectiveness Illustration: RFMO Compliance Practice*

As De Bruyn et al indicate, RFMOs have taken measures that address in important ways some of the effectiveness limitations mentioned in the preceding paragraphs: measures include more or less comprehensive reference points for conservation and management, transhipment restrictions, and enhancements to flag State jurisdiction via the implementation of scientific programmes, data reporting protocols and verification controls and other monitoring mechanisms, and capacity building schemes.[170] A comprehensive review of compliance measures established across the tuna RFMOs by Koehler include reporting duties and obligatory data verification, participation in observer programs, implementation of landing reports, and cross-checking of transhipment reports.[171] Although the quality of the rules across RFMOs varies, as does compliance among the member States,[172] the evidence indicates that these RFMO measures make a valuable contribution to compliance mechanisms, reaching beyond what is established in the UNFSA, and reaching also beyond the limits of UNFSA ratification. This is so because some contracting parties of RFMOs,

---

170 P de Bruyn et al, 'The Precautionary Approach to Fisheries Management: How This is taken into account by Regional Fisheries Management Organisations (RFMOs)' (2013) 38 *Marine Policy* 397–406, 403.

171 Koehler (2013) at 35, supra at 156.

172 Koehler (2013) at 36–37, supra at 156.

including some with large distant water fleets such as China, have not ratified or acceded to the UNFSA.[173]

One area where the activity of RFMOs has been instrumental in catalysing an important area where the UNFSA has developed the older and less detailed LOSC obligations: high seas fishing compliance. LOSC Article 119.2 requires States to exchange catch and fishing effort data, and other relevant scientific data, either directly or through international organisations as appropriate. By contrast, UNFSA Article 7.8 indicates that States fishing on the high seas shall regularly inform each other, either directly or through appropriate subregional or regional fisheries management organizations or arrangements, or through other appropriate means, of the measures they have adopted for regulating the activities of vessels flying their flag which fish for such stocks on the high seas. The UNFSA provision clearly develops Article 119.2, and adds a substantive and procedural dimension that can perform the function of basic compliance standard.

Further, the UNFSA also introduces a change in emphasis: it suggests that information is not merely collected following each State's interpretation of its own international conservation duties, but is collected for the relational purpose of cooperating with other State parties of the UNFSA, including through the cooperative framework of RFMO s, in a manner that serves the collective purposes of those institutions, and serves a collective objective of coordination. Arguably, the structure of the obligation to cooperate is given shape by the collective conservation, management, and compliance needs as determined via the institutional decision-making processes of the RFMO s. This and other obligations established by the UNFSA seek to ensure specific cooperation outcomes, which transcend the individualist State perspective of self-administration that is characteristic of the LOSC.

The compliance significance of Article 7.8 of the UNFSA becomes fully apparent when the practices of RFMO institutions are considered. For instance, the Commission for the Conservation of Antarctic Marine Living Resources (CCAMLR) and the Indian Ocean Tuna Commission (IOTC), compile estimations of the number of vessels operating in their management areas, including vessels operating with no or inappropriate authorisation, and instances of misreporting and non-reporting. These reports are then contrasted with information reported by their member States.[174] Similarly, the International

173 China is a member State of the International Commission for the Conservation of Atlantic Bluefin Tuna, but has not ratified the UNFSA [accessed on 20 March 2021 via https://www.iccat.int/en/contracting.html and http://www.un.org/depts/los/reference_files/chronological_lists_of_ratifications.htm].

174 GRWG, at 40.

Convention for the Conservation of Atlantic Tunas (ICCAT), relies on a statistical documentation scheme, with which it is able to identify unreported fishing in respect of bluefin tuna.[175] Some organisations also contrast the data provided by members with data provided by third parties, such as NGOs,[176] or scientific institutions.[177] A study carried out by Gilman and Kingma concerning the compliance processes of the Western and Central Pacific Fisheries Commission (WCPFC), highlights the availability of information accessible by the institutions of the RFMO, containing compliance knowledge on whether States have taken action under RFMO conduct rules, as well as under the LOSC and the UNFSA. Here, cooperation depends on openness regarding State compliance with regard to issues such as the identification of fishing vessels and operators, tracking of fishing activities through traditional or electronic monitoring and surveillance methods, identification of infractions, and enforcement action.[178]

2.8.2 *Governance Effect of the IUU Fishing Interpretive Lens*

It follows from the above that the combined effect of the UNFSA compliance rules and the regulatory action of the RFMOs confers on the latter the potential to carry out a supervisory and evaluative role. It is further recalled that the extra-legal regulatory margin implied by the non-legal aspect of the unregulated fishing filter of the IUU fishing interpretive lens creates a margin in the lens's interpretive space whereby rules that are not legally binding on some States can nevertheless be positioned to display certain pragmatic effects on them. This will concern States whose vessels operate in the regulated area, but who are neither parties to the UNFSA, nor RFMO members. In this respect, the practical effect of the IUU fishing interpretive lens closely resembles the intended effect of certain UNFSA provisions, but with the caveat that the unregulated element in the IUU fishing lens impacts on non-UNFSA parties.

175 V Restrepo, 'Estimation of Unreported Catches by ICCAT' in *Fish Piracy: Combating Illegal, Unreported and Unregulated Fishing* (OECD, 2004) 155–157, 156.

176 See for example the assessment carried by the International Seafood Sustainability Foundation carried out for the Western and Central Pacific Fisheries Commission: ISSF, Position Statement for WCPFC12 (2015). Further, see Commission for the Conservation of Antarctic Marine Living Resources (CCAMLR), Rules of Procedure of the Commission, Rule 34.

177 See North East Atlantic Fisheries Convention (1959) 486 UNTS 157, Article 14(1).

178 See E Gilman and E Kingma, 'Standard for Assessing Transparency in Information on Compliance with Obligations of Regional Fisheries Management Organizations: Validation through Assessment of the Western and Central Pacific Fisheries Commission' (2013) 84 *Ocean & Coastal Management* 31–39, 35 and 36.

In particular, this concerns UNFSA Articles 17.1 and 17.2, whereby States that do not agree to join the competent RFMO or apply its rules and CMMs are identified as 'not discharged' from the duty to cooperate in the conservation and management of the stock, and shall not authorise vessels to fish for stocks that are the subject of such CMMs. The provisions of the UNFSA are only applicable to State parties,[179] which by virtue of these provisions accept the regulatory role of RFMOs irrespective of membership. Thus, it can be argued that at least one effect of the IUU fishing lens is to adopt the UNFSA framework as an objective blueprint, with the net effect of extending the regulatory effect of RFMO rules to any flag State whose vessels operate in the relevant regulated area. This effect is far from negligible: as discussed in the previous section, the cooperation implications of the UNFSA have substantially developed those of the LOSC, and have important implications for the regulatory conduct of States in matters concerning straddling and highly migratory fishery management.

Some commentators may argue that this effect of the IUU fishing lens has the pragmatic advantage of extending useful, well-defined rules specifically developed to improve fishery management. Whist this may be true, at same time it should be noted that reliance on this pragmatic effect of the IUU fishing lens has implications that could be undesirable. For example, other mechanisms with the potential to assist in the interpretation and implementation international obligations, and the elaboration or progressive definition of GAIRS, may be neglected and fall into disuse. This trend, if left uncontrolled, may result in the IUU fishing lens favouring the creation of a governance space that *de facto* operates quite independently from international law. As Simma and Pulkowski caution, actors that rely on regulatory autonomy may believe they are able to disengage from the obligations established in the general legal framework within which those actors are actually situated.[180] The degree to which instances of such disengagement may have occurred in the context of high seas fisheries, and their implications, is investigated and discussed in Chapter 4.

2.9 Conclusion

This chapter has set out the results of an analysis on the international obligations emanating from customary and treaty law that are relevant to the

179 Franckx (2000) at 81, supra at 93.

180 B Simma, and D Pulkowsky, 'Of Planets and the Universe: Self-Contained Regimes in International Law' (2006) 17(3) European Journal of international Law 483–529, 485.

regulatory duties of flag States in respect of IUU fishing. The focus of the analysis has been to evaluate rule effectiveness, understood as functional adequacy, by reference to the empirical realities discussed in the preceding chapter. The framework of State obligations under the LOSC including the customary provisions that it contains, the Compliance Agreement and the UNFSA, as well as the existence and effect of GAIRS and RFMO measures has been subjected to analysis, and their relevance to IUU fishing control have been set out. The manner in which each agreement contributes to addressing the regulatory shortfalls whereby States enable the perpetuation of IUU fishing activities has been identified. The limitations of each instrument have been scoped, and the effect of instrument interaction broadly analysed in order to define effectiveness strengths and limitations.

In summary, it has been found that although flag State duties as contained in the LOSC are considered deficient for effectively addressing IUU fishing activities, they establish certain red lines and *de minimis* requirements. The Compliance Agreement and in particular the UNFSA have made invaluable contributions to facilitate the implementation of those obligations, in respect of regulatory actions by States IUU fishing control. The innovative cooperation blueprint established by the UNFSA is particularly valuable, placing participation and decision-making in RFMO s at the centre of high seas fisheries management. Neither the LOSC, the UNFSA nor the Compliance Agreement have been universally ratified, and the general obligations contained in the LOSC remain residually applicable to States that are not parties to any of those treaties. Though international tribunals and legal commentators have assisted in the interpretation of those general obligations, the absence of well-defined rules and conduct standards means that some uncertainties persist. This can also be said of many of the obligations established in the LOSC.

The recent arbitral award in the case of the South China Sea as analysed by leading legal commentators supports the view that the general obligations set out in the LOSC, and in particular the duty to protect the marine environment as per Article 192, may be systemically interpreted in accordance with objective standards, as well as other rules derived from other international agreements of which a State is a party. The case also opens the possibility that egregious acts of destruction capable of damaging the ecosystem, and of which the flag State had knowledge, may be considered breaches of the LOSC. Yet, the damage threshold is perhaps too high to capture most IUU fishing instances, and the LOSC is silent as to how the flag State is to avail itself of the information it needs to become aware of the mentioned acts of destruction. Further, the due diligence nature of the obligation means that the regulatory conduct of the

State needs to be examined before any conclusions can be drawn in respect of a breach.

The UNFSA has made significant contributions in these regulatory areas, and has had the effect of creating a more effective cooperation framework. RFMOs have been placed in a position to perform a coordinating role in respect of fishery management, and even a supervisory role with regard to compliance. Voids left by the UNFSA include the absence of unauthorised transhipment as a serious infraction, although the Port State Measures Agreement has corrected this void in respect of its State parties.[181] A significant contribution of the UNFSA is its implication of acceptance of the role of RFMOs by all UNFSA parties, irrespective of their RFMO membership. Yet, this is somewhat counterbalanced by the lack of definition of 'real interest', which is a crucial concept to establish the conditions for RFMO membership, and therefore is directly relevant to the effectiveness of RFMO measures.[182]

The effectiveness of IUU fishing as interpretive lens is very much connected to the regulatory output of RFMOs, and the degree to which the lens has the potential to condition the regulatory conduct of States that remain outside of the scope of the UNFSA, and are not RFMO members. In a pragmatic sense, those States can nevertheless be identified as something akin to regulatory subjects via the IUU fishing lens in respect of the unregulated fishing activities of their vessels, should they be perceived as undermining RFMO measures. The practical effect of this is akin to the operationalisation the RFMO rules as if they were objective standards of conduct for States with regard to their respective regulated ocean regions and/or species, irrespective of not having binding force vis-à-vis such States. This effect occurs against a backdrop of a lack of development of GAIRS. Arguably, the advent of the IUU fishing lens and its effect of invigorating the reach of RFMO rules could yet slow such development further. In this chapter, a number of trends with the potential to crystallise into GAIRS have been identified, namely the imposition of sanctions able to deprive perpetrators of illicit gains, the ban on large-scale driftnetting, and the assignation of IMO numbers to vessels of 100 GT or more. In these cases, more specific research to ascertain the existence of such rules as GAIRS is desirable, and arguably a similar effort should be undertaken in respect of VMS requirements for distant water fishing vessels.

181 Agreement on Port State Measures to Prevent, Deter and Eliminate Illegal, Unreported and Unregulated Fishing (2009), UN Registration Number 54133.

182 See 1969 Vienna Convention on the Law of Treaties (VCLT), 1155 UNTS 331, Articles 34 to 37.

PART 2

IUU Fishing as Compliance Mechanism

CHAPTER 3

Compliance and State Responsibility

Introduction

With this chapter, the enquiry first undertaken into exploring IUU fishing as interpretive lens moves in a different direction: its potential to ensure rule compliance, including an assessment of how it fares compared with international law. The first step in this exploration involves insight into the international legal framework and its relationship with the notion of compliance. The relationship is important, because the effectiveness of a legal regime is not limited to the factors that were explored in the previous chapter, namely the existence, clarity, and adequacy of the rules that it contains. Arguably, it also encompasses the potential to ensure compliance with those rules. Thus, the aim of this chapter is exploring the degree to which international law can live up to this, by ensuring compliance with international legal rules. In particular, this chapter sets out the results of an enquiry into the features of State responsibility, and the extent to which it can ensure State compliance with their international obligations with the conservation and management of high seas fisheries, beyond the specific boundaries of the special fisheries treaties discussed in the previous chapter.

Leading commentators have discussed the limitations of the rules of State responsibility to provide an adequate foundation for the promotion of State compliance in environmental matters.[1] A number of contributions have also tracked the emergence of treaty mechanisms dealing with compliance by their State parties with treaty obligations, including in the context of international fisheries management.[2] The notion that State responsibility is insufficient as

---

1 See J Brunnee, 'Multilateral Environmental Agreements and the Compliance Continuum' in Winter (Ed) *Multilevel Governance of Global Environmental Change* (Cambridge University Press, 2006) 387. B Kingsbury, 'The Concept of Compliance as a Function of Competing Conceptions of International Law' (1998) 19(2) *Michigan Journal of International Law* 345–379. A Chayes, and AH Chayes, *The New Sovereignty: Compliance with International Regulatory Agreements* (Harvard University Press, 1998) 17. HH Koh, 'Why do Nations Obey International Law?' (1997) 106(8) *Yale Law Journal* 2599–2660.

2 See R Wolfrum, 'Means of Ensuring Compliance with and Enforcement of International Environmental Law' (1999) 272 *Recueil des Cours* 9–154. C Carr, 'Recent Developments in Compliance and Enforcement for International Fisheries' (1997) 24 *Ecology Law Quarterly* 847–860. G Handl, 'Compliance Control Mechanisms and International Environmental Obligations, (1995) 5 *Tulane Journal of International Law* 29–50.

 | DOI:10.1163/9789004463219_005

a discipline for ensuring effective living marine resource administration by States beyond the specific compliance mechanisms found in specific fishery treaty regimes is widely supported: arguments vary, with some indicating that responsibility is valid *per se* but requiring complementary support mechanisms,[3] and others that responsibility simply lacks the intrinsic characteristics necessary to encourage appropriate self-rationing by States.[4] Indeed, it is clear from the discussion in Chapter 1 that State responsibility has not prevented the proliferation of IUU fishing activities, or their intensification in some marine areas in recent decades. Identifying the reasons for this failure is the main objective of this chapter.

3.1 State Responsibility as Compliance Mechanism

The principle of sovereignty is the fundament whereby States can exercise power over the persons and resources under their jurisdiction.[5] There is also an external dimension to sovereignty, which ensures a formal status of State equality,[6] and determines that States only assume international legal obligations to which they give their consent.[7] The principle of sovereignty, thus understood, implies that compliance is an unwelcome guest to the essentially horizontal inter-State relations that characterise the international landscape. Compliance, as a normative concept whereby it is desirable that obligations are observed *by all to whom they are relevant*, and by extension enforcement as operational guarantor of compliance, are not natural companions to this vision of international life. As Schachter said with regard to legal work conducted within the context of the United Nations (UN):

3 R Rayfuse, 'Countermeasures and High Seas Fisheries Enforcement' (2004) *Netherlands International Law Review* 41–76, 50. MA Fitzmaurice and C Redgwell, 'Environmental Non-Compliance Procedures and International Law' (2000) 31 *Netherlands Yearbook of International Law* 35–65, 36. R Rayfuse, and M Wilder, 'International Fisheries and Sustainability: Dealing with Uncertainty' (2000) 14 *Ocean Yearbook* 114–137, 124.

4 J Wakefield, *Reforming the Common Fisheries Policy* (Edward Elgar, 2016) 32. RA Barnes, 'Fisheries and Marine Biodiversity' in Fitzmaurice, Ong and Merkouris (Eds) *Research Handbook on International Environmental Law* (Elgar, 2010) 545.

5 RA Barnes, 'The Law of the Sea 1850–2010' in Starkey and Heidbrink (Eds) *A History of the North Atlantic Fisheries, Volume 2* (German Maritime Museum, 2012) 179.

6 See P Malanczuk, *Akehurst's Modern Introduction to International Law* (Routledge, 1997) 17.

7 H Bull, *The Anarchical Society: A Study of Order in World Politics*, Fourth Edition (Palgrave Macmillan, 2012) 147. See Vienna Convention on the Law of Treaties (1969) 1155 UNTS 331. See Articles 19–22 on the subject of Reservations, and 34–38 on the subject of third parties to a treaty.

> For a long time compliance and enforcement were on the margins of UN concern. Like somewhat backward members of a family, their place was vaguely recognized, but not much was expected from them. (…) Some prominent lawyers dismissively referred to enforcement as political matter outside the law.[8]

Indeed, if at all, compliance was being understood simply as the cessation of the act or acts whereby a State had breached its international obligations.[9] State responsibility is a construct of international law, which has historically been associated to the need to foster peaceful diplomatic relations between States.[10] It is predicated on the idea of States as sovereign equals,[11] whereas a normative notion of compliance implies submission to rules which, if set by others, would carry hierarchical connotations. For sovereign States, as ultimate arbiters over matters within their legal control, international obligations are usually understood to be binding only insofar as they have been expressly agreed by each of them with one another.[12] Logically, this means that international law formally establishes a horizontal, reciprocal structure of inter-State interaction and dispute settlement as its only binding compliance function,[13] as befitting actors subject to no oversight by a hierarchical superior.

Indeed, international responsibility has been developed by States on the basis that controls over sovereign States are entered into by necessity, and are exceptional.[14] The Permanent Court of International Justice (PCIJ) in its *obiter dictum* in the *Lotus* judgment underscored such conception of sovereignty, indicating that 'restrictions upon the independence of States cannot therefore be presumed'.[15] In this traditional conception of international obligation, the

8 O Schachter, 'United Nations Law' (1994) 88 *American Journal of International Law* 1–24, 9.

9 D Shelton, 'Righting Wrongs: Reparations in the Articles on State Responsibility' (2002) 96 *American Journal of International Law* 833–858, 836.

10 J Crawford, and M Koskenniemi, 'Introduction' in Crawford and Koskenniemi (Eds) *The Cambridge Companion to International Law* (Cambridge University Press, 2012) 1.

11 M Koskenniemi, 'A History of International Law Histories' in Fassbender and Peters (Eds) *The Oxford Handbook of International Law* (Oxford University Press, 2012) 943.

12 C Tomuschat, 'Obligations Arising for States Without or Against their Will' (1993) *Recueil des Cours* 241 209.

13 C Chinkin, 'Dispute Resolution and the Law of the Sea: Regional Problems and Prospects: in Crawford and Rothwell (Eds) *The Law of the Sea in the Asian Pacific Region* (Martinus Nijhoff, 1995) 244.

14 CJ Tams, 'Individual States as Guardians of Community Interests' in Fastenrath et al (Eds) *From Bilateralism to Community interests: Essays in Honour of Bruno Simma* (Oxford University Press, 2011) 383.

15 *The Case of the SS Lotus (France v Turkey)* Judgment [1927] PCIJ Publications Series A No 10, page 18.

State has freedom to act for the potential of what it considers to be its own domestic interests, which it is entitled to guard and promote, within the limits determined by the sovereignty of other States.[16] It is therefore not surprising that invocations of State responsibility have had, at best, an intermittent presence as a method for the purposes of evaluating State conduct.[17] As Handl points out, this situation has been echoed in the context of fisheries conservation and management, where invocations of responsibility have been infrequent,[18] specially when considering the ubiquity of fishing activities.

3.2 State Responsibility and International Rules and Actors

The law of State responsibility has undergone a process of codification conducted by the International Law Commission ('ILC') in its Articles of State Responsibility for Internationally Wrongful Acts (ARSIWA).[19] The ARSIWA rules have in some aspects developed the principle of responsibility,[20] as well as having consolidated it in positive international law.[21] ARSIWA Articles 1 and 2 succinctly encapsulate the meaning of State responsibility, stipulating that responsibility is activated by an internationally wrongful act by a State, which occurs when by that State has by action or omission attributable to it breached an obligation under international law.[22] Thus, responsibility requires the existence of an international legal duty establishing a prohibition or an obligation of conduct onto the State.[23] As a principle that

16 G von Glahn and JL Taulbee, *Law Among Nations: An Introduction to Public International Law* (Routledge, 2016) 21.

17 P Allott, *Eunomia: New Order for a New World* (Oxford University Press, 1990) 296.

18 G Handl, 'Flag State Responsibility for Illegal, Unreported and Unregulated Fishing in Foreign EEZs' (2014) 44(1–2) *Environmental Policy and Law*, 158–169, 159.

19 International Law Commission (ILC), 'Articles of State Responsibility for Internationally Wrongful Acts' (2001) UNGA A/RES/56/83 [ARSIWA]. Also, J Crawford, 'The ILC's Articles on Responsibility of States for Internationally Wrongful Acts' in ILC, Report of the International law Commission on the Work of Its Fifty-third Session No 10 (2001) 43, UN A/56/10. Some authors maintain that the ILC has developed the pre-existing law of responsibility through ARSIWA in some respects. See in particular Rayfuse (2004) at 44, supra at 3.

20 Shelton (2002) at 833, supra at 9.

21 J Crawford, *Brownlie's Principles of Public International Law* (Oxford University Press, 2012) 81.

22 ARSIWA Articles 1 and 2.

23 See *Responsibilities and Obligations of States Sponsoring Persons and Entities with respect of Activities in the Area*, Advisory Opinion of 1 February 2011, paras 66 and 71.

is implicit in every international obligation,[24] State responsibility is considered to be a matter of customary law.[25] This affords it a general character that makes it relevant to all States, as subjects of international law.[26] It is therefore the case that, for the purposes of enabling and regulating the participation of nationals in high seas fisheries, responsibility in principle concerns all flag States.

The law of State responsibility is 'concerned with the legal consequences attaching to the violation of states' primary international law obligations'.[27] An internationally wrongful act implies the infringement of an obligation characterised as such by international law,[28] binding on a State at the time the breach occurs.[29] ARSIWA therefore sets out the system of secondary rules, which are concerned with the determination of the circumstances in which the breach of a primary rule constitutes an internationally wrongful act, when such act is attributable to a State, the circumstances in which other States may invoke a right to a remedy against that State, and the defences available in respect of that breach.[30] This has a number of implications, all of which are relevant to the IUU fishing context.

3.2.1 *Exclusion of Rules and Actors*

In accordance with Article 2 of ARSIWA, international responsibility arises when an internationally wrongful act is attributable to a State *and* constitutes a breach of an international obligation assumed by that State. As discussed in previous chapter, a State that has not formally agreed to a treaty is not bound by its obligations.[31] This is significant because, other than in the case of obligations of a customary character, the international obligations that are relevant to IUU fishing control have been set out in treaties, and they do not have

24 *Case Concerning the Difference Between New Zealand and France Concerning the Interpretation or Application of Two Agreements Concluded on 9 July 1986 Between the Two States and which Related To The Problems Arising from the Rainbow Warrior Affair* Award [1990] Reports of International Arbitral Awards, Vol XX 215, para 75.

25 R McCorquodale and P Simons, 'Responsibility Beyond Borders: State Responsibility for Extraterritorial Violations by Corporations of International Human Rights Law' (2007) 70(4) *Modern Law Review* 598–625, 601.

26 Crawford (2012) at 384, supra at 21.

27 V Roeben, 'Responsibility in International Law' (2012) 16 *Max Planck Yearbook of United Nations Law* 99–158, 103.

28 ARSIWA Article 3.

29 ARSIWA Articles 12 and 13.

30 Crawford (2012) at 540, supra at 21.

31 See Vienna Convention on the Law of Treaties, Articles 19–22 and 34–38, 1155 UNTS 331.

legal force vis-à-vis third parties.[32] In the context of IUU fishing, any measures established by regional fishery management organisations and similar bodies (collectively, RFMOs) in respect of States that have not assumed a legal obligation to comply with them cannot generate State responsibility. Neither can do so any voluntary rules that, such as those set out in the voluntary instruments discussed in the previous chapter, do not possess an intrinsically legal nature. This is so, irrespective of how important or apposite they might seem.[33]

Just as not every international rule can trigger State responsibility when infringed, neither can responsibility be invoked in respect of all international actors. Indeed, the responsibility regime generally excludes non-State actors from participating in its mechanisms.[34] This typically prevents the international responsibility of actors such as fishing companies, irrespective of how destructive their actions. It also prevents invocation by actors who, like specialist non-governmental organisations, may have key knowledge of IUU fishing activities, but lack a legal basis to invoke the responsibility of States in respect of the causation or perpetuation of those activities.

3.2.2 *Responsibility and Due Diligence Obligations*

As already explained, State obligations associated with the oversight over fishing vessels in the high seas are not obligations to obtain a specific result, but are due diligence obligations.[35] This type of obligation refers to State conduct. They appear at first sight well suited to the fisheries context: they do not establish prohibitions or limits on the State, but imply *inter alia* a 'responsibility to ensure' on the part of States. This includes ensuring that appropriate domestic laws and regulations are adopted, and that there is vigilance in regard to their compliance, backed by enforcement mechanisms to address infractions.[36] In principle, this means that the existence of discrete illegal or unregulated fishing activities do not always imply that a due diligence obligation has been

32 E Franckx, 'Pacta Tertiis and the Agreement for the Implementation of the Straddling and Highly Migratory Fish Stocks provisions of the United Nations Convention on the Law of the Sea' (2000) 8 *Tulane Journal of International and Comparative Law* 49–82, 62.

33 See T Sato, 'Legitimacy of International Organizations and Their Decisions: Challenges that International Organizations Face in the 21st Century' (2009) 37(15) *Hitotsubashi Journal of Law and Politics* 11–30, 29.

34 See J Brunnee, 'International Legal Accountability through the Lens of the Law of State Responsibility' (2005) 36 *Netherlands Yearbook of International Law* 3–38, 22.

35 *Responsibilities and Obligations of States with Respect to Activities in the Area*, Advisory Opinion [2011] ITLOS Reports 10, paras 110–112.

36 *Request for an Advisory Opinion Submitted by the Sub-Regional Fisheries Commission*, Advisory Opinion, ITLOS Reports 2015, paras 129, 137 and 138 [SRFC].

breached, and that in each case the actual conduct of the State has to be enquired into. In the review of international legal obligations conducted in Chapter 2, a number of areas of uncertainty in the scope of the legal obligations were highlighted, and it is not always straightforward to assess whether there has been a breach.[37]

A breach of a due diligence obligation requires the offending course of action or inaction to be attributable to the organs of a State, to be part of the exercise of State authority, and/or part of a conduct controlled by or on behalf of a State.[38] Yet, despite this recognition, breaches of due diligence obligations concerning the protection of the marine environment and its resources can be difficult to demonstrate, in the absence of evaluation benchmarks against which the conduct of States may be assessed.[39] For example, under the LOSC, States are only duty-bound to establish a system of domestic laws and exert vigilance in their application. In general, they are not bound to specific *outcomes* as a result of adopting those measures. Hence, outside of the specialist treaty frameworks discussed in the previous chapter, and in the absence of well-established generally established international rules and conduct standards (GAIRS), assessments of State conduct and any ensuing attempt to the determination of a breach of a due diligence obligation contained in Parts VII or XII of the LOSC can be problematic. Especially for the purposes of addressing unregulated fishing, the analysis of the relevant international duties, undertaken in the previous chapter, suggests that, arguably, only wilfully unconcerned and uncooperative behaviours by States might enable the engagement of responsibility.[40]

It can be deduced from the above that well defined conduct rules, such as those typically established in special treaties, are fundamental for the interpretation of State conduct and the determination of potential breaches. This includes also the interpretation of more open textured or even general obligations. For example, in the underlying factors that underpinned the actions of the ITLOS in the Bluefin Tuna provisional measures case. Here, ITLOS had ordered the suspension of extraordinary activities, and the return by all parties

---

37 See *In the Matter of the South China Sea Arbitration (Republic of the Philippines v Peoples' Republic of China)* Award [2016] PCA Case No. 2013–19 [South China Sea].

38 Respectively ARSIWA Articles 4, 5, 6 and 8.

39 See Y Tanaka, *The International Law of the Sea* (Cambridge University Press, 2012) 367.

40 This limitation is enhanced by the fact that international court approaches to breaches of procedural duties have not always been robust. See J Brunnee, 'International Environmental Law and Community Interests: Procedural Aspects' in Benvenisti, Nolte and Yalin-Mor (Eds) *Community Interests Across International Law* (Oxford University Press, 2018) 158.

in the dispute to the ordinary quota of bluefin tuna previously established by virtue of a special international agreement.[41] Hence, the factor that enabled the tribunal to adopt an interim decision lied in the existence of stock allocations previously agreed by the parties, from which specific conduct expectations could be ascertained. Even more insightful is the South China Sea award, which also highlights the importance of treaty law, as well as other rules of international law such as GAIRS, in furnishing general obligations with appropriate content,[42] so that breaches can be determined from State actions, and responsibility claims activated.

3.3 Reciprocal Structure of State Responsibility and Its Implications

To fully appreciate the difficulties of associating responsibility to any notion of compliance, it is important to fully understand its functionality. As explained in the first section of this chapter, responsibility occurs in the context of international relations between States that have formally equal status. Hence, invocations of State responsibility are typically associated to claims concerning breaches of international legal obligations owed by one State to another. The reciprocal nature of these juridical relationships means that, normally, claims arise when an action or inaction by a State has resulted in some damage or injury to another State.[43] Hence, responsibility implies that the determination of a breach may carry the potential to result in some form of liability.[44]

This function of responsibility is specified in ARSIWA Article 42, which addresses the entitlement of States to invoke responsibility in cases where they have suffered some form of injury. In the words of Crawford and Watkins:

41 For commentary on the strengthening effect of the Bluefin Tuna provisional measures upon the regional cooperation agreement previously entered into by the parties to the dispute see T Stephens, 'The Limits of International Adjudication in International Environmental Law: Another Perspective on the Southern Bluefin Tuna Case' (2004) 19(2) *International Journal of Marine and Coastal Law* 177–198, 183 and 186.

42 South China Sea, para 941.

43 *Reparations for Injuries Suffered in the Service of the United Nations*, Advisory Opinion [1949] ICJ Reports 174, para 181. See also *Trail Smelter Arbitration* (*United States of America v Canada*) Award [1941] United Nations Reports of International Arbitral Awards Vol III 1903, page 1965.

44 Responsibilities in the Area paras 66 and 70. *Case Concerning the Factory at Chorzow* (*Claim for Indemnity*) Jurisdiction [1927] Publications of the permanent Court of International Justice Series A 1, page 21 [Chorzow Factory].

> To the extent that one regime stands out in terms of institutional refinement, it is the regime of liability that States trigger when they violate an international rule.[45]

According to Article 42(a), a State that has been injured may invoke the responsibility of another State that owes it the obligation that has been breached. Under Article 42(b), responsibility may also be invoked where the obligation is owed to 'a group of States including that State, or the international community as a whole, and the breach of the obligation (i) specially affects that State, or (ii) is of such character as radically to change the position of all the other States to which the obligation is owed with respect to the further performance of obligations'. Under Article 42, a bilateral structure characterised by breaches of 'obligations owed to another' emerges as a central feature of responsibility.

According to Ago, this structure is necessarily reciprocal, and is characterised by 'the correlation between a legal obligation (...) and a subjective right'.[46] In addition, any responsibility invocation under Article 42 has to meet a further requirement: the need for injury or damage caused by the internationally unlawful act.[47] In this respect, the responsibility regime could arguably be understood as being similar to domestic laws established to regulate delictual injury between persons.[48] This function is not solely related to situations where there is a need for reparation: responsibility invocations in respect injurious acts often simply seek breach declarations, or orders for the cessation of the activity that constitutes the breach.[49] In all these circumstances, whether injury is material or to a right, or whether reparation, cessation, or declaration is sought, State responsibility is activated by or on behalf of an injured State, operating akin to a mechanism of civil justice.[50]

This has adverse implications for the operation of responsibility in the context of IUU fishing control. The area of the ocean demarcated as high seas by the LOSC is a 'public' space, in the sense that all States are entitled to a right whereby their nationals may utilise high seas resources, over which no

45 J Crawford and J Watkins, 'International Responsibility' in Besson and Tassioulas (Eds) *The Philosophy of International Law* (Oxford University Press, 2010) 285.

46 R Ago, Second Report of the ILC, *Yearbook of the International Law Commission* 2 (1970) 192 para 46.

47 Chorzow Factory, at 21.

48 R Wright, 'The Grounds and Extent of Legal Responsibility', (2003) 41 *San Diego Law Review* 1, 3.

49 Shelton (2002) at 836, supra at 9.

50 D Alland, 'Countermeasures of General Interest' (2002) 13 *European Journal of International Law* 1221–1239, 1226.

individual State can claim sovereignty.[51] Yet, despite enabling this type of universal access, high seas protections are rooted in poorly defined obligations, especially outside of the specific fishery treaties previously discussed.[52] Public spaces such as the high seas are often relegated by States when it comes to prioritising investment in environmental security concerns, in favour of areas over which they have sovereignty or sovereign rights, and that are less remote.[53] Often, international proceedings where the conservation of high seas stocks has been argued by claimants, are usually related to claims intending to expand is some way the jurisdiction that States enjoy over fisheries inside their exclusive economic zones (EEZ). In the face of such claims, the individual rights of flag States to keep the high seas open to fishing have been vigorously defended. As Boyle indicates:

> Compulsory dispute settlement clauses may be intended to have a certain antiseptic quality, deterring states from making unilateral claims to 'creeping jurisdiction'. (…) The few attempts to extend coastal State fisheries jurisdiction beyond 200 miles have not succeeded. The EU's robust response in the Swordfish case stopped Chile in its tracks and the dispute was eventually settled. Canada successfully contested ICJ jurisdiction in its dispute with Spain over regulation of high seas fishing, but thereafter dropped its unilateral claims and settled.[54]

Further to the cases to which this quote refers, namely *Swordfish* (*Chile v European Community*) case,[55] and the *Fisheries Jurisdiction* (*Spain v Canada*) case,[56] the background circumstances giving rise to an international arbitration saw attempts by China to claim exclusivity over areas of the South China Sea extending beyond its EEZ.[57] Similarly expansionist claims can be observed in older cases involving activities in the high seas, prior to the adoption of the LOSC.[58] In all

---

51 LOSC Article 89 and 116.

52 See Chapter 2, sections 2.3.1, 2.4.1 and 2.5.1.

53 CD Stone, 'Defending the Global Commons' in Sands (Ed) *Greening International Law* (Earthscan, 1993) 35 and 36.

54 A Boyle, 'UNCLOS Dispute Settlement and the Uses and Abuses of Part XV' (2014) 47(1) *Revue Belge de Droit International Belgian Review of International Law* 182–204, 185.

55 *Case Concerning the Conservation and Sustainable Exploitation of Swordfish Stocks in the South-Eastern Pacific Ocean* (*Chile v European Community*) [2000] ITLOS Reports 13.

56 *Fisheries Jurisdiction* (*Spain v Canada*) [1998] ICJ Reports 432.

57 South China Sea, at 495.

58 See *Fisheries Jurisdiction Cases* (*United Kingdom of Great Britain and Northern Ireland v Iceland*) (*Federal Republic of Germany v Iceland*) [1974] ICJ Reports 3.

these cases, the binary character of ocean division is a salient dispute feature: the open character of the highs seas is protected versus some type of jurisdiction claim, which would if successful have entailed a *prima facie* foreclosure, conditioning or limitation to the extractive activities of fishing vessels flagged to other States. It is thus the case that the reciprocal structure of State responsibility, at least from the perspective of Article 42, appears to offer less to the protection of the living resources of the high seas than to the protection of the access and exploitation rights of States.

3.4 Responsibility and *erga omnes* Obligations

The law of State responsibility has been said to contain the potential to perform a public function aiming towards the preservation of the integrity of the legal order, transcending the above-discussed role of enabling private justice.[59] This public function is arguably provided by ARSIWA Article 48.1(b),[60] which refers to obligations being 'owed to the international community as a whole'. This provision appears to open the door of responsibility, in a seeming acknowledgement of the rise in State obligations that transcend mere bilateral reciprocity,[61] in order to protect collective interests.[62] *Prima facie*, the protection afforded by Article 48.1(b) might be understood to, for example, extend to breaches of the obligations enshrined in Articles 94 and 192 of the Convention, in respect of the exercise of flag State jurisdiction in the high seas and the preservation of the marine environment and its living resources.[63] Being general in character, these obligations apply to all States for the purposes of high seas fishing, irrespective of whether a State is a party to a fisheries treaty. Hence, the characterisation of these duties as omnes obligations is particular important

59 A Nollkaemper, 'Constitutionalization and the Unity of the Law of International Responsibility' (2009) 16(2) *Indiana Journal of Global Legal Studies* 535–564, 536. See also CJ Tams, *Enforcing Obligations Erga Omnes in International Law* (Cambridge University Press, 2005) 6.

60 See J Crawford, *Brownlie's Principles of Public International Law* (Oxford University Press, 2008) 539.

61 E Stein, 'Bruno Simma, The Positivist?' in Fastenrath, et al (Eds) *From Bilateralism to Community interests: Essays in Honour of Bruno Simma* (Oxford University Press, 2011) 22. HLA Hart, in Raz and Bullock (Eds) *The Concept of Law* (Clarendon Press, 1994) 250.

62 Save for issues of State responsibility, the law of treaties provides the secondary rules applicable to treaty-derived obligations. See Vienna Convention on the Law of Treaties, 1155 UNTS 331, Articles 19–22, 34–38, and 60 [VCLT].

63 J Klabbers, *International Law* (Cambridge University Press, 2013) 42.

for the establishment of State responsibility in the context of marine fisheries and, in particular, for addressing unregulated fishing.

A number of influential authors such as Allott and Benvenisti have supported the operation of responsibility beyond reciprocal rights and duties.[64] However, the notion of duties owed to the international community as reflected in Article 48.1(b) of ARSIWA arguably has the most synergy with scholarship by Simma in 'From Bilateralism to Community Interests in International Law'.[65] Simma's contribution drove the idea of States as protectors of the international community on the basis of the evolution of the structure of general obligations,[66] which he associated to an international recognition of 'community interests'.[67] At the centre Simma's formulation is a type of obligation in respect of which the entire international community has an actionable right: the *erga omnes* (omnes) obligation. With omnes obligations, Simma saw in the protection of the shared interests, such as the natural environment, the need for solidarity, transcending the reciprocal structure of responsibility based on individual rights and duties. At the same time, he was concerned with a 'universal' community comprising of States, but also possibly of non-State actors, including not only international organisations, but also human beings.[68]

The principle behind the special character of omnes obligations was alluded to in the famous *obiter dictum* by the ICJ in the case of the *Barcelona Traction Light and Power Company*:

> In particular, an essential distinction should be drawn between obligations of a State towards the international community as a whole and those arising *vis-à-vis* another State in the field of diplomatic protection.[69]

---

64 P Allott, *Eunomia: New Order for a New World* (Oxford University Press, 1990) 296. R Ago, 'Second Report on State Responsibility' (1970) 2(1) *Yearbook of the International Law Commission* 177–198, 192. E Benvenisti, 'Sovereigns as Trustees of Humanity: on the Accountability of States to Foreign Stakeholders' (2013) 107(2) *American Journal of International Law* 295–333, 299.

65 B Simma, 'From Bilateralism to Community Interest in International Law' (1994) IV *Recueil des Cours*, 217–384.

66 Simma (1994) at 256 and 259, supra at 65.

67 Simma (1994) at 233, supra at 65.

68 See B Kingsbury and E Donaldson, 'From Bilateralism to Publicness' Fastenrath et al (Eds) From Bilateralism to Community interests: Essays in Honour of Bruno Simma' (Oxford University Press, 2011) 82.

69 *Case Concerning The Barcelona Traction, Light and Power Company Limited (Belgium v Spain)* Judgment [1970] ICJ Rep 3, para 33.

This passage was influential in the development of the omnes doctrine, and of the Article 48.1(b) drafting.[70] This ARSIWA provision appears to establish a right of States to invoke responsibility when an obligation breached was owed to the international community as a whole. There is in it, however, a lack of clarity as to whether there is a need for a protected right that States can rely on as the basis for a responsibility claim. The hesitation in the text of the provision may stem from a lack of clarity in other jurisprudence of international tribunals in this regard. Indeed, shortly after the *Barcelona Traction* case was decided, the ICJ denied two States, Liberia and Ethiopia, the possibility of claiming under the responsibility regime on the basis that neither had a 'material interest' in the breach by South Africa of a public interest.[71] This interest did not amount to a general interest, as it did not benefit the entire international community, but simply a particular human group in South Africa.[72] Would the outcome be any different in the event of breach of a general obligation that protects an interest that all States possess, such as the obligation to protect the marine environment under LOSC Article 192, upon which the fishing freedom of the high seas is balanced? A few considerations are pertinent before the question can be answered.

In the *Nuclear Tests Case*,[73] Australia, New Zealand and the Republic of Fiji had initially raised a complaint against France as a result of atmospheric nuclear testing by France, over the potential for nuclear fallout, endangering high seas areas of the Pacific Ocean *inter alia*.[74] At the time, Tiewul indicated:

> Nuclear test explosions on the high seas violate the doctrine of the freedom of the high seas, inasmuch as they interfere with two of its most crucial incidents: the freedoms of navigation and of fishing.[75]

According to Tiewul, the activities constituted an abuse of rights by France, resulting in the erosion of the rights of other States concerning their utilisation of the high seas.[76] In their complaint before the ICJ, the claimant States

70 Tams (2005) at 94, supra at 59.

71 *South West Africa Cases* (*Ethiopia v South Africa*) (*Liberia v South Africa*) Judgment [1966] ICJ Reports 6, para 44.

72 ILC, 'Third Report on State Responsibility, by Mr. James Crawford, Special Rapporteur' (2000) document A/CN.4/507 39, para 85.

73 *Nuclear Tests* (*Australia v France; New Zealand v France*) Interim Measures order of 22 June [1973] ICJ Reports 99 [Nuclear Tests].

74 Nuclear Tests, para 22.

75 SA Tiewul, 'International Law and Nuclear Test Explosions on the High Seas' (1974) 8(1) *Cornell International Law Journal* 45–64, 47.

76 *Ibid.*

sought to base their claim on the breach by the respondent of such an obligation to protect the environment, as well as on a breach of the obligation to respect their high seas freedoms.[77] However, the ICJ, in its interim order of 22 June 1997, did not extend the provisional measures requesting France to avoid nuclear test fallout over the high seas.[78] In fact, the court was reluctant to recognise that the claimants had a generic right conferring onto them the power to claim responsibility in order to ensure the protection of the high seas environment.[79] Later, in the *Nuclear Tests Re-Examination* case, the court did not shed any further clarity, as it indicated that, without prejudice to the primary obligation of States to protect the marine environment, the claimant did not have a claim to have the case re-examined, given the affirmation of the defendant to abide by such obligation.[80] Hence, whilst the existence of the general obligation to protect the marine environment was not denied, the court failed to clarify the precise parameters of any possible recourse over the breach of such obligation.

So far, undisputed recognition of omnes obligations has been afforded only in a very narrow category of norms, namely the right of peoples to self-determination,[81] the freedom of human beings from slavery, and protection against genocide.[82] From this jurisprudential perspective, the key requirement for an obligation to be understood as deserving of the omnes protection appears to be therefore in the fundamental nature of the rights protected. In line with Simma's original intention, the expression 'international community as a whole' may be seen to refer to the entire human community, beyond States and their interactions.[83] Certainly, the issue of transcendence beyond States was also a reflection made by the ICJ dictum in *Barcelona Traction*.[84] Arguably, thus, erga omnes obligations may be protecting certain human rights considered essential in nature:[85] those that are universally shared and protectable

77 Y Shigeta, 'Obligation to Protect the Environment in the ICJ's Practice: To What Extent Erga Omnes?' (2012) 55 *Japanese Yearbook of International Law* 176–207, 190.

78 Nuclear Tests, para 35.

79 Nuclear Tests, paras 29 to 31.

80 Nuclear Tests, Order of 22 September 1995, para 64.

81 *Case Concerning East Timor (Portugal v Australia)* Judgment [1995] ICJ Reports 90, para 29.

82 Armed Activities on the Territory of the Congo (New Application: 2002) (Democratic Republic of the Congo v Rwanda) (Jurisdiction and Admissibility) [2006] ICJ Reports 6, para 32. See also Barcelona Traction, para 34.

83 See Simma (1994) at 357, supra at 65. Tams (2011) at 379, supra at 14. Kingsbury and Donaldson (2011) at 80, supra at 68.

84 Barcelona Traction, para 33.

85 This is not a universally accepted position amongst legal scholars, although an overlap between both concepts is often acknowledged. See, respectively in favour and

across the entire international community, including international organisations,[86] and individuals.[87] This suggests an association that is closely connected with humanity and universality, and thus with the category norms usually referred to as *ius cogens*.[88] These are rights generally understood to protect against harms of a particular egregious nature.[89] These rights are universal as well as individual, and generate a duty of respect by each individual State: they thus offer the foundation for a bilateral claiming structure which is in line with the structure of State responsibility.[90] To the extent that these type of rights are protected by erga omnes obligations, this justifies their inviolable character.[91] By contrast, as seen in *Nuclear Tests*, duties concerning the protection of high seas freedoms are not inviolable, and the rights they protect are therefore not absolute. Allowances have to be made for the utilisation of the high seas by other States, including uses such as fishing, that may be destructive by their very nature.[92]

Despite this, the rights associated to the freedom of fishing, as established in LOSC Article 87 and qualified in Article 116 of the Convention, do pertain in principle to all States. The ICJ in the Icelandic *Fisheries Jurisdiction* case, referred to the duty as an interest of all States, as follows (emphasis added):

---

against: Tams (2005) supra at 96, and D Tladi, Third Report on Perempltory Norms of General International Law (just cogens), UNGA Doc A/CN.4/714, 12. *P Birnie, A Boyle, C Tedgwell, International Law and the Environment* (Oxford University Press, 2009) 387.

86 J Crawford, J Peel and S Olleson, 'The ILC's Articles on Responsibility of States for Internationally Wrongful Acts: Completion of the Second Reading' (2001) 12(5) *European Journal of International Law* 963–991, 973.

87 AA Cançado Trindade, *International Law for Humankind: Towards a New Ius Gentium* (Martinus Nijhoff, 2005) 316. B Simma, 'Universality of International Law from the Perspective of a Practitioner' (2009) 20 *European Journal of International Law* 265–297, 265.

88 D Shelton, 'Hierarchy of Norms and Human Rights: Of Trumps and Winners' (2002) 65(2) *Saskatchewan Law Review* 301–332, 323.

89 VCLT Article 51. For further discussion, see E Wyler, 'From State Crime to Responsibility for Serious Breaches of Obligations under Peremptory Norms of General International Law' (2002) 13(5) *European Journal of International Law* 1174–1160.

90 See Tams (2005) at 135, supra at 59. Also, G Fitzmaurice, Second Report: Draft Article 19(1) (iv) (1957) II *Year Book of the International Law Commission* 16–70, 31.

91 Questions have been raised as to whether practice supports the existence of rules formally declared as fundamental. See J Brunnee and SJ Toope, *Legitimacy and Legality in International Law* (Cambridge University Press, 2010) 270. Also, Shelton (2002) at 326, supra at 10.

92 Nuclear Tests, paras 29 to 31.

> It is on of the advances in maritime international law, resulting from the intensification of fishing, that the former laissez-faire treatment of the living resources of the sea in the high seas has been replaced by a recognition of a duty to have due regard to the rights of other States and the needs of conservation *for the benefit of all.*[93]

But 'for the benefit of all' in this context may not mean that these interests are of sufficient importance to be always protected by omnes obligations. One problem is that the rights associated to the freedom of the high seas do not appear to have a clearly established reciprocal relationship with the obligations established for the conservation of high seas resources.[94] Further, the rights and freedoms that have been established by the Convention in favour of all States,[95] but they do not automatically extend to all human beings, since they require mediation by the regulating State. This factor distinguishes them from rights that possess a universal nature.[96] Actual access to fishery resources depends on a wide variety of socio-economic and development conditions, and historical factors, neither of which is distributed equally across States or their nationals.[97] Therefore, the freedom to fish the high seas and the conditional right of exploitation that gives it meaning is characterised by interests that do not possess a universal character, other than as potential to exercise such freedom.

In her commentary concerning the arbitration case of the South China Sea, Oral highlights the award as a possible turning point for omnes obligations. Indeed, the award chastises the failure by a flag State to adopt rules and measures to prevent the harvesting of endangered species, and the destruction of fragile marine habitats that was a breach of its general due diligence obligation under Articles 192, as well as the more defined duty concerning fragile ecosystem protection under LOSC 194(5).[98] Oral argues that the award may be paving the way for the formulation of this general obligation as one of an *erga omnes*

---

93 *Fisheries Jurisdiction (UK v Iceland)* Judgment [1974] ICJ Reports 3, para 64.

94 Y Tanaka, 'Protection of Community Interests in International Law: The Case of the Law of the Sea' (2011) 15 *Max Plack Yearbook of United Nations Law* 329–375, 364.

95 Such as second generation human rights. See JD Van der Vyver, 'State Sovereignty and the Environment in International Law" (1992) 109(3) *South African Law Journal* 472–495, 481.

96 See A Telesetsky, 'Fishing Moratoria and Securing TURFs: Creating Opportunities for Future Marine Resource Abundance in the Face of Scarcity in Western Africa' (2013) 42(1) *Georgia Journal of International and Comparative Law* 35–68, 49.

97 See FAO, 'State of World Fisheries and Aquaculture' (2016) 81.

98 South China Sea, para. 960–961, 966, and 984.

character.[99] However, this possibility should be approached with caution: the reliance of the tribunal on the general obligation arising from Article 192 of the LOSC to find China responsible for the destruction of reefs and endangered marine species is indeed interesting. Nevertheless, it ultimately concerned areas where Philippines had sovereign rights that had been encroached on, and that it was entitled to defend. Hence, its invocation of State responsibility respected the bilateral structure that is characteristic of this international legal institution.[100] Logically, claims for flag State responsibility in respect of high seas illegal or unregulated fishing by vessels under its jurisdiction would also need to be based on an infringement of an obligation and the injury caused by the breach to a State right. The question of whether State rights can be associated to the obligation established in LOSC Article 192 regarding the protection of the marine environment and the conservation of its living resources is addressed in section 3.6.

3.5 Responsibility and *erga omnes partes* Obligations

The International Law Commission introduced in ARSIWA 48.1(a) a development in the law of responsibility, whereby injury to a subjective right of the claimant was not an explicit requirement for invocation. Instead, the provision indicates that the obligation breached must be owed to a group of States for the protection of a collective interest of the group, and that the claimant State must form part of that group. In its commentary to Article 48, the ILC suggests that this particular provision refers to arrangements made by States by treaty, including those established for the protection of the natural environment and its resources.[101] Under Article 48.1(a), *erga omnes partes* (idem, or partes) obligations appear to involve an ongoing shared management dimension that cannot easily be addressed via the reciprocal claim structure that has traditionally been

99 N Oral, 'The south China Sea Arbitral Award: A Triumph for Part XII of UNCLOS and the Protection and Preservation of the Marine Environment' in Jayakumar, Koh, Beckman, Davenport and Phan (Eds) The South China Sea Arbitration: The Legal Dimension (Elgar, 2018) 223.

100 See South China Sea, paras 815 et seq. and 950. The case gravitates around the destructive harvesting activities of Chinese fishing vessels in respect of marine features that, although disputed by China and Taiwan, are in principle located in the EEZ of Philippines, thus concerning sovereign rights in respect of the breach of which Philippines is entitled to invoke responsibility.

101 ILC Commentary to Article 48, paragraph 7.

characteristic of the law of responsibility.[102] Hence, unlike in the case of erga omnes obligations, which as already discussed are not suitable for invocation in matters concerning the conservation of natural resources,[103] partes obligations may at first appear ideally suited. The key implication of Article 48.1(a) appears to be that an erga omnes partes obligation protects a collective interest, yet it should be noted that the text of paragraph 1 also requires injury to a State in the group, with such injury being the factor that permits a responsibility claim by any other group member with an interest in addressing the breach, and ensuring and perpetuating the acts whereby obligations to the group are met. Or in other words, ongoing compliance with the duties established by the treaty.

As Fitzmaurice explains, the invocation of responsibility erga omnes partes was attempted by Australia in the Whaling in the Antarctic Case, on the proviso that it was acting on behalf of the collective interests of the State parties to the treaty in ensuring mutual compliance.[104] As the same author also indicates, the Whaling case might have been interpreted as a continuation of a trend commenced by the ICJ in 2009 with Questions relating to the Obligation to Prosecute or Extradite (Belgium v. Senegal) to favour standing in omnes partes contexts,[105] were it not for the fact that the court remained silent on the nature of the obligations at stake. It follows from the above that the importance of the existence of rights and obligations as defined in treaty frameworks establishing collective interestscannot be overstated, given their critical function for the purposes of responsibility under ARSIWA Article 48.1(a).

3.6 Responsibility and Injury to Rights

It follows from the above sections that ARSIWA Article 42 and Article 48, establish distinct approaches to enable State responsibility invocations, depending

102 Stephens (2004) at 178, supra at 41. For further discussion, see E Brown Weiss, 'Invoking State Responsibility in the Twenty First Century' (2002) 96 *American Journal of International Law* 798–816.

103 See M Fitzmaurice, *Whaling and International Law* (Cambridge University Press, 2015) 112. See also H Sakai, 'After the Waling Case: Its Lessons from a Japanese Perspective' in Fitzmaurice and Tamada (Eds) *Whaling in the Antarctic: The Significance and the Implications of the ICJ Judgment* (Brill Nijhoff, 2016) 308. See also See Third Report of the Special Rapporteur on State Responsibility (2000) para 06(b) A/CN.4/507/Add.3.

104 Fitzmaurice (2015) at page 110, supra at 103.

105 See Fitmaurice, 112, and C Tams, 'Roads not Taken, Opportunities Missed: Procedural and Jurisdictional Questions Sidestepped in the Whaling Judgment' in Fitzmaurice and Tamada (Eds) *Whaling in the Antarctic: The Significance and the Implications of the ICJ Judgment* (Brill Nijhoff, 2016) 193.

on the type of injury that has been caused, and on who is entitled to claim. Specifically, Article 42(a) requires injury to the rights of the individual claimant State, whereas 42(b) responds to the existence of injury either to universal rights of the international community as a whole, which specially affect the claimant State, or otherwise radically change the position of the States in a group to which the obligation is owed in respect of future performance. If these criteria are met, then the injured State can claim responsibility and resort to the full spectrum of remedies, or in the case of invocation within the parameters of Article 48, another State may claim on its behalf.[106] A responsibility claim under Article 42(b) would require the claimant State to prove injury to a subjective right under a treaty for the performance of the collective obligation being breached, a situation that can be contextualised to high seas fishing.

The freedoms and rights enshrined in Articles 87.1(e) and 116 of the LOSC, respectively concern the freedom of high seas fishing, and the right by States to confer onto their nationals access to high seas fishing, albeit subject to meeting their conservation and management obligations under the LOSC.[107] In the protection of those closely associated freedoms and rights, States can and do take action, as proven for example by the claim brought by Spain before the ICJ in the Canadian Fisheries Jurisdiction ICJ case.[108] It has been argued that, in the context of a violation of a well established right, there may be no need to prove more than the existence of an encroachment upon that right.[109] However, as already explained, the rights associated to the high seas fishing freedom are not absolute, given that such rights are conditioned, as a minimum by general duties that require the exercise of jurisdiction over national vessels, the protection of the marine environment and its living resources, and the duty to cooperate, as well as due regard for the rights of other States. Taking those conditioning factors into account, an injury to the right to fish the high seas

106 The ILC Commentary on Article 42 indicates that the provisions in this article are closely connected to Article 60 of the VCLT, on the subject of material breaches of a treaty. Under paragraph (b) of this article, dealing with obligations that are not reciprocal in character, States are injured where they are affected by the breach in a manner that distinguishes them from the remaining States to which the obligations are owed, or affects each State to which the obligation is owed individually.

107 See R Barnes and C Massarella, 'High Seas Fisheries' in Morgera and Kulovesi (Eds) *Research Handbook on International Law and Natural Resources* (Edward Elgar, 2016) 369.

108 *Fisheries Jurisdiction* (*Spain v Canada*) Judgment [1998] ICJ Reports 432, para 84. Nevertheless, the parties in this dispute operated in the context of a fisheries convention. For a discussion on the possible omnes rationale behind the ICJ decision, see Shigeta (2012) at 193, supra at 115.

109 EJ de Arechaga, *International Law in the Past Third of a Century* (Martinus Nijhoff, 1978) 29.

can still exist, although largely reduced to a binary question of the possibility of accessing a target stock.

Indeed, without such core right to enable nationals to harvest high seas stock, provided that it is done in compliance with applicable international obligations (eg. in an appropriately regulated and cooperative manner), the freedom of fishing would be rendered meaningless. As such, the rights associated with the freedom of fishing, namely rights to enable nationals to have the opportunity of harvesting stock, is opposable against any State that may be preventing another in a legally unjustified manner to engage in the exercise of such right.[110] This scenario thus falls within the spectrum of ARSIWA 42(a) as well as (b)(i), insofar as a breach of such right might be interpreted as harming the fishing State individually, or harming it specially within a group of fishing States. Thus, it seems that such scenario can in principle provide a basis for a responsibility claim.

It can also be said that the perpetuation of this core freedom is in the interest of all States. In this regard, the ILC stated as follows:

> Any freedom that is to be exercised in the interests of all entitled to enjoy it, must be regulated. Hence, the law of the high seas contains certain rules (...) designed not to limit or restrict the freedom of the high seas, but to safeguard its exercise in the interests of the entire international community.[111]

The nature of obligations to safeguard those general interests in respect high seas fisheries were examined in the context of the ITLOS case in its Southern Bluefin Tuna Preliminary Measures Order of 27 August 1999.[112] In this case, the claimants failed to prove that the injurious acts that they attributed to the respondent State entailed the curtailment of their opportunities for harvesting. In this case, the claimants' fleets had continued fishing, despite claims of grievous damage to the stock by the actions of the respondent. It was apparent that their right to fish had not been in a binary sense extinguished, and continued in existence. From this perspective, it is arguable that only the

110 For a challenge to the characterisation of the freedom of fishing as a State right, see T Henriksen, 'Revisiting the Freedom of Fishing and Legal Obligations on States Not Party to Regional Fisheries Management Organizations' (2009) 40(1) *Ocean Development and International Law* 80–96.

111 ILC, Draft Articles on the Law of the Sea (1956) Commentary 9, pages 253 and 278, as referred to in D Guilfoyle, 'The High Seas' in Rothwell et al (Eds) *The Oxford Handbook of the Law of the Sea* (Oxford University Press 2015) 206.

112 *Southern Bluefin Tuna Cases* (*New Zealand v Japan*) (*Australia v Japan*) Provisional Measures [1999] ITLOS Reports 280, para 67 [Bluefin Tuna].

disappearance of the possibility to target the stock (namely, the commercial extinction of said stock) could have eliminated the claimants' opportunity to exercise the freedom of fishing in the context of that fishery. To cause the commercial extinction of the target stock would have extinguished that right, and would have been *de facto* equivalent to an act of access closure. Yet, commercial extinction is an incredibly high standard for claiming responsibility, and an exorbitant collective price to pay in both biological and economic terms. Thus, whilst State responsibility invocation may be viable as a last resort to stop a stock from disappearing completely, or at least suffering such damage as to effectively cause the closure of the fishery, it must be recognised that it possesses little value from a conservation *and management* perspective.

3.7 Other Factors Limiting the Effectiveness of State Responsibility

As discussed in Chapter 1, IUU fishing is a highly prevalent activity, and that its presence in the high seas is on the increase.[113] The occurrence of international litigation concerning high seas conservation and management hardly reflects the scale of the problem.[114] The reasons for this are probably manifold and complex, but at least one explanation is that the reciprocal structure of State responsibility is not conducive to environmental protection claims. Orrego Vicuna has argued that the costs associated to the determination of liabilities under a responsibility claim might operate as a deterrent for States that may want to avoid the consequences of a breach.[115] Nevertheless, it can also be argued that, if the responsibility mechanism induces any compliance at all, it is confined to situations where there is a well-defined subjective right.[116] By contrast, when the objective is solely the protection of the resources or their environment, claimants face considerable difficulties.[117]

113 DC Dunn et al, 'Empowering High Seas Governance with Satellite Vessel Tracking Data' (2018) *Fish and Fisheries* 729–740, 730.

114 Beyond the cases discussed in the previous section, other international fisheries cases before the ITLOS, the International Court of Justice, and the Permanent Court of Arbitration concern activities in the EEZ.

115 F Orrego Vicuna, 'Responsibility and Liability for Environmental Damage Under International Law: Issues and Trends' (1997) 10 *Georgia International Environmental Law Review* 279.

116 A Bleckmann, 'The Subjective Right in Public International Law', (1985) 28 *German Yearbook of International Law* 144. B Simma, 'Reciprocity' in Bernhardt (Ed) *Encyclopedia of Public International Law* Vol IV (North Holland Publishing, 2009) 29.

117 F Orrego Vicuna, 'Responsibility and Liability for Environmental Damage Under International Law: Issues and Trends' (1997) 10 *Georgia International Environmental Law Review* 279–308, 284.

Firstly, the dependency of State responsibility on a breach of due diligence obligations means that its effectiveness may be marred by certain non-legal factors. For example, as Boyle points out, the implementation of due diligence obligations is conditioned by considerations of foreseeability.[118] This means State responsibility may not be engaged simply because a single IUU fishing event has occurred, unless shortfalls in the domestic regime can be clearly established. Serdy has further argued that there may also be a reluctance by States in calling out such shortfalls, considering that their own domestic systems may be far from perfect.[119] Secondly, the so-called 'problem of many hands' is illustrative of the challenges that may be faced in the context of high seas stocks protection.[120] The problem of many hands occurs where actions of multiple actors whose activities are not coordinated or well defined, but are all potentially part of the cause of a harmful outcome, giving rise to a diffusion of responsibility.[121] In this context, the individual responsibility of each actor becomes very difficult to ascertain and delimit,[122] and may even be impossible, particularly when there is a lack of visibility of the individual harmful action.[123] This phenomenon, which is characteristic of situations where damage to collective interests is involved,[124] adequately describes circumstances in which harm to the high seas' living resources by vessels operating in an uncoordinated manner, variously regulated under different flags, can unfold.

ARSIWA Article 47 acknowledges the possibility of shared responsibility between two or more States. Yet, as Okowa has noted, there are problems associated with this provision, to the extent that it may be insufficient to establish a right to claim joint and several responsibility from two or more States.[125] Nollkaemper indicates that 'such responsibility does not fall on these states

---

118 AE Boyle, 'Globalising Environmental Liability: The Interplay of National and International Law' (2005) 17 *Journal of Environmental Law* 3–12, 8.

119 A Serdy, *The New Entrants Problem in International Fisheries Law* (Cambridge University Press, 2016a) 145.

120 The phrase was coined by DF Thompson, 'Moral Responsibility of Public Officials: The Problem of Many Hands' (1980) 74 *American Political Science Review* 905.

121 A Nollkaemper, *The Problem of Many Hands in International Law* (Amsterdam Center for International Law, 2015) 12.

122 M Bovens, '*The Quest for Responsibility: Accountability and Citizenship in Complex Organisations*' (Cambridge University Press, 1998) 46.

123 H Nissenbaum, Accountability in a Computerised Society' (1996) 2(25) *Science and Engineering Ethics* 29.

124 Brunnee (2018) at 153, supra at 40.

125 PN Okowa, *State Responsibility for Transboundary Air Pollution in International Law* (Oxford University Press) 200.

as a collective, but falls on each of them as individual States'.[126] However, of the three types of scenarios where shared responsibility may arise according to Nollkaemper, namely where a State commits a wrongful act in conjunction with another State, where one wrongful act is attributed to two or more States, or where two independent wrongs are attributed to two States, only the last one might typically be relevant to IUU fishing control. This is because the individual regulatory relationship between a flag State and its fishing vessels, established under Articles 91.1 and 92.1 of the LOSC respectively on nationality of ships and genuine link, and exclusive jurisdiction of the flag State, would normally preclude the other two.

There are, in addition, a number of possible knowledge barriers capable of preventing responsibility invocations. The costs inflicted by IUU fishing, even when foreseeable and attributable to a particular flag State, can nevertheless be difficult to ascertain due to the furtive nature of the activity. Often, the calculation of economic damage and associated liabilities is fraught with difficulty.[127] A study by Serdy on the liability potential of responsibility in the context of regionalised high seas fisheries conservation suggests that knowledge barriers are such for the calculation of costs, that the liability potential of State responsibility to ensure appropriate reparation appears remote.[128] In the absence of knowledge about damage, or the opportunity of reparation, there is little to encourage responsibility invocation. These empirical knowledge obstacles are exacerbated by the fact that the claimant carries the responsibility for proving the existence injury.[129] These non-legal factors converge with the structural features of State responsibility, resulting in a lack of opportunities and incentives for States to engage responsibility claims for the purposes of protecting the living resources of the high seas.

---

126 A Nollkaemper, *Issues of Shared Responsibility before the International Court of Justice* (Amsterdam Center for International Law, 2011), referring to L May, *Sharing Responsibility* (University of Chicago Press, 1992) 38.

127 See AE Boyle, 'Remedying Harm to International Common Spaces and Resources: Compensation and Other Approaches' in Wetterstein (Ed) *Harm to the Environment: The Right to Compensation and the Assessment of Damages* (Clarendon Press, 1997) 83.

128 Serdy (2016a) at 375, supra at 119.

129 *Case Concerning Pulp Mills on the River Uruguay (Argentina v Uruguay)* Judgment [2010] ICJ Reports 14, para 164: 'Regarding the arguments put forward by Argentina on the reversal of the burden of the proof and on the existence (...) of an equal onus to prove under the 1975 Statute, the Court considers that while a precautionary approach may be relevant (...) it does not follow that it operates as a reversal of the burden of proof'.

3.8 Conclusion

This chapter has set out and analysed the functional role of the rules of State responsibility as a compliance mechanism in matters of IUU fishing control. The discussion is largely aligned with other literature, regarding the limitations of the rules of State responsibility as a foundation for ensuring compliance in matters of environmental protection. Arguably, the law of responsibility has not had the effect of conferring effective protection to collective interests of an environmental character,[130] such as the protection of high seas fishing resources.

In particular, the operation of responsibility around the due diligence obligations that characterise the international legal framework for high seas fisheries regulation purposes is problematic: The indeterminacy of State conduct standards outside of the scope of the specialist fishery treaties means that potential breaches are difficult to determine, despite documented instances of IUU fishing. The potential of open textured due diligence obligations to provide a basis for responsibility invocations is thus generally weak. Additionally, the reciprocal structure of responsibility can also prevent invocation, and appears better suited to protect well established rights of high seas utilisation. Reciprocity affords State responsibility a limited functionality that can be understood as akin to a private justice mechanism, and which is inadequate for the protection of public spaces and resources.

Further, the successful invocation of responsibility requires certain formal qualifying conditions, which generally exclude non-State actors, as well as non-legal rules. This, combined with the problem of many hands, combine to undermine the effectiveness of State responsibility as a compliance mechanism. Further, despite recent developments in the law of responsibility supporting erga omnes obligations, this chapter has explained that this type of obligation is better equipped to protect universal rights, rather than the rights associated to conservation and management of high seas fisheries. Nevertheless, it has been noted that some of the rights associated to the freedom of fishing in the high seas are in principle able to provide a basis for responsibility claims, and that this may be sufficient, although only as a final line of defence, to prevent

130 See PW Birnie, EA Boyle, and C Redgwell, *International Law and the Environment* (Oxford University Press, 2009) 211. I Scobbie, 'The Invocation of Responsibility for the Breach of Obligations under Peremptory Norms of General International Law' (2002) 13(5) *European Journal of International Law* 1201–1220, 1210 and 1211. P Okowa, 'Environmental Dispute Settlement: Some Reflections on Recent Developments' in Evans (Ed) *Remedies in International Law* (Hart, 1998) 158.

the extinction of high seas species as a result of fishing activity. More appropriate protections can be provided via *erga omnes partes* obligations, linked to the existence of collective interests protected by treaty. Hence, the importance of treaty frameworks, alongside other international rules such as GAIRS, through which State conduct standards can be ascertained for the purposes of responsibility assessments, cannot be overestimated.

CHAPTER 4

IUU Fishing as Compliance Mechanism

Introduction

This chapter builds on the previous analysis concerning the compliance potential of the international legal responsibility and treaty framework. It turns its attention to the compliance and enforcement elements that complement the illegal, unreported and unregulated (IUU) Fishing interpretive lens, and which together result in a fully formed compliance mechanism. By exploring this compound mechanism, a number of problematic areas attain visibility. Some of the problems discussed in this chapter have been identified or intuited in pre-existing literature. This chapter reviews and evaluates these critiques in order to clarify causes of concern, and understand their features and impacts. This enquiry into the compliance and enforcement dimension of the IUU fishing paradigm completes the effectiveness study initiated in Chapter 2, whereby the effectiveness contribution of the IUU fishing paradigm is contrasted with the effectiveness of the international legal framework of the high seas. This final part of the study aims to shed light into the costs that are incurred to sustain the perceived effectiveness of IUU fishing as a full compliance mechanism, and the ways in which such costs impact upon international law.

4.1 States and Compliance with International Obligations

As seen in the previous chapter, State responsibility has significant shortcomings. This is especially problematic in cases where relevant treaty rules are not binding on States due to their status as non-parties, but by no means the only issue. Although treaty obligations are assumed by States via formal acts like ratification or accession,[1] cases of non-compliance by States in respect of the LOSC,[2] and its satellite fisheries treaties, are far from uncommon.[3] In recent

1 1969 Vienna Convention on the Law of Treaties, 1155 UNTS 331, Article 12 [VCLT].

2 United Nations Convention on the Law of the Sea (1982) 1833 UNTS 3 [LOSC].

3 R Rayfuse, 'Regional Allocation Issues Or Zen And The Art Of Pie Cutting' in 'FAO Sharing the Fish: Allocation Issues in Fisheries Management' (FAO, 2006) 101. R Churchill, 'The Persisting Problem of Non-Compliance with the Law of the Sea Convention: Disorder in the Oceans' (2013) 27 *International Journal of Marine and Coastal Law* 813–820, 813.

 | DOI:10.1163/9789004463219_006

decades, concerns have steadily risen with the realisation that important environmental impacts are being caused due to a failure by States to comply with international legal obligations.[4] Yet, the notion of 'State compliance' and the creation of robust mechanisms to ensure it are controversial. Chayes and Chayes have argued that State compliance is a relative matter, which should be conditioned to considerations of reasonableness under the parameters of applicable treaties.[5] The famous Henkin quote, setting out the widespread assumption that 'almost all nations observe almost all principles of international law and almost all of their obligations almost all the time',[6] is re-affirmed by Chayes and Chayes, arguing that compliance cannot, and should not, be validated empirically or subjected to a strictly binary application of the law.[7] This position has synergy with the implications of due diligence obligations, which preclude considerations of compliance that are tied to objective, measurable results. Yet, keeping compliance a relative concept, perpetually situated in the shadow of uncertainty, has important effectiveness costs.

4.2 The Compliance and Enforcement Dimensions of the IUU Fishing Paradigm

Over the past few decades international fisheries law has been developed in response to the need for international cooperation in matters of shared stock management.[8] The UNFSA in particular has contributed to the transformation of cooperation in the management of straddling and highly migratory stock, as has the consolidation of the governance authority of RFMOs. Their rules and measures, particularly in matters of target stock management and IUU fishing vessel identification and surveillance, have acquired significant impact over time. In addition, the intended effect of the IUU fishing lens has resulted in a kind of 'legally hybrid' regulatory space, in which the governance output of RFMO has become relevant to States with vessels operating in the RFMO regulatory areas, in ways that are important from a governance perspective, but that can be denuded of legal significance.

4 O Schachter, 'United Nations Law' (1994) 88 *American Journal of International Law* 1–24, 10.
5 A Chayes and AH Chayes, 'On Compliance' (1993) 47(2) *International Organization* 175–205, 176.
6 L Henkin, *How Nations Behave* (Columbia University Press, 1979) 47.
7 Chayes and Chayes (1993) at 177, supra at 5.
8 Y Takei, *Filling Regulatory Gaps in High Seas Fisheries: Discrete high Seas Fish Stocks, Deep-sea Fisheries and Vulnerable Marine Ecosystems* (Martinus Nijhoff, 2013) 33.

This governance system has developed around a series of objectives, key amongst which is the capability to influence the economic drivers that propel undesirable fishing activity, and to operationalise them in order to foster compliance with the RFMO governance system.[9] The success of these mechanisms has been attained as a result of their ability to complement and/or even replace regulatory tools that, though available to flag States, are often under-utilised.[10] There is an important trend in the adoption of economic measures, which are usually exercised via the ports where fishing vessels need to stop for victualing and trade.[11] These mechanisms are articulated through the establishment of measures that have the effect of excluding vessel operators suspected of engaging in IUU fishing activities from port services and trading opportunities.[12]

4.2.1 *Extraterritorial Port State Controls*

With increasing awareness of the potential role of ports in identifying and addressing IUU fishing activity,[13] attention has been turned to the potential of ports to exercise types of governance in ways that are not comprehensively covered by the LOSC.[14] When it comes to establishing port State measures in respect of high seas fishing by vessels flagged to third States, a right by States to exercise extraterritorial jurisdiction may exist in customary international law.[15] According to Molenaar, this right may exist, and may not be related to

9 One exception to this is the provision of subsidies to IUU fishing operators, in respect of which States have not yet developed a meaningful set of global or regional rules. For further commentary, see Y Cho, 'The Concept of "Developing Countries" in the Context of the WTO Fisheries Subsidies Negotiation' (2018) 9(2) *Beijing Law Review* 137–152.

10 See OS Stokke, Management Options for High Seas Fisheries: Making Regime Compliance More Effective, in Caddell and Molenaar (Eds) Strengthening International Fisheries Law in an Era of Changing Oceans (Hart, 2019), 51.

11 See J Swan, 'Port State Measures to Combat IUU Fishing: International and Regional Developments' (2006) 7 *Ocean & Fisheries Law* 38–43, 41. EJ Molenaar, 'Port State Jurisdiction: Toward Comprehensive, Mandatory and Global Coverage' (2007) 38(1–2) *Ocean Development and International Law* 225–257, 226. E Witbooi, 'Illegal, Unreported and Unregulated Fishing on the High Seas: The Port State Measures Agreement in Context' (2014) 29 *International Journal of Marine and Coastal Law* 290–320, 293. J Swan, Port State Measures: From Residual Port State Jurisdiction to Global Standards' (2016) 31 *International Journal of Marine and Coastal Law* 395–421, 396.

12 See D Vidas, 'IUU Fishing or IUU Operations? Some Observations on Diagnosis and Current Treatment' in DD Caron and HN Scheiber (Eds) *Bringing New Law to Ocean Waters* (2004) 127 and 131.

13 GA Petrossian, 'Preventing Illegal, Unreported and Unregulated (IUU) Fishing: A Situational Approach' (2015) 189 *Biological Conservation* 39–48, 39.

14 LOSC Article 218.

15 Molenaar (2007) at 226, supra 11. See also CJ Tams, *Enforcing Obligations Erga Omnes in International Law* (Cambridge University Press, 2005) 9.

specific standards for the evaluation of vessel conduct established in the fisheries treaties. There is, Molenaar argues, an established practice involving certain port State controls related to common State interests in the protection of the environment. This practice may have evolved from overlapping standards established via a wide variety of practices and treaty sources, which include measures such as access to port notices, denying permission to land, tranship, or process cargo, and denying the opportunity to use other port services or facilities, other than the provision of humanitarian assistance in cases of emergency.[16] Measures involving vessel inspections in port may be subsumed into this general right to ultimately reject cargo before it is unloaded in port, as they form part of an increasingly established set of practices carried out for reasons of domestic security.[17]

To add specificity, it is worth pointing out that the exercise of port jurisdiction in respect of foreign ship inspections is supported by the following instruments: In the Paris Memorandum of Understanding,[18] it is contemplated in recognition that sub-standard ships can bring significant amount of safety and environmental risks to States. The International Labour Organization (ILO) also fosters the adoption of standards verifiable through port controls over undesirable crew employment practices and potentially dangerous cargo transportation respectively.[19] Other instruments that support the extraterritorial jurisdiction of the State in respect of vessels seeking port services have been adopted for environmental and safety purposes by the IMO.[20] In regard to matters that overlap with vessel safety and seaworthiness, these include the 1974 International Convention for the Safety of Life at Sea (SOLAS),[21] and the 2012 Cape Town Agreement, incorporating the 1977 International Convention for the Safety of Fishing Vessels and its 1993 Torremolinos Protocol.[22] This agreement, which deals specifically with fishing and fisheries support vessels, differs

16 Molenaar (2007) at 229, supra at 11.

17 *Ibid.*

18 Paris Memorandum of Understanding on Port State Control (1982).

19 ML Mc Connell, 'Darkening Confusion Mounted Upon Darkening Confusion: The Search for the Elusive Genuine Link' (1985) 16 *Journal of Maritime Law and Commerce* 365–395, 378.

20 A Boyle, 'Further Development of the 1982 Convention on the Law of the Sea: Mechanisms for Change' in Freestone, Barnes and Ong (Eds) *The Law of the Sea: Progress and Prospects* (Oxford University Press, 2006) 41. Y Tanaka, *The International Law of the Sea* (Cambridge University Press, 2012) 154.

21 International Convention for the Safety of Life at Sea (1974) 1184 UNTS 278 [SOLAS].

22 Cape Town Agreement on the Implementation of the Provisions of the 1993 Torremolinos Protocol Relating to the 1977 International Convention for the Safety of Fishing Vessels (2012).

from SOLAS, since fishing vessels often acquire cargo at sea, rather than in port, and require the observance of safety conditions concerning capture, processing and storage equipment that is unique to the industry. Other standards that may address some of the most damaging cost-cutting aspects of IUU operations, such as the mistreatment of crews,[23] derive from other instruments, such as the International Convention on Standards of Training, Certification and Watchkeeping for Fishing Vessel Personnel,[24] and the Work in Fishing Convention,[25] that are not directly concerned with stock management issues. The existence of these mutually supporting standards adds strength to the argument that there is a general right to exercise port State measures in order to protect environmental interests by withholding port services and carrying out pre-emptive inspection.

In the specific context of port States measures in matters of high seas fisheries regulation, the UNFSA has reinforced the authority of the port State over the provisions of the LOSC by establishing not only a right, but also a duty to inspect vessels suspected of having undermined the rules and measures of RFMOs.[26] UNFSA Article 23.4 does not limit the customary elements that underpin the right to exercise port State jurisdiction, as it specifically preserves the residual jurisdiction of the port State derived from other treaty and non-treaty sources.[27] In addition, the UNFSA contributes with considerable clarity to the substance of conducts that may be considered IUU fishing activities, as Article 21.11 of the UNFSA lists specific actions that State parties should treat as 'serious infractions'. The list in this UNFSA provision permits an objective evaluation of vessel activities, and promotes the elaboration and application of port State measures in a coherent manner across State parties.

A number of State conduct guidelines have also been defined in the IPOA IUU.[28] These included guidelines for States to establish duties on vessel masters to notify port State authorities of their intention to utilise the port in

23 See Doumboya et al, 'Assessing the Effectiveness of Monitoring Control and Surveillance of Illegal Fishing: The Case of West Africa' (2017) 50(4) *Frontiers in Marine Policy* 1–10, 7.

24 International Convention on Standards of Training, Certification and Watchkeeping for Fishing Vessel Personnel (1995), deposited with the IMO.

25 Work in Fishing Convention (2007) ILO Registration No. 188.

26 UNFSA Article 23.2.

27 For instance, the 1989 Convention for the Prohibition of Fishing with Long Drift-Nets in the South Pacific, 29 ILM 1449. In respect of ship-to-ship activity, which includes transhipment, see IMO International Ship and Port Facility Security (ISPS) Code (2002) Part B paras 4.38 SOLAS/CONF.5/34.

28 FAO International Plan of Action to Prevent, Deter and Eliminate Illegal, Unreported and Unregulated Fishing (2001) [IPOA IUU].

advance as a condition for access.[29] The vessel, along with catch, licences and other documents, and vessel gear, may be inspected once the vessel is in port, and the information may be shared with other States and with RFMOs when there are indications of IUU fishing.[30] If evidence of IUU fishing activity is found during an inspection in port, the port State is encouraged to report the incident to the relevant RFMOs, relevant coastal States, and the vessel's flag State.[31] The IPOA sets out some of the ways in which the port State may make use of its powers, including declining access to ports,[32] as well as permission to land or tranship.[33]

The State parties to the UNFSA, at the 2006 Review Conference of the treaty, sought the adoption of a legally binding agreement on port State measures, in order to crystallise into law the content of an existing voluntary instrument, the Model Scheme on Port State Measures to Combat Illegal, Unreported and Unregulated Fishing.[34] In 2009, the PSMA was adopted.[35] This agreement makes explicit reference to IUU fishing, as per paragraph 3 of the IPOA IUU. As a consequence, State parties to the PSMA assume the expanded meaning of regulation that includes not only acts that imply a breach of domestic law or international responsibility, but also fishing activities that may not breach but do undermine the conservation and management measures of RFMOs.

PSMA measures incorporate a need for inspection of catch as well as authorisation and licensing information, and vessel monitoring and tracking data.[36] Many PSMA measures seek to facilitate regulatory action by port States pursuant to IUU fishing presumptions.[37] The main achievement of the PSMA is to formalise the transposition of the burden of proof onto the persons responsible for vessel operations if IUU fishing is suspected. If the absence of IUU fishing activity cannot be proven, inspections or simply vessel exclusion from the

---

29 IPOA IUU paragraph 54 and 55.

30 IPOA IUU paragraph 58.

31 IPOA IUU paragraph 59.

32 Except in cases of distress or *force majeure*, as per IPOA IUU paragraph 54.

33 IPOA IUU paragraph 56.

34 A Fabra, V Gascon and R Werner, as cited in ER Agoes, 'Development Toward the Adoption of the FAO Agreement on Port State Measures to Prevent, Deter and Eliminate Illegal, Unreported and Unregulated Fishing' (2010) 8 *Indonesian Journal of International Law* 202–218, 209.

35 Agreement on Port State Measures to Prevent, Deter and Eliminate Illegal, Unreported and Unregulated Fishing (2009), UN Registration Number 54133.

36 PSMA Annex B (d).

37 See Molenaar (2006) at 242, supra at 15.

port may ensue.[38] These actions are extraterritorial, in the sense that the presumed IUU fishing activities of the vessels under suspicion could have taken effect in any part of the ocean. In essence, the agreement has crystallised into treaty law the fisheries related port State standards that had previously been contained in the voluntary text of the IPOA IUU.[39]

Many of the enforcement cooperation measures established by RFMOs are synergistic with the measures established by the PSMA.[40] For example, several RFMOs have compiled blacklists of vessels identified whilst fishing without authorisation,[41] usually referred to as 'IUU lists', which can then be relied on by port States to withhold port services to the featured vessels.[42] There are logistical and economic advantages likely to promote the increasing exercise of port State jurisdiction, over other measures. For example, the costly and controversial,[43] at-sea boarding and inspection scheme premised under the UNFSA is,[44] by contrast, underutilised. Port State measures concern non-punitive provisions, such as inspections at port, unloading bans, withholding of port services, and information exchange protocols between the flag State, the port State, and RFMOs where relevant. In general, sanctions or punitive enforcement measures, such as fines or detention, which are not supported by international practice.[45] Overall, there is evidence of a consolidation of port State measures as a compliance strategy to ensure that the undesirable activities interpreted to be IUU fishing lens are discouraged and, where possible, disrupted.[46] The

38 Molenaar (2007) at 229, supra at 15. Witbooi (2014) at 293, supra at 11. Swan (2016) at 396, supra at 11.

39 J Doulman and J Swan, 'A Guide to the Background and Implementation of the 2009 FAO Agreement on Port State Measures to Prevent, Deter and Eliminate Illegal, Unreported and Unregulated Fishing' (2012) FAO Fisheries and Aquaculture Circular No 1074, 5.

40 T Lobach, 'Combatting IUU Fishing: Interaction of Global and Regional Initiatives' in Vidas (Ed) *Law, Technology and Science for Oceans in Globalisation: IUU Fishing, Oil Pollution, Bioprospecting, Outer Continental Shelf* (Martinus Nijhoff, 2010) 111.

41 The tuna RFMOs operate a consolidated IUU list accessible through the following shared website: www.tuna-org.org [accessed on 20 March 2021].

42 Lobach (2010) at 112, supra at 40.

43 For a favourable opinion on the viability of high seas boarding and inspection of foreign vessels flagged to States outside the UNFSA framework, see R Rayfuse, 'Countermeasures and High Seas Fisheries Enforcement' (2004) 51 *Netherlands International Law Review* 41–76, 43. Against this view, see D Guilfoyle, 'Interdicting Vessels to Enforce the Common Interest: maritime Countermeasures and the Use of Force' (2007) 56(1) *International and Comparative Law Quarterly* 69–82, 70.

44 UNFSA Articles 21 and 22.

45 See Case C-286/90 *Public Prosecutor v PM Poulsen and Diva Navigation Corp* [1992] ECR I-6019, paras 28 to 34.

46 Swan (2006) at 39, supra at 11. Molenaar (2007) at 229, supra at 11.

net effect of this is to confer on IUU fishing an increasing importance as an effectiveness-driven interpretive and compliance model.

4.2.2 *Extraterritorial Market Suspensions*

In recent years, port-based measures have been adapted to operate not only to address the suspected IUU fishing activities of individual vessels, but also as barrier to trade against entire national fishing fleets, as flag States become suspects of tolerating undesirable fishing practices. Compliance with the rules of the international organisation established to regulate global trade, the WTO,[47] is required to avoid bias in the operation of international market mechanisms, and WTO compliant market measures are envisaged in the IPOA IUU.[48] These measures require an approach to regulation that takes into consideration the interaction between the legal framework of the WTO on the one hand, and the LOSC and the fisheries treaties on the other.[49]

The WTO's Appellate Body decision in the Shrimp/Turtle case is relevant to the operationalisation of market measures when a State is suspected of permitting or enabling IUU fishing by its vessels.[50] The Appellate Body clarified that the establishment of market exemptions associated to the protection of common environmental concerns is permitted, provided by that it meets certain due process requirements in order to prevent bias. In particular, Article XX of the General Agreement on Tariffs and Trade (GATT),[51] states as follows (emphasis added):

> General Exceptions: Subject to the requirement that such measures are not applied in a manner which would constitute a means or *arbitrary or unjustifiable discrimination* between countries where the same conditions prevail, or a *disguised restriction* on international trade, nothing in this Agreement shall be construed to prevent the adoption or enforcement by any contracting party of measures: (…) (b) necessary to protect human, animal or plant life or health; (…) (g) relating to the conservation

---

47 Agreement Establishing the World Trade Organization [1994] 1867 UNTS 154.

48 IPOA IUU, paragraphs 65 to 76.

49 M Tsamenyi et al, 'The European Council Regulation on Illegal, Unreported and Unregulated Fishing: An International Fisheries Law Perspective' (2010) 25(1) *International Journal of Marine and Coastal Law* 5–32, 30. A Serdy, *The New Entrants Problem in International Fisheries Law* (Cambridge University Press, 2016a) 264.

50 For commentary on the case, see JH Jackson, 'Comments On Shrimp/Turtle And The Product/Process Distinction' (2000) 11(2) *European Journal of International Law* 303–307, 303.

51 General Agreement on Tariffs and Trade (1947) 55 UNTS 194.

of exhaustible natural resources *if such measures are made effective in conjunction with restrictions on domestic production or consumption.*

It is clear from its wording that the Article XX exemption does not require that the community interest being protected by the trade measure be associated to the existence of a breach of international legal obligations. The exemption nevertheless requires that they are not arbitrary, or cause unjustifiable discrimination, which means they must not be adopted in a manner that gives rise to bias.

A small number of RFMOs has played a leading role in addressing IUU fishing through the coordination of market measures by their member States. Some RFMOs, namely the International Commission for the Conservation of Atlantic Tunas (ICCAT), the Commission for the Conservation of Southern Bluefin Tuna (CCSBT), and the institutional fishery management arm of the Commission for the Conservation of Antarctic Marine Living Resources (CCAMLR) have elaborated a process known as the 'catch documentation scheme' (CDS). The CDS is a statistical mechanism able to record and clarify the traceability of certain types of catch, particularly bluefin tuna and toothfish.[52] Beyond the critically important function of introducing transparency to the species' supply chain, the CDS has another advantage: it is able to identify the States that participate in the RFMO capture scheme, but that fail to regulate their vessel operations in accordance with the conditions of the CDS, which include substantive capture restrictions established by the competent RFMO.[53] Of the mentioned RFMOs, ICCAT has established sanctions against non-member flag States in connection with instances of IUU fishing activities by their vessels, identified via the CDS procedures, to which it has responded by rolling out trade-restrictive measures.[54] This approach was initially met with resistance, but proved ultimately successful, with the targeted States eventually joining the RFMO as members.[55] Currently, all the tuna RFMOs that have introduced measures involving trade restrictions, benefit suspensions, or rolling quota deductions, apply them in respect of member as well as non-member States.[56]

52 G Hosch, 'Trade Measures to Combat IUU Fishing: Comparative Analysis of Unilateral and Multilateral Approaches' (2016) Issue Paper 6 of the International Centre for Trade and Sustainable Development, 1 and 3.

53 *Ibid.*

54 ICCAT, Recommendation 06–13 Concerning Trade Measures (2006).

55 Hosch (2016) at 1, supra at 52.

56 P de Bruyn, H Murua, and M Aranda, 'the Precautionary Approach to Fisheries Management: How This Is Taken into Account by Regional Fisheries Management Organisations (RFMOs)' (2013) 38 *Marine Policy* 397–406, 402.

The perceived effectiveness of these measures has seen the perpetuation of market restrictive approaches. In 2008, the European Union (EU) adopted a Regulation establishing market measures in order to combat IUU fishing, named Council Regulation (EC) 1005/2008 (the IUU Regulation), which entered into force in January 2010.[57] The EU is in prime position to implement market measures, due to the fact that it is the world's largest seafood market, accounting for circa 40% of global imports.[58] An empirical data collection system for the purposes of identifying and verifying IUU fishing operates under the IUU Regulation via a specially designed mechanism, the 'catch certification scheme' (CCS).[59] Crucially, data entered in the CCS form by the fishing vessel master has to be validated by the competent flag State, as the country where the exportation originates.[60] This process of validation results in the provision to the EU and its member (port and market) States of a flag State assurance of the legality of the catch. If the flag State fails to adequately verify the veracity of the CCS form, this may be discovered via the port inspection procedures established in the IUU Regulation.[61] Where this occurs, the importation of the relevant consignments can be refused, and other measures taken against the implicated vessel.[62] In addition, the IUU Regulation sets out a further procedure for the flag State to follow: this is a detailed mechanism of conduct justification whereby the European Commission can demand answers from the flag State, in accordance with the criteria set out in Article 32 of the IUU Regulation. If the justifications given are not found to be satisfactory under a set of parameters established in Article 31 of the same instrument, the European Commission may proceed to the identification of the flag State as 'non-cooperating', which in turn prompts its inclusion in a public list.[63] The State in question may also receive a trading suspension of all fishery products originating from that State,[64] until rectifications in its approach to fishing vessel governance are undertaken,

57 Council Regulation 1005/2008/EC of 29 September 2008 Establishing a Community System to Prevent, Deter and Eliminate Illegal, Unreported and Unregulated Fishing, Amending Regulations (EEC) No 2847/93, (EC) No 1936/2001 and (EC) No 601/2004 and repealing Regulations (EC) No 1093/94 and (EC) No 1447/1999 [2008] OJ 286/1 (CR 1005/2008) [IUU Regulation].

58 C Elvestad and I Kvalvik, 'Implementing the EU IUU Regulation: Enhancing Flag State Performance through Trade Measures' (2015) 46(3) *Ocean Development and International Law* 241–255, 242.

59 A model of the CCS is set out at EC 1005/2008, Annex II.

60 IUU Regulation, Article 17.

61 IUU Regulation, Articles 9 to 11.

62 IUU Regulation Article 18, and Chapter V dealing with IUU fishing vessel lists.

63 IUU Regulation Article 35.

64 IUU Regulation Article 38.

which enables the State to resume trading, and to be removed from the public list of non-cooperating States.[65] The market restrictive mechanisms of the IUU Regulation can therefore be seen as a complement to the IUU fishing lens, with each operating as two sides of the same coin. On the one hand, the IUU fishing lens determines what parameters conform undesirable fishing, enabling EU States to interpret IUU activities accordingly, and take port State measures as a reaction. Where it becomes apparent that these problems are systemic, and where attempts to resolve the situation do not produce improvements, the European Commission can then implement market suspensions against said flag States, restricting the entrance of fishery products until the problem is solved. With these two dimensions acting together and in coordination, IUU fishing works effectively as a complete compliance system.

4.2.3 *Section Conclusion*

In this section, it has been discussed how port and trade measures ensure that flag States are brought into a regulatory space in which economic and operational pressures are applied as a response to systemic IUU fishing practices. The aim of such responses is no longer just to ensure that the undesirable fishing practices of individual vessels, as interpreted through the IUU fishing lens, are disincentivised or disrupted. Trade suspensions can have significant impact on the economic viability of entire fleets, as a result of perceived failures by the flag State. Such trade suspensions may ensue even if no instances of international responsibility are identified, via the 'unregulated fishing' filter of the IUU fishing lens. The innovative nature and perceived effectiveness of port and market controls in addressing IUU fishing have been generally well received in international fishery policy circles.[66] In respect of the largest and most impactful of the mechanisms reviewed in this section, the EU IUU Regulation, its potential for enhancing IUU fishing regulatory controls by third countries as well as member States of the EU has been noted by civil society,[67] as well as some scholars.[68]

---

65 IUU Regulation Article 34.

66 In respect of the RFMOs, see D Calley, *Market Denial and International Fisheries Regulation: the Targeted and Effective Use of Trade Measures Against the Flag of Convenience Fishing Industry* (Martinus Nijhoff Publishers, 2011) 103. In respect of the IUU Regulation, see A Leroy et al, 'The EU Restrictive Trade Measures Against IUU Fishing' (2016) 64 *Marine Policy* 82–90.

67 Environmental Justice Foundation (EJF), 'The EU IUU Regulation: Building on Success EU Progress in the Global Fight Against Illegal Fishing' (EJF, 2016) [accessed on 20 March 2021 via https://ejfoundation.org/reports/the-eu-iuu-regulation-building-on-success-eu-progress-in-the-global-fight-against-illegal-fishing].

68 AM Miller, SR Bush, and AP Mol, 'Power Europe: EU and the Illegal, Unreported and Unregulated Fisheries Regulation in the West and Central Pacific Ocean' (2014) 45 *Marine*

4.3 Critiques to IUU Fishing as a Compliance Mechanism

The review of the IUU fishing compliance paradigm would not be complete without investigating the concerns raised by its critics. Such concerns revolve around issues of perceived effectiveness, legality, and legitimacy. These are assessed in turn in the following paragraphs.

4.3.1 *Effectiveness Critique*

As stated, one of the effectiveness claims associated to IUU fishing as a compliance system is the inclusion of rules adopted by RFMOs in a *sui generis* regulatory space where they are afforded the potential for triggering responses against non-compliance, including in situations where they are not capable of displaying legal force. This occurs in a context where the output of RFMOs as centres for decision-making in matters involving conservation and management has attracted considerable criticism, due *inter alia* to a poor track record of conservation and management achievements.[69] Failures are related to multiple factors, but at least partly related to the manner in which these organisations engage in decision-making. Most RFMOs tend to take decisions through consensus,[70] but decision-making methods are not uniform across all RFMOs. Some may take some decisions through qualified and even simple majorities.[71] Substantive decisions, such as total allowable catch, season length, approach to managing effort, and other important decisions will be adopted pursuant to those processes.[72] Consensus decision-making by State participants is

---

Policy 138–145, 141. I Lutchman, S Newman and M Monsanto, 'an Independent Review of the EU Illegal, Unreported and Unregulated Regulation' (IEEP, Undated) [accessed on 20 March 2021 via http://minisites.ieep.eu/assets/858/IEEP_Independent_Review_of_the_EU_IUU_Regulations.pdf].

69 S Cullis-Suzuki, and D Pauly, 'Failing the High Seas: A Global Evaluation of Regional Fisheries Mangement Organizations' (2010) 34(5) *Marine Policy* 1036–1042, 1036.

70 J Swan, 'Decision-Making in Regional Fishery Bodies or Arrangements: The Evolving Role of RFBs and International Agreement on Decision-Making Processes' FAO Fisheries Circular No. 995 FIPL/C995(en) at 21 [accessed 21 December 2018 via file:///G:/Desktop/Swan%20RFMO%20processes.pdf].

71 TL McDorman, 'Implementing Existing Tools: Turning Words Into Actions: Decision-Making Processes of Regional Fisheries Management Organizations (RFMOs)' (2005) 20(3–4) *International Journal of Marine and Coastal Law* 423–458, 429 and 430. See also Western and Central Fisheries Commission Rules of Procedure as adopted at the Inaugural Session in Pohnpei, Federated States of Micronesia, 9–10 December 2004 (2006) at 10 [accessed on 21 March 2021 via https://www.wcpfc.int/system/files/Rules_of_Procedure.pdf].

72 See HS Schiffman, 'The Evolution of Fisheries Conservation and Management: A Look at the New South Pacific Regional Fisheries Management Organization in Law and Policy' (2011) 28(2) *Thomas L Cooley Law Review* 181–188, 183.

generally preferred. However, this type of decision-making may water down conservation and management measures, soften the standards applicable to member States, or sometimes prevent important decisions to be taken altogether. This is a side-effect of the compromises being made among the different State participants.[73] On the other hand, in cases where decisions are taken by simple or qualified majority, members may object, and exempt themselves from the effects of the decision.[74] As Serdy has noted, when this occurs, it is akin to unregulated fishing on the part of the RFMO's own members, placing them on a par with non-members that let their vessels undermine the governance output RFMO.[75] Further, under Articles 8.4 and 17.2 of the UNFSA State parties have duties to ensure that they regulate their vessels in a manner that is compatible with the RFMO rules, and that they report catch and other critical data in accordance with the established institutional processes, irrespective of whether they are members of the RFMO or not. This means that there is an expectation that non-members who are UNFSA parties meet rules that the members themselves, under a self-exemption, may not meet. The resulting incoherence casts a shadow over the integrity of those decision-making processes. Even if infrequently invoked, the possibility of self-exclusion, and the inability of consensus decision-making to ensure appropriate conservation and management outcomes undermine the effectiveness perception of the IUU fishing lens.

Objectivity in RFMO decision-making is critical to address these weaknesses. For example, rule-making processes may be informed by actors who possess particular expertise in matters of fishery conservation, or IUU fishing control. This is important because the impacts of fishing, and the *modi operandi* of those who fish illegally can be obscure. Evidence materials and scientific data may sometimes be contributed by third parties, rather than from flag States. Independent actors, such as NGO s, can participate in certain RFMO processes. They have the potential to contribute significant input in the development of responses to IUU fishing, as well as enhancing transparency in decision-making mechanisms by reinforcing observer presence.[76] A study

73 R Warner, *Protecting the Oceans Beyond National Jurisdiction: Strengthening the International Legal Framework* (Martinus Nijhoff, 2009) 125.

74 McDorman (2005) at 443–446, supra at 76. Food and Agriculture Organization (FAO) State of World Fisheries and Aquaculture (FAO, 2016) 8.

75 Serdy (2016a) at 153, supra at 49.

76 Communication from the Commission to the European Parliament, the Council, the European Economic and social Committee and the Committee of the Regions on the External Dimension of the Common Fisheries Policy (2001) 8, COM/2011/424/final.

by Wiser,[77] in which transparency was evaluated in twelve RFMOs, utilised institutional transparency indicators derived from the Convention on Access to Information, Public Participation in Decision-Making and Access to Justice in Environmental Matters (Aarhus Convention).[78] These standards included *inter alia* public access to applicable conduct standards, access to information on data collection methods, and availability of compliance reports.[79] The study concluded that quality in the implementation of the access and publication rules varied, with only a small number of individual institutions ranking highly in respect of decision-making openness to expert independent observers: a mixed picture that has been similarly reflected in later studies.[80] RFMO processes that are either biased to non-members or exclude transparency to independent observer or expert participation, have the potential to result in a lack of clarity and objectivity in the adopted rules.[81]

RFMO decision-making processes were explored by Koehler, in an overview of five RFMOs that regulate tuna fisheries,[82] namely ICCAT, IOTC, WCPFC, the Inter-American Tropical Tuna Commission (IATTC), and the Commission for the Conservation of Southern Bluefin Tuna (CCSBT). Her study adopted a method whereby the identification of conduct rules, the conduct assessment processes, and the transparency of the evaluations and their outcomes, are identified. The study reveals considerable heterogeneity in practices, with at least one RFMO not permitting external observers at the time the study was carried out, resulting in a breach of the RFMO's own rules.[83] Those restrictions are no longer in operation, but at the time they would have been incompatible

77 GM Wiser, 'Transparency in 21st Century Fisheries Management: Options for Public Participation to Enhance Conservation and Management of International Fish Stocks' (2001) 4(2) *Journal of International Wildlife Law and Policy* 95–129.

78 1998 Convention on Access to Information, Public Participation in Decision-Making and Access to Justice in Environmental Matters, 2161 UNTS 447.

79 Wiser (2001) at 103, supra at 77.

80 Wiser (2001) at 123, supra at 77. NA Clark, JA Ardron, and LH Pendleton, 'Evaluating the Basic Elements of Transparency of Regional Fisheries Management Organizations' (2015) 15 *Marine Policy* 158–166, 163 and 164.

81 The presence of bias in RFMO decision-making was also highlighted by T Henriksen, and A Hoel, 'Determining Allocation: From Paper to Practice in the Distribution of Fishing Rights between Countries' (2011) 42(1) *Ocean Development & International Law* 66–93, 66.

82 HR Koehler, 'Promoting Compliance in Tuna RFMOs: a Comprehensive Baseline Survey of the Current Mechanics of Reviewing, Assessing and Addressing Compliance with RFMO Obligations and Measures' (International Seafood Sustainability Foundation, 2013) 6–16 [accessed on 20 March 2021 via http://citeseerx.ist.psu.edu/viewdoc/download?doi=10.1.1.433.9664&rep=rep1&type=pdf].

83 *Ibid.*

with UNFSA Article 12.2, whereby RFMOs are required to afford the opportunity to representatives from other organisations. The study also notes that, even in the presence of independent observers, confidentiality conditions and certain limitations on access to documentation have at times been imposed, so as to ensure that discussion of identified compliance matters is kept within the RFMO.[84] This would have raised similar issues of inconsistency UNFSA Article 12, resulting in considerable opacity. A recent NGO report indicates that substantial flaws in transparency still exist across RFMOs when it comes to stakeholder inclusivity, compliance mechanisms, and the reasons behind objections.[85] Similarly, problems have been identified in respect of catch data voids and avoidance of reporting procedures, as well insufficiency and inconsistency of sanctions as a response to know infractions.[86]

4.3.2 *Legality Critique*

As already discussed, the UNFSA contains important cooperation provisions, particularly Article 8.3 stipulating that RFMOs should be open to the participation of all States 'with a real interest', and Article 8.4, conditioning access to stocks to RFMO membership. For UNFSA State parties, these provisions might *prima facie* be understood as part of their regime for the implementation of the cooperation and conservation obligations established in Articles 118, 119, 192, and 197 of the LOSC. However, the potential for the UNFSA to be interpreted as a source of objective standards for LOSC State parties that are not also parties to the UNFSA is problematic. As Harrison has pointed out, Articles 8.3 and 8.4 of the UNFSA represent a significant development from the open access high seas fisheries regimes established by the LOSC.[87] This means that the UNFSA cannot simply be interpreted as a standard for the implementation of the high seas fisheries provisions contained in the LOSC: it reaches further, establishing a system whereby a collective rationalisation for high seas resources utilisation may progressively replace the conditional freedom regime and arguably

84 *Ibid.*

85 EJF, Oceana, The Nature Conservancy, Pew, and WWF, 'Achieving Transparency and Combating IUU Fishing in RFMOs: Reinforcing the EU's Multilateral Actions to Promote Best Practices' (2019) 14 and 17 [accessed on 21 March 2021 via http://www.iuuwatch.eu/wp-content/uploads/2020/07/RFMO-2019-Paper-2020-Annexes-EN.pdf].

86 *Ibid.* See also ICCAT, 'Report of the Independent Performance Review of ICCAT' (2009) 86 [accessed on 21 March 2021 via https://www.iccat.int/Documents/Other/PERFORM_%20REV_TRI_LINGUAL.pdf].

87 J Harrison, *Making the Law of the Sea: A Study in the Development of International Law* (Cambridge University Press, 2011) 106.

more rudimentary cooperation provisions established by the LOSC.[88] UNFSA is therefore not merely an implementing tool for State parties of the LOSC, which has a much higher level of ratifications and accessions.[89] As a special agreement, the legal effect of the UNFSA is constrained by the *pacta tertiis* principle to its treaty parties.[90]

On the basis of some limited State practice concerning treaty law establishing a regime for the Aaland Islands, arguments might be attempted to assign the force of an objective regime to the UNFSA.[91] Yet, these run aground when the acceptance of objective regimes in general practice is considered,[92] and when the generality requirements of objective regimes are placed in context,[93] and contrasted with the peculiarities of the UNFSA.[94] It has also been suggested that increasingly, practices of cooperation with RFMOs by States that are not parties of the UNFSA with regard to seeking membership, cooperating non-member Status, or non-authorisation of fishing outside membership, may be crystallising into custom.[95] However, the reliance of the UNFSA on RFMO decisions *in lieu* of objective standards as a conditioning for the determination of substantive fishing standards has given rise to questions about whether Article 8.4 possesses the required objectivity to crystallise into custom.[96]

---

88 Harrison (2011) at 109, supra at 92.

89 DOALOS, Chronological List of Ratifications, Accessions and Successions to the Convention and The Related Agreements [accessed on 20 March 2021 via http://www.un.org/depts/los/reference_files/chronological_lists_of_ratifications.htm].

90 P Orebech, K Sigurjonsson, and TL Mc Dorman, 'The 1995 United Nations Straddling and Highly Migratory Fish Stocks Agreement: Management, Enforcement, and Dispute Settlement' (1998) 13 *International Journal of Marine and Coastal Law* 119–142, 123.

91 But see in respect of the Aaland Islands and other post-colonial arrangements SP Subedi, 'The Doctrine of Objective Regimes in International Law and the Competence of the United Nations to Impose Territorial or Peace Settlements on States' (1994) 37 *German Yearbook of International Law* 162–207, 173.

92 MA Fitzmaurice, 'Third Parties and the Law of Treaties' (2003) 6 *Max Planck Yearbook of the United Nations* 37–138, 82 and 111.

93 R Barnes, 'Objective Regimes Revisited' [2004] 9 *Asian Yearbook of International Law* 97–146, 105.

94 R Rayfuse, 'United Nations Agreement on Straddling and Highly Migratory Fish Stocks as an Objective Regime: A Case of Wishful Thinking?' (1999) 20 *Australian Yearbook of International Law* 253–278, 277.

95 RG Rayfuse, *Non-Flag State Enforcement in High Seas Fisheries* (Martinus Nijhoff, 2004) 373.

96 M Rosello, 'Cooperation and Unregulated Fishing: Interactions Between Customary International Law, and the European Union IUU Fishing Regulation' (2017) 84 *Marine Policy* 306–312, 310.

The reasons whereby the above is relevant to the IUU fishing lens have been identified by Serdy, who has denounced what he refers to as the 'concept' of IUU fishing as a mechanism where the *pacta tertiis* principle is circumvented through what he sees as an intentional confusion of unregulated and illegal fishing.[97] It should be noted that the controversy highlighted by Serdy with regard to encroachment on the *pacta tertiis* principle should over time become less significant. This is in part, as Rayfuse has pointed out, through the increasing number of ratifications of the various fisheries treaties and ensuing internalisation of treaty law within the domestic laws of State parties.[98] It is also a consequence of the ongoing development of new treaties, such as the PSMA, in which the IUU fishing lens is an operative element of the treaty, and in respect of which ratifications and accessions have increased exponentially in the past two years.[99] In respect of remaining States, namely those that are not bound by internal or international law to assimilate the IUU fishing lens via the internalisation of the rules established by the UNFSA or the PSMA, it should be recalled that considerations of international responsibility, whilst not always easy to determine and often dependent on contextual factors, are also related to general legal norms, to which they are bound.

As discussed in Chapter 2, LOSC Article 119.2 establishes a duty, which at first sight is reasonably clear, whereby States are to exchange catch information in order to ensure the conservation of high seas stocks. This provision of the Convention establishes a cooperation objective that is in principle apt to at least outline the basis of responsibility by a State in matters of high seas fisheries management, which would imply the need to reveal certain aspects of the fishing activity of their vessels to the affected RFMO. This position is supported by Serdy, as a possible avenue through which State parties to the LOSC may be asked to cooperate with RFMO conservation and management, irrespective of their membership status.[100] Yet, Article 119.2, when examined closely, is characterised by a number of subjective considerations resulting in a degree of indeterminacy. This may result in the provision falling short of the specificity that is required of a cooperation standard. As Kim points out, one of the problems with RFMO practice is bias, which injures the equality of States, and which can only be combatted with the articulation of procedural frameworks

97 A Serdy, 'Pacta Tertiis and Regional Fisheries Management Mechanisms: The IUU Fishing Concept as an Illegitimate Short-Cut to a Legitimate Goal' (2017) 48(3) *Ocean Development & International Law* 345–364, 345 and 354.

98 Rayfuse (2004) at 373, supra at 94.

99 FAO, Parties to the Port State Measures Agreement (2017) [accessed on 20 March 2021 via http://www.fao.org/fishery/psm/agreement/parties/en].

100 Serdy (2016a) at 154, supra at 49.

that ensure objectivity. If this is accepted as the main obstacle, it also means that possible mechanisms of RFMO cooperation in conservation and management do not need, in principle, to be circumscribed solely to the contribution of set fishery data, but could also incorporate other procedures established to ensure objectivity in cooperation, so that State equality is respected.[101]

Tanaka has shed further light into why objectivity is required: The absence or indeterminacy of legal parameters to take important decisions may be usurped by 'an ideology to justify a policy of a particular State', encroaching on rights and freedoms of other States in their exercise of jurisdiction.[102] Tanaka expresses concern in respect of the community interest argumentations developed by Simma.[103] It is recalled that these were explored in Chapter 3, and found to have been insufficient defined by international jurisprudential practice outside of interests established by treaty, and otherwise relating to a very small number of *jus cogens* obligations that are not applicable to fisheries. Tanaka, relying in part on Scelle's theory of the law of 'dedoublement fonctionnel',[104] argued that States exercising jurisdiction in manners that might impact the rights of third parties are required to act in an objective manner. The premise is based on Scelle's assertion that the decentralised nature of international law requires State organs to perform a public function that is carried out not in their sole interests, but on behalf of the generality of States.[105] Tanaka's solution, which is the legalisation via treaty of standards defining the precise manner in which community interests should be protected,[106] is progressively being realised. Indeed, the increase in ratifications and accessions to the UNFSA and the PSMA in recent years means that perhaps one day in the future, port and market measures will be articulated around standards recognised in law, and the IUU fishing lens and its reliance on RFMO measures decontextualized from the international legal framework will cease to be useful. At that point, the required conduct standards will have instead been established by

101 HJ Kim, 'The Return to a Mare Clausum Through Regional Fisheries Management Organizations' (2013) 44(3) *Ocean Development & International Law* 205–218, 206.

102 Y Tanaka 'Protection of Community Interests in international Law: The Case of the Law of the Sea' in Von Bogdandy and Wolfrum (Eds) *Max Planck Yearbook of United Nations Law Vol 15* (Koninklijke, 2011a) 354.

103 B Simma, 'From Bilateralism to Community Interest in International Law' (1994) VI *Recueil des Cours* 217–384.

104 Y Tanaka (2011a) at 350, supra at 102.

105 G Scelle, 'Le Phénomène Juridique du Dédoublement Fonctionnel' in Schatzel (Ed) *Rechtsfragen der Internationalen Organisation, Festschrift für Hans Wehberg zu Seinem Gebrutstag* (1956) 342.

106 Y Tanaka (2011a) at 350, supra at 102.

international law. However, as that time has not yet arrived, it can be argued that the IUU fishing lens is occupying a space that exists due to the development of treaty, general international law, and general objective standards able to support open textured obligations being still insufficient to support, develop and maintain an acceptable level of high seas fisheries governance.

4.3.3 *Legitimacy Critique*

The problematic relationship between the UNFSA and the decision-making processes of RFMO s stems in part from flaws in the UNFSA itself. As Molenaar has indicated, the indeterminacy of the 'real interest' test established in UNFSA Article 3 has permitted the development of a range of biased practices.[107] Serdy has identified a number of examples, in which would be new entrants to RFMO s have been excluded from participation in the fishery.[108] McDorman has noted another problem: that the UNFSA confers upon States a considerable margin of autonomy in RFMO decision-making,[109] and rules and processes established by them in the decision-making fora of the RFMO s may sometimes deviate from the full range of obligations, including those that are established in the UNFSA.[110] These flaws in the UNFSA in appropriately defining the parameters of RFMO decision-making perpetuate a problem that is not unique to fisheries, and in respect of which scholars engaged in broader aspects of international institutional law have issued warnings: that a lack of transparency and objectivity in institutional decision-making may lead to cases of undue dominance by certain actors, and/or otherwise resulting in inadequate and potentially biased decisions being adopted.[111] Such warnings on poorly designed decision-making procedures have also been made in respect of RFMO s.[112]

107 Molenaar (2000) at 499, 507 to 522, and 530 supra at 11.

108 Serdy (2016a) at 5, 96, and 154, supra at 49.

109 McDorman, at 427, supra at 74.

110 McDorman, at 423, supra at 74.

111 On the subject of porosity to interpretive preferences in institutional contexts, see J Black, 'Says Who? Liquid Authority and Interpretive Control in Transnational Regulatory Regimes' (2017) 9(2) *International Theory* 286–310. For the influence of law in fluid institutional decision-making dynamics, see N Krisch, 'Liquid Authority in Global Governance' (2017) 9(2) *International Theory* 237–260.

112 See T Polacheck, 'Politics and Independent Scientific Advice in RFMO Processes: A Case Study of Crossing Boundaries' (2012) 36(1) *Marine Policy* 132–141. E Gilman and E Kingma, 'Standard for Assessing Transparency in Information on Compliance with Obligations of Regional Fisheries Management Organizations: Validation through Assessment of the Western and Central Pacific Fisheries Commission' (2013) 84 *Ocean & Coastal Management* 31–39.

The flaws of the UNFSA and the indeterminacy of the LOSC obligations concerning high seas fisheries have driven commentators to refer to conduct parameters that lie in the penumbral space between law and policy. The porosity of this location is demonstrated in work by Serdy, who in spite of making a critique of the IUU fishing 'concept' that is juridical in nature, nevertheless refers to the 'IUU fishing concept as an illegitimate shortcut to a legitimate goal'.[113] Another commentator, Kim, has also focused on the uncertain borderland whereby the customary legal right to fish the high seas meets considerations of cooperation and conservation outside the boundaries of specialist treaty law.[114] In attempting to explore this space, he focuses on the formal as well as informal practices of RFMOs in respect of two different dimensions: formalised practices allowing participation in decision-making procedures of the relevant RFMO, and the often informal practices of new entrant participation in substantive matters of allocation.[115] As Kim explains, non-members that cooperate with RFMOs have less rights than members, and often gain privileges by invitation only. Further, the possibility of invitation, especially regarding stock access, is often restricted to non-member States with vessels that already fish the regulated area, as a method to regularise actual IUU fishing, whereas would-be entrants that, by definition, have not engaged in IUU fishing, are paradoxically excluded from the fishery as they lack 'real interest'.[116] Due to the obscure meaning of this term, this review and critique of RFMO decision-making mechanisms, which concerns in particular the unregulated fishing prong of the IUU fishing lens, may be more fruitfully situated in the realm of legitimacy.

Legitimacy is a broad and contested concept, which is discussed in further detail in the next section of this book. However, in the context of public international law,[117] as well as more specifically the environmental law literature,[118] legitimacy is generally discussed by reference to seminal work

---

113 A Serdy, 'Pacta Tertiis and Regional Fisheries Management Mechanisms: The IUU Fishing Concept as an Illegitimate Short-Cut to a Legitimate Goal' (2017) 48(3) *Ocean Development & International Law* 345–364, 345 and 354.

114 Kim (2013) at 212, supra at 101.

115 *Ibid.*

116 Kim (2013) at 111 and 216, supra at 101.

117 See A Boyle and C Chinkin, *The Making of International Law* (Oxford University Press, 2007) 27.

118 M Fitzmaurice, 'Legitimacy of International Environmental Law. The Sovereign States Overwhelmed by Obligations: Responsibility to React to Problems Beyond National Jurisdiction?' (2017) 77 *Zeitschrift für ausländisches öffentliches Recht und Völkerrecht* 339–370, 341.

by Franck.[119] According to this author, there are four key indicators of legitimacy: determinacy, coherence, adherence to the existing normative hierarchy, and symbolic validation by formal production mechanisms.[120] As Fitzmaurice indicates, these conditions for legitimacy converge upon the existence of a framework of formal requirements establishing how conduct rules are to be made, applied, and interpreted in a fair manner.[121] According to Fitzmaurice, the requirement of coherence is closely associated to the inherent generality of a rule, namely its capacity to be applied in an objective manner by analogy to the same set of circumstances across many contexts.[122] A lack of generality may be observed, for example, in the rules adopted by RFMOs in respect of which some States have achieved self-exemptions, or which permit other forms of bias.

It may be inferred from the above that legitimacy informs the mechanisms of formation of conduct rules, insofar as legitimacy refers to the procedures whereby they come into existence, and extends into considerations that may predate 'made law'. To illustrate this point, the provision in UNFSA Article 8.3 whereby States may become members of RFMOs if they have a 'real interest' in the fishery lacks clarity and determinacy. As a treaty provision, Article 8.3 was produced via processes that are objective, clearly articulated, that have been formalised positive law.[123] As a legal provision that forms an integral part of the UNFSA, it therefore does not lack legitimacy. However, as a mechanism that establishes a procedure for certain actors to make important decisions, the indeterminacy of the provision weakens its ability to ensure that the decisions adopted, and any conduct duties or expectations they establish, are legitimate. Hence, legitimacy in the manner in which it is presented by Franck has a finality: the making of legitimate conduct rules, particularly in respect of rules that have an intended legal force.

4.3.4 *Illustration: The Cambodia Case*

As stated, port and market measures for IUU fishing control have been subjected to analysis by a number of international trade law scholars, and have been found to be in principle compliant with the requirements of the WTO.[124]

119 TM Franck, 'Legitimacy in the International System (1998) 82(4) *American Journal of International Law* 705–759. Also, TM Franck, *Fairness in International Law and Institutions* (Oxford University Press, 1995).

120 Franck (1998) at 712, supra at 119.

121 Fitzmaurice (2017) at 367, supra at 118.

122 *Ibid.*

123 VCLT Articles 6 to 25.

124 See Calley (2011) at 103, supra at 71. MA Young, 'International Trade Law Compatibility of Market-Related Measures to Combat Illegal, Unreported and Unregulated (IUU) Fishing' (2016) 69 *Marine Policy* 209–219, 209.

Nevertheless, these studies did not take into account the specific legitimacy concerns raised above, and were based on the general design of the legal provisions, rather than the specific issues of bias that can be raised in their implementation. The measures in question concern States and several international organisations including some RFMO s, but the following paragraphs are focused on the IUU regulation, given its vast potential impact on third States.[125] This section contains a case study illustrating that, when the operationalization of the IUU Regulation is subjected to scrutiny, a number of legitimacy shortfalls may be observed, along the lines discussed above.

Under the IUU Regulation, the European Commission adopted a trading suspension against Cambodia in March 2014. Cambodia was not at the time a party to the LOSC, the UNFSA, or any of the RFMO treaties mentioned in the Commission Decision.[126] In this case, the discussion held between the Commission and Cambodia at the time between the verification of IUU fishing events and the identification of Cambodia as a non-cooperating State have not been made public. Nevertheless, the Commission published in writing the justification of its own decision to enforce with a trade suspension against Cambodia a number of unspecified RFMO decisions concerning IUU fishing by Cambodian vessels' unregulated fishing standards.[127] In this document, the Commission rightly attempted to argue the decision on several legal bases that do not require treaty ratification, ranging from the rules of the IUU Regulation, to the duties of customary law enshrined in the LOSC. It also indicated that Cambodian vessels had engaged in unauthorised operations in the ICCAT and CCAMLR management areas, and might have been in breach of legal obligations binding on it by virtue of the customary nature of Article 94.2 of the LOSC to exercise administrative control over its vessels. The implication of the Commission's decision was that the Cambodian vessels were obliged to operate within the framework of the conservation rules of the RFMO s, despite the fact that Cambodia was neither a member of ICCAT, nor a party to the UNFSA. Beyond the legal merit or demerit of the justifications published by Commission for its decision against Cambodia, arguments of legitimacy might

---

125 J He, 'The EU Illegal, Unreported, and Unregulated Fishing Regulation Based on Trade and Market-Related Measures: Unilateralism or a Model Law?' (2017) 20(2) *Journal of International Wildlife Law & Policy* 168–197, 197.

126 Rosello (2017) at 308, supra at 69.

127 Commission Decision of 15 November 2012 on notifying the third countries that the Commission considers as possible of being identified as non-cooperating third countries pursuant to Council Regulation (EC) No 1005/2008 establishing a Community system to prevent, deter and eliminate illegal, unreported and unregulated fishing (2012) para 92, OJEU 55 C 354/13.

have been used to support the decision, but they were absent. Such arguments would have been particularly appropriate, as the RFMO rules were dealt with as a separate category from the international legal obligations that were alleged to have been breached by Cambodia.[128] Firstly, it is noteworthy that the individual RFMO decisions allegedly being undermined were not quoted or identified. In principle, the legitimacy critique discussed above would suggest that the RFMO decisions in question should be identified, so that minimum safeguards of openness may provide some assurances as to their legitimacy and appropriateness to context.

4.3.5 *Implications of the Legitimacy Critique*

If it is accepted that accurate and transparent catch data contributions are the substantive undercarriage of the general duty to cooperate in matters of high seas fishery management. Any additional demands must be approached either as part of the UNFSA framework where applicable, or by objective decision-making in RFMO fora. If this is accepted, it may then be concluded that the legitimacy critique is arguably the most far-reaching of the two critiques raised against IUU fishing. The legitimacy critique may be synthesised as follows: Individual RFMO decisions may lack transparency and objectivity. If it is evident that they lack the latter, it is therefore likely that they are flawed from a legitimacy perspective, particularly in cases where they have also failed to meet conservation and management objectives. A perception of illegitimacy can mean that they are likely to become less effective in ensuring the conservation and management mandate of the RFMO under the LOSC and the UNFSA. Such decisions may then be uncritically enforced against the RFMO and UNFSA parties and non-parties alike via powerful market mechanisms.[129] Further, under the wording of Article XX of the GATT, market measures are protected by the exemptions established by Article XX upon considerations of objectivity that are directly relevant to the legitimacy guarantees that have been discussed as possessing shortfalls in the above paragraphs. It is evident that some of the issues highlighted in the effectiveness critique are also problematic from a legitimacy perspective, because the effectiveness loss is derived from the indeterminacy and room for bias contained in the decision-making processes of the mentioned RFMO s. Henriksen and Hoel have warned of the risk that objective decisions may not be forthcoming when decision-making processes enable sufficient room for the application of power pressures by

---

128 *Ibid.*

129 Serdy (2016a) at 141 and 154, supra at 49. Serdy (2017) at 351, supra at 113.

some RFMO members, indicating that this has the potential to erode the effectiveness of RFMO decision.[130] These considerations demonstrate that legitimacy forms the backbone of the IUU fishing critique, especially as problems of effectiveness are closely linked to legitimacy flaws. The port and market State controls, although generally praised for enhancing effectiveness, do not address the legitimacy flaws of individual RFMO decisions and may, in fact, enhance through enforcement their possible bias.

4.4 Correcting the Legitimacy Flaws of the IUU Fishing Compliance Paradigm

It may be concluded from the discussion in this chapter that the principal flaw affecting the IUU fishing regulatory model is not intrinsic to its design. It in fact lies in the potential for perpetuating certain pre-existing legitimacy flaws in RFMO decision-making processes, which it is unable to discern, and to correct. In the worst case scenario, opaque, inappropriate, or biased decisions by RFMOs may be enforced against States in respect of which those decisions have no legal force, enhancing any potential lack of objectivity or fairness. The failure to establish an objective blueprint for RFMO decision-making has been identified as a limitation of the UNFSA, and specially its lack of clarity in defining 'real interest'. Nevertheless, the IUU fishing compliance system unlocks and potentially magnifies the effects of this flaw, as it does not contain safeguards equivalent to those of international law in respect of third State autonomy.

Given that legitimacy is a key factor in the deficiencies found through the IUU fishing compliance mechanism critique conducted above, adopting a strictly legal approach in any efforts to rectify its shortfalls appears to be self-limiting, beyond issues of treaty and general practice development already covered in the literature.[131] Rather, in addressing the flaws of the IUU fishing paradigm, another avenue appears more appropriate and potentially fruitful: that the IUU fishing paradigm should be appraised from the perspective of accountability. Accountability is widely acknowledged to be necessary to ensure effectiveness as well as neutrality in decision-making.[132] Accountability concerns

130 Henriksen and Hoel (2011) at 84, supra at 81.

131 See Tanaka (2011) at 350, supra at 102. Molenaar (2007) at 226, supra 11.

132 M Koenig-Archibugi, 'Accountability in Transnational Relations: How Distinctive Is it?' (2010) 33 *West European Politics* 1142–1164. J Koppell, 'Accountable Global Governance Organizations' in Bovens, Gooding and Schillemas (Eds) *The Oxford Handbook of Public Accountability* (Oxford University Press, 2014) 371.

are traceable to contexts characterised by considerable change in institutional decision-making, and the blurring of authority lines.[133] Accountability has emerged as a suitable mechanism to demonstrate the integrity of multilateral institutions and their decisions, and fidelity in their endeavours to the actors they represent, as well as those they impact.[134]

The relevance of accountability to the IUU fishing regulatory model has not been subjected to analysis, but it has nevertheless been intuited by scholars: critics of the IUU Fishing regulatory model have themselves acknowledged the desirability of State accountability in effective high seas fishery management.[135] The intuited implications of their critique is that the IUU fishing paradigm embodies the wrong type of accountability. Logically and necessarily, any reassessment under the accountability lens would have to be sensitive to the need for preserving the effectiveness elements that are supposed to be the stregth of the paradigm: the ability to support lawful and objective responses vis-à-vis flag States that are obviously failing to address IUU fishing activities by vessels flying their flag in the high seas. The degree to which the IUU fishing compliance paradigm may be conceptualised as a mechanism of flag State accountability that is able to catalyse the IUU claim to effectiveness, whilst addressing the legitimacy flaws that undermine it, is put to the text in the following chapters.

4.5 Conclusion

This chapter has finalised the evaluation of the claim to effectiveness of the IUU fishing regulatory model. It has done so via exploration of the enforcement mechanisms that complement and reinforce the effect of the IUU fishing

133 See C Hood, 'The New Public Management in the 1980s: Variations on a Theme' (1995) 20(2/3) *Accounting, Organizations and Society* 93–109. C Pollitt, 'Justification by Works or by Faith? Evaluating the New Public Management' (1995) 1(2) *Evaluation* 133–154, 134. C Pollitt, 'The New Public Management in International Perspective: an Analysis of Impacts and Effects' in McLaughlin and Osborne (Eds) *Current Trends and Future Prospects of Public Management: A Guide* (Routledge, 2002) 285 and 288.

134 RO Keohane, 'Multilateralism: An Agenda for Research' (1990) 45(4) *Journal of Global Policy Analysis* 731–764, 731. RO Keohane, 'Global Governance and Democratic Accountability' in Held and Koenig-Archibugi (Eds) *Globalization: Frontiers of Governance* (Polity, 2003) 31.

135 See Serdy, (2016a) at 145 and 147, supra at 54; and ER van der Marel 'An Opaque Blacklist: the Lack of Transparency in Identifying Non Cooperating Countries under the EU IUU Regulation' in Martin, Salonidis and Hioueras (Eds) *Natural Resources and the Law of the Sea* (Juris, 2017) 237–256, 256.

interpretive lens. The chapter has covered the increasing utilisation of extraterritorial port State controls, and their foundation in customary law in respect of non-punitive port State measures. The contribution of RFMO practices to the development and appropriate implementation of the UNFSA and general duty to cooperate in matters of high seas fisheries management as the juridical buttress of extraterritorial market measures has been discussed. Their application to the protection of the objectivity of rules brought into the high seas regulatory space by the IUU fishing lens has been contextualised to the operation of WTO exceptions to trade restrictions under the GATT.

Considerations of legitimacy have been found to be important in the application of market measures for the purposes of upholding general international legal duties and WTO law. The manner in which the RFMOs and the EU have operationalized market measures has also been discussed, and their contribution to effectiveness identified. In particular, the EU IUU Regulation has been highlighted as a powerful regulatory instrument for the purposes of articulating the functionality of IUU fishing as a compliance paradigm. It enhances the effect of regional RFMO rules and measures, and is capable of conditioning the conduct of flag States. The combination of these instruments has afforded the IUU fishing compliance paradigm a global dimension, and potentially a high effectiveness value.

To complete the above assessment, existing critiques to the concept and operation of IUU fishing have been evaluated and expanded upon. Findings have identified that the very claim to effectiveness that is the leitmotif of IUU fishing as a compliance paradigm should be qualified by a number of considerations. It has been pointed out that the paradigm does not operate in a vacuum, as it exists in the midst of a lattice of legal norms and rules. Yet, the IUU fishing lens can obscure such rules, and divert efforts from their development and/or the clarification of legal conduct standards. Further, IUU fishing as a compliance paradigm has the effect of enforcing RFMO rules and measures, potentially against any flag State irrespective of membership. Decision-making flaws have been identified, that have the potential to generate legitimacy shortfalls that can affect the substance and coherence of RFMO regulation. These flaws are a symptom of RFMO weakness, enabling States to muscle in exceptions in the decision-making process that have undesirable results, and that the framework of the UNFSA has not been able to pre-empt. The IUU fishing lens is unable to discern rules and measures affected by legitimacy shortfalls from perfectly valid and objective rules, and it therefore has the potential of enforcing and amplifying the effects of those flaws rules and measures.

The study suggests that in order to address this problem, emphasis should not be placed exclusively on a possible incompatibility with the *pacta tertiis* principle. Both the legality and legitimacy critique completed here suggest that efforts should instead be constructively be re-directed towards finding mechanisms to identify and correct the legitimacy flaws that have been identified. With an appropriate methodology, the IUU fishing system could be transformed into a mechanism able to encourage objective decision-making in international fora. This is important, because objective rule-making has the potential to form the basis for the development of conduct standards, able to clarify and promote the implementation of, and confer definition and practicality to, existing open-textured obligations. This chapter has highlighted the need for a strategy able to reformulate the paradigm in a manner capable of supporting this objective. This strategy has been identified as a re-conceptualisation of the IUU fishing compliance paradigm as a flag State accountability paradigm.

PART 3

IUU Fishing as Flag State Accountability Paradigm

CHAPTER 5

IUU Fishing and State Accountability

Introduction

The preceding chapter has identified the concept of accountability as potentially possessing certain characteristics that may be useful in addressing legitimacy concerns, in the context of imperfect international organisation decision-making processes.[1] The relevance of accountability to institutional practices involving the idea of IUU fishing has been intuited by scholars, but not subjected to comprehensive analysis.[2] Evaluating whether the legitimacy flaws identified in the analysis of the IUU fishing compliance paradigm can be addressed from an accountability perspective is the objective of this chapter. The study carried out as part of this endeavour takes into consideration not only the need to address potential legitimacy flaws, but also the need to preserve the effectiveness features that have afforded the IUU fishing idea its popularity and endurance. This implies the rejection of an understanding of the IUU fishing idea as an intrinsically illegitimate concept.[3] Yet, it is acknowledged that the paradigm is blind to, and has the potential to perpetuate and enhance, the effects of RFMO decisions that in some cases may be considered biased or, at least, lacking in objectivity.

As no prior studies exist that either characterise the IUU fishing idea as a complex compliance framework, or that subject it to analysis from an accountability perspective, this chapter commences with an exploration of the meaning of accountability, and follows with its contextualisation in the realities of high seas fisheries governance. As part of this analysis, two factors have been considered: firstly, whether accountability is apt as a perspective from which to evaluate the features that are characteristic of the IUU fishing compliance framework. Secondly, the degree to which accountability is able to facilitate

1 RO Keohane, 'Multilateralism: An Agenda for Research' (1990) 45(4) *Journal of Global Policy Analysis* 731–764, 731. RO Keohane, 'Global Governance and Democratic Accountability' in Held and Koenig-Archibugi (Eds) *Globalization: Frontiers of Governance* (Polity, 2003) 31.

2 See A Serdy, *The New Entrants Problem in International Fisheries Law* (Cambridge University Press, 2016a) 145 and 147.

3 For the opposite view, see A Serdy, 'Pacta Tertiis and Regional Fisheries Management Mechanisms: The IUU Fishing Concept as an Illegitimate Short-Cut to a Legitimate Goal' (2017) 48(3) *Ocean Development & International Law* 345–364, 354.

 | DOI:10.1163/9789004463219_007

an interpretation of that framework in a manner that serves to address the legitimacy shortfalls previously identified, whilst protecting its effectiveness features. Findings reveal a high degree of synergy between accountability and the IUU fishing compliance framework, and help explain accountability as a multifaceted governance mechanism relevant to effectiveness,[4] as well as legitimacy.[5]

5.1 A Conceptual Analysis of Accountability

Accountability scholarship has developed alongside exploration of legitimacy and effectiveness questions situated in institutional contexts, and is therefore not a concept that pertains exclusively to the discipline of international law. It is, however, a concept that is relevant to any situation where there are actors that either govern or are governed, and as such it is ubiquitous. As Dubnick explains, accountability research has seen a meteoric rise in matters concerning public institutions since the early 1980s, and a direct consequence of this many accountability definitions have proliferated.[6] Accountability has been associated with desirable attributes of good governance,[7] becoming an objective of its own, and this has somewhat diminished its visibility and appeal as an analytical framework. Thus, to understand the essential attributes of accountability, a classic conceptual method, as first proposed by Sartori.[8] This approach is a qualitative method widely utilised across the social sciences,[9] as a mechanism through which the idiosyncratic features of a concept can be ascertained.[10] According to this method, a concept must first be extricated

4 M Dubnick, 'Accountability and the Promise of Performance: in Search of the Mechanisms (2005) 28(3) *Public Performance & Management Review* 376–417, 377.

5 K Yang, 'Further Understanding Accountability in Public Organizations: Actionable Knowledge and the Structure-Agency Duality' (2012) 44(3) *Administration and Society* 255–284, 272.

6 MJ Dubnick, 'Accountability as a Cultural Keyword' in Bovens, Goodin and Schillemans (Eds) *The Oxford Handbook of Public Accountability* (Oxford University Press, 2014) 24.

7 M Bovens, 'Two Concepts of Accountability: Accountability as a Virtue and as a Mechanism' (2010) 33(5) *West European Politics* 946–967, 948.

8 G Sartori, *Social Science Concepts: A Systematic Analysis* (Sage Publications, 1984).

9 See D Collier and J Gerring, *Concepts and Method in Social Science: The Tradition of Giovanni Sartori* (Routledge, 2009) 5. D Collier and S Levitsky, 'Democracy with Adjectives: Conceptual Innovation in Comparative Research' (1997) 49(3) *World Politics* 430–451, 431. For a partial critique of the method, see D Collier and JE Mahon, 'Conceptual "Stretching" Revisited: Adapting Categories in Comparative Analysis' (1993) 87(4) *American Political Science Review* 845–855.

10 Sartori (1984) at 15, supra at 8.

from its empirical, historical, and theoretical context, so that its 'core' characteristics can be identified. Only then can it be re-contextualised in a specific reality.[11]

To commence with, studies in English concerned with the meaning of accountability have been identified. Many can be traced to a time of considerable change in institutions of government, involving the blurring of parameters for the exercise of public authority.[12] They often involve the delivery of public services in situations of a perceived lack of legitimacy safeguards associated to traditional institutional architectures and associated hierarchies.[13] This resulted in calls for the activities of public authorities to be subjected to enhanced scrutiny, in order to ensure that decisions were made appropriately.[14] The need to ensure that controls are placed over institutional decisions is relevant to international fisheries governance. Such concerns have for example been raised by Serdy,[15] and Henriksen and Hoel,[16] specifically concerning decision-making within RFMO s.

Understanding accountability requires processing a great deal of divergent descriptions and conceptualisations. In many ways, the distortions undergone by the IUU fishing concept itself as a consequence of its perceived usefulness are not dissimilar to how accountability is perceived. Illustrating this point, Sinclair has referred to accountability as 'chameleonic',[17] and Mulgan as 'ever-expanding'.[18] This expansion and dilution of meaning will be familiar to IUU

---

11 Sartori (1984) at 29, *supra* at 8.

12 See for example V Bekkers et al, 'Governance and the Democratic Deficit: An Evaluation' in Bekkers, Dijkstra, Edwards and Fenger (Eds) *Governance and the Democratic Deficit* (Aldershot, 2007) 308. I Bache and R Chapman, 'Democracy Through Multilevel Governance? The Implementation of the Structural Funds in South Yorkshire' (2008) 21 *Governance: An International Journal of Policy, Administration and Institutions* 397–418. J Torfing and P Triantafillou, 'What's in a Name? Grasping New Public Governance as a Political-Administrative System' (2013) 18(2) *International Review of Public Administration* 9–25.

13 MS Haque, 'Significance of Accountability under the New Approach to Public Governance' (2000) 66(4) *International Review of Administrative Sciences* 599–617, 599.

14 Haque (2000) at 600, supra at 15. T Erkkilä, 'Governance and Accountability: A Shift in Conceptualization' (2007) 31(1) *Public Administration Quarterly* 1–38.

15 Serdy (2017) at 345 and 354, supra at 3.

16 T Henriksen, and A Hoel, 'Determining Allocation: From Paper to Practice in the Distribution of Fishing Rights between Countries' (2011) 42(1) *Ocean Development & International Law* 66–93, 66.

17 A Sinclair, 'The Chameleon of Accountability: Forms and Discourses' (1995) 20(2) *Accounting, Organizations and Society* 219–237, 219.

18 R Mulgan, 'Accountability: An Ever-Expanding Concept?' (2000) 78(3) *Public Administration* 555–573, 555.

fishing scholars and students alike. The ability of accountability to inhabit different meanings depending on the perspective from which it is approached can be illustrated with recent international law literature. Here, scholars comment on a project involving the normativity of soft law (referred to throughout the referenced text as 'IN-Law'):

> IN-Law's openness and appreciation of the many dimensions of accountability, however, leads to a certain conceptual ambiguity, which may be owed to the project's empirical rather than normative pretence. IN-Law in some regards claims to be adopting a narrow version of accountability, eg by focusing on accountability mechanisms as such and those that are governed by formal rules or procedures. Yet the project considers *ex ante*, ongoing, and *ex post* forms of accountability, and includes, for example, responsiveness-promoting measures. In this sense, it seems that IN-Law rather follows a very broad concept of accountability, drawing it near to more comprehensive notions of legitimacy.[19]

The above quotation is of particular interest because it suggests that accountability and legitimacy are closely intertwined, inviting efforts to address their interaction and boundaries. As Rached argues, 'conceptual clarification, thus, is indispensable whenever once comes across such multifaceted umbrella terms.[20] A number of authors have carried out reviews of pre-existing literature with just this objective in mind. A brief synthesis of their work is offered in the following paragraphs.

5.1.1 *Meta-analysis of Accountability Definitions*

One of the most frequently cited definitions of accountability was provided by Mulgan,[21] who attempted to define it by identifying its essential attributes,

---

19 P Dann and M von Engelhardt, 'Legal Approaches to Global Governance and Accountability: Informal Lawmaking, International Public Authority, and Global Administrative Law Compared' in Pauwelyn, Wessel and Wouters (Eds) *Informal International Lawmaking* (Oxford University Press, 2012) 116.

20 DH Rached, 'The Concept(s) of Accountability: Form in Search of Substance' (2016) 29(2) *Leiden Journal of International Law* 317–342, 317.

21 This definition by Mulgan is contained in the reference cited at footnote 20, which at the time of writing had received over 1,400 citations. It has been cited, amongst many others, in the following contributions to the accountability literature in the political science and international legal scholarship: D Curtin, and A Nollkaemper, 'Conceptualizing Accountability in International and European Law' (2005) 36(1) *Netherlands Yearbook of International Law* 3–20, 4. Dubnick (2005) at 382, supra at 12. J Black, 'Constructing and Contesting Legitimacy and Accountability in Polycentric Regulatory Regimes'

relying upon previous attempts at definition made by other authors in the field of public administration. Mulgan stated (emphasis added):

> One sense of 'accountability', on which all are agreed, is that associated with the process of being called 'to account' to some authority for one's actions. Indeed, this sense may fairly be designated the original or core sense of 'accountability' because it is the sense with the longest pedigree in the relevant literature and in the understanding of practitioners. Such accountability has a number of features: it is external, in that the account is given to some other person or body outside the person or body being held accountable; it involves social interaction and exchange, in that one side, that calling for the account, seeks answers and rectification whilst the other side, that being held accountable, responds and accepts sanctions; it implies rights of authority, in that those calling for an account are asserting rights of superior authority over those who are accountable, including the rights to demand answers and to impose sanctions. The inclusion of sanctions in the core of accountability is contestable on the grounds that it may appear to go beyond the notion of 'giving an account'. On the other hand, 'calling to account', as commonly understood, appears incomplete without a process of rectification. [22]

In his review, Mulgan thus identifies accountability as an apparently simple concept with a small number of features, revolving around a process of conduct disclosure between two actors.[23] This has been summarized by Harlow, an international legal scholar, who argues that the element of 'narration' or 'justification' of conduct is probably a constant in all accountability perspectives.[24] Mulgan's work in seeking to clarify accountability is not dissimilar in approach

---

(2008) 2(2) *Regulation & Governance* 137–164, 148. M Bovens, 'Two Concepts of Accountability: Accountability as a Virtue and as a Mechanism' (2010) 33(5) *West European Politics* 946–967, 946.

22 Mulgan (2000) at 555, supra at 18.

23 For precedents containing similar characterizations, see also H Finer in 'Administrative Responsibility and Democratic Government' (1941) 1 *Public Administration Review* 335–350, 338; GE Caiden, 'The Problem of Ensuring the Public Accountability of Public Officials' in Jabbra and Dwivedi (Eds) *Public Service Accountability* (Kumarian, 1988) 25. GW Jones, 'The Search for Local Accountability' in Leach (Ed) *Strengthening Local Government in the 1990s* (Longman, 1992) 73. M Dubnick, 'Clarifying Accountability: an Ethical Theory Framework' in Sampford and Preston (Eds) *Public Sector Ethics* (Routledge, 1998) 69.

24 C Harlow, 'Accountability and Constitutional Law' in Bovens, Goodin and Schillemans (Eds) The Oxford Handbook of Public Accountability (Oxford University Press, 2014) 195 to 197.

to that of other authors, whose contributions highlight the basic framework of accountability as a relationship. Actors relate to each other due to their participation in a process featuring elements of authority to which at least one of them has to respond.[25] However, beyond this simple central element, the complexities of accountability soon emerge. Mulgan situates accountability in a social context where actors are compelled to disclosure their conduct, so that it can be evaluated by others with the right or authority to do so. Mulgan, despite acknowledging the effectiveness of hierarchical accountability, has also highlighted a vulnerability: the risk that the actor occupying the upper echelon in the hierarchical structure may, through inaction, deactivate the accountability process.[26] Although Mulgan questions a necessary association of accountability with sanctions, there is a closeness between the hierarchical context and the possibility of sanction. As Thynne and Goldring explain, accountability occurs 'in the context of a relationship with an institution or person (…) 'in a position to *enforce* their responsibility by calling them to account' (emphasis added).[27]

Lindberg has contested the conduct assessment approach to accountability, suggesting there is a nuanced but important distinction. The main aim of accountability, he argues, is behaviour disclosure, rather than conduct evaluation by a hierarchical superior.[28] Schillemans has criticised this viewpoint, indicating that the association of accountability with an *ex post* conduct assessment is dominant in the pre-existing literature.[29] As part of this literature, some influential definitions can be identified, which shed further light. Firstly, from the discipline of international relations, an often-quoted definition of accountability by Grant and Keohane,[30] encapsulates accountability as follows:

---

25 See BS Romzek and MJ Dubnick, 'Accountability' in Shafritz (Ed) *International Encyclopedia of Public Policy and Administration* (Westview Press, 1998) 6.

26 R Mulgan, One Cheer for Hierarchy-Accountability in Disjointed Governance (2003) 55(2) *Political Science*, 6–18.

27 I Thynne, and J Goldring, *Accountability and Control: Government Officials and the Exercise of Power* (LBC Information Services, 1987) 8. See also, H Koontz and C O'Donnell, *Principles of Management* (McGraw-Hill, 1972) 62.

28 S Lindberg, 'Mapping Accountability: Core Concept and Subtypes' (2013) 79(2) *International Review of Administrative Sciences* 202–226, 209.

29 In particular, see T Schillemans, The Public Accountability Review: A Meta-Analysis of Public Accountability Research in Six Academic Disciplines (2013) Working Paper, Utrecht University School of Governance, 2 [accessed on 20 March 2021 via https://dspace.library.uu.nl/handle/1874/275784].

30 RW Grant and RO Keohane, 'Accountability and Abuses of Power in World Politics' (2005) 99 *American Political Science Review* 29–43, 30.

> Accountability (...) implies that some actors have the right to hold other actors to a set of standards, to judge whether they have fulfilled their responsibilities in light of these standards, and to impose sanctions if they determine that these responsibilities have not been met.[31]

Grant and Keohane highlight the procedural dimension of accountability, and the compulsion to participate in the accountability process being due to the possibility of enforcement. They also indicate the presence of conduct standards under which the conduct assessment will be made are important. Secondly, another definition, this time by Bovens, an author often cited by legal scholars with an interest in accountability,[32] proposes accountability as:

> (a) social relationship in which an actor feels an obligation to explain and to justify his or her conduct to some significant other.[33]

In these definitions, a difference in emphasis is clearly detectable: in Bovens', the accountability-bound actor 'feels an obligation' to explain conduct, whereby in Grant and Keohane's a subordinate actor is 'made to disclose' conduct, to be evaluated against standards. Bovens' definition suggests that the compulsion on an actor to participate in an accountability process may not always derive from external hierarchical or enforcement pressures, but form an internal feeling of compulsion. According to this perspective, the actor wants to give account because there is a motive for it, which may exist even in the absence of sanction. This understanding is one whereby accountability can occur across equals, and outside hierarchical structures, and is therefore compatible with the formally horizontal international legal order of States. Research at the domestic and international levels has traced the

---

31 The definition of accountability by Grant and Keohane has been cited, *inter alia*, in the following articles: Curtin and Nollkaemper (2005) at 4, supra at 2. Lindberg (2009) at 203, supra at 28. J Steffek, 'Public Accountability and the Public Sphere of International Governance' (2010) 24(1) *Ethics and International Affairs* 45–67, 49 and 52. Rached (2016) at 320 and 327, supra at 20.

32 See E Hüpkes, M Quintyn, and MW Taylor, 'The Accountability of Financial Sector Supervisors–Principles and Practice' (2005) 16(6) *European Business Law Review* 1575–1620, 1581. D Curtin, *Executive Power of the European Union: Law, Practices, and the Living Constitution* (Oxford University Press, 2009) 253. EM Busuioc, *European Agencies: Law and Practices of Accountability* (Oxford University Press, 2013) 48 and 55.

33 M Bovens, 'The Concept of Public Accountability' in Ferlie, Lynn and Pollitt (Eds) *The Oxford Handbook of Public Management* (Oxford University Press, 2005) 184. Previously in M Bovens, 'The Quest for Responsibility: Accountability and Citizenship in Complex Organisations' (Cambridge University Press, 1998) 23.

relative success of certain accountability strategies in institutional structures where relationships among the actors are predominantly horizontal, rather than hierarchical.[34] In those structures, the focus is predominantly placed on collaborative information-sharing, specially for the purposes of facilitating learning outcomes.[35] In this type of accountability framework, emphasis will normally be placed on the nature, depth and format of the disclosures, so as to ensure the delivery of the desired level of information and comprehension.[36] Bovens has associated this functionality to an ability to enable some forms of institutional learning, in what he, quoting Luhman, calls 'autopoiesis'.[37] This perspective also confers upon accountability a potential to reach beyond the bilateral hierarchical relationship between the two key accountability actors, transcending an *ex post* conduct assessment function, and opening up spaces that are vital to organisational life across social, political, and other institutional spectra.[38] Lastly, as indicated by Harlow, the information-sharing dimension of accountability is also associated to mechanisms of knowledge production and inclusion into institutional processes, such as those that ensure information and participation in decision-making procedures.[39] It may be inferred from the above that the concept of accountability, although bilateral in its minimum core expression, is also significant in broader organizational or institutional contexts, where it can play an important role as a result of its information-production nature and ability to enable collective learning.

---

34 AJ Meijer, 'Publishing Public Performance Results on the Internet: Do Stakeholders Use the internet to Hold Dutch Public Service Organizations to Account?' (2007) 24 *Government information Quarterly* 165–185. T Erkkilä, *Government Transparency: Impacts and Unintended Consequences* (Palgrave Macmillan, 2012).

35 T Schillemans, 'Accountability in the Shadow of Hierarchy: The Horizontal Accountability of Agencies' (2008) 8 *Public organization Review* 175–194, 180. See also T Schillemans, 'Remedies for the Accountability Deficit of Agencies: Does Horizontal Accountability Work?' (2011) 43 *Administration and Society* 387–416.

36 R Gray, 'Accounting and Environmentalism: An Exploration of the Challenge of Gently Accounting for Accountability, Transparency and Sustainability' (1992) 17(5) *Accounting, Organizations and Society* 399–425. PJ Birkinshaw, 'Freedom of Information and Openness: Fundamental Human Rights' (2006) 58 *Administrative Law Review* 177–218.

37 M Bovens, 'Analysing and Assessing Public Accountability: A Conceptual Framework' (2006) European Governance Paper No. C-06-01, 26. N Luhmann, 'The Autopoiesis of Social Systems' (1986) 6(2) *Sociocybernetic Paradoxes* 172–192.

38 See MJ Dubnick, 'Move Over Daniel, We Need Some "Accountability Space"' (2011) 43(6) *Administration & Society* 704–716, 708.

39 Harlow (2014) at 197, supra at 24.

5.2 Beyond the Core Concept: Social Dimension of Accountability

The collective or 'community' dimension of accountability is identifiable, and can be seen in further detail through a brief historical analysis, where a public performance function joins accountability as a part of institutional life.[40] The following paragraphs offer a brief synthesis of historical material found in respect of accountability, and of an etymological study conducted by Dubnick.[41] Firstly, historical literature in respect of public fiscal practices in ancient Egypt suggests that public accounting rituals served to legitimise the role of government authorities, and that these practices had an effect beyond the merely functional, insofar as they would have ultimately contributed to sustaining government controls over distant provinces.[42] Public, disclosure-mediated practices in the public administration are also identifiable in other time periods. In ancient Greece, the work of Athenian public officials may have been expected to be performed with a degree of visibility, and may sometimes have included ritualised processes in which questions of rectitude were publically asked by prominent citizens in order to verify or affirm certain priorities amongst officials.[43] Similarly, accountability can be associated to the evolution of public accounting and its imposition by law as part of the organisation of government from the middle ages.[44] A ritualised process, if very different in substance, is identifiable in the Middle Ages in Britain: here, political curtailments were placed on the immunity of the sovereign, and such processes involved public rituals acting out rule acceptance, openly recognising the authority of other actors as a limit to the King's own power.[45]

According to Dubnick, the etymological root of accountability may date from the late thirteenth century, from the old French *comptes a rendre*, emerged during the reign of William I at the time when the Doomsday Books were compiled.[46] The surveys took part as a necessary post-conquest

---

40 See Sartori (1084) at 41, supra at 8, with regard to the historical 'spirit' of concepts.

41 MJ Dubnick, 'Seeking Salvation for Accountability' (2002) *Annual Meeting of the American Political Science Association* 1–30.

42 M Ezzamel, 'Accounting, Control and Accountability: Preliminary Evidence from Ancient Egypt' (1997) 8(6) *Critical Perspectives on Accounting* 563–601, 763.

43 DD von Dornum, 'The Straight and the Crooked: Legal Accountability in Ancient Greece' (1997) *Columbia Law Review* 1483–1518, 1483.

44 See Harlow (2014), at 196, citing FW Maitland, *Constitutional History of England* (Cambridge University Press, 1908), supra at 27.

45 G Seidman, 'The Origins of Accountability: Everything I Know about the Sovereign's Immunity, I Learned from King Henry III' (2004) 49(2) *Louis University Law Journal* 393–492, 401.

46 Dubnick (2002) at 8, supra at 41.

accounting exercise upon which the new kingdom gained important knowledge upon which to elaborate a new government. In particular, they required property holders to 'render a count' of the details of their possessions in the terms dictated by the new administrators. Apart from their financial functionality, these surveys also served to provide a public performance or ritual through which the incoming ruling order and those under its authority communicated their respective status and intentions. In the words of Dubnick, 'what it involved was the performative enactment of a governance system through the creation of a moral community based on sworn oaths of obedience. It was the first modern enactment of accountability as a foundation of governance'.[47] The case is not exclusive to England, as in the Norman conquest of Sicily, and in France, similar record-making and ritualised processes of compliance have been documented.[48]

Hence, seen through this historical lens, accountability reveals itself as an instrument that reflects the understandings of participants in the power structures and expected conduct parameters of their place and time.[49] Through the ages, accountability has been at once animated by the intent and interaction of the key actors in the process, but has been equally dependent on institutional and social drivers, compelling those actors to take part and submit to the process.[50] The broad significance of the social dimension of accountability has been succinctly captured in this quote by Dubnick and Yang:

> Accountability is transcendent in reflecting the centuries old dilemma defined by the need to reconcile human potential for autonomy with the requirements of social order.[51]

The contemporary relevance of the performance element of accountability has been recently highlighted by Busuioc and Lodge, who observe accountability's value from the perspective of the account-giving actor as a mechanism for the public signalling of connection to a desirable social order, as follows:

---

47 *Ibid.*

48 See N Vincent, 'Review: 'The Holy Bureaucrat: Eudes Rigaud and Religious Reform in Thirteenth-Century Normandy' (2007) 30 *Biography* 389–392, 389.

49 For a top-down view of accountability as a response to the differing ideologies of incoming powers through different time periods in the United States, see EP Weber, 'The Question of Accountability in Historical Perspective: From Jackson to Contemporary Grassroots Ecosystem Management' (1999) 31(4) *Administration and Society* 451–494.

50 A similar conclusion is discussed by Rached (2016) supra at 20.

51 MJ Dubnick, and K Yang, 'The Pursuit of Accountability: Promise, Problems and Prospects' in Menzel and H White (Eds) *The State of Public Administration* (Sharpe, 2011) 180.

> Accountability – in terms of both holding and giving – is about managing and cultivating one's reputation vis-à-vis different audiences. It is about being seen as a reputable actor in the eyes of one's audience(s), conveying the impression of competently performing one's (accountability) roles, thereby generating reputational benefits.[52]

Despite their importance, these insights into accountability in community contexts are often obscured in more analyses where individual drivers take centre stage. They have been addressed in a voluminous part of the literature dealing with rational choices, both in community contexts, and in respect of the bilateral relationship only.

5.2.1 *Rational Drivers to Participation*

The study of accountability has been marked by the ubiquity of institutionalised hierarchies of conduct evaluation by the actor in authority.[53] Principal-agent theory has been one of the dominant approaches, premised on the divergence between the strategic interests of a principal and a subordinate agent, resulting in a need to restrain the agent's autonomy through incentives and sanctions.[54] The principal-agent perspective assumes that conduct expectations established by a principal for an agent may, in the absence of some form of hierarchy or other incentive or disincentive, be insufficient to guarantee agent compliance.[55] The value of conduct rules or standards lies predominantly in their instrumental function to further the strategic interests of the participants in accordance with existing incentives and disincentives.[56] Typically, these strategies rely on a logic based upon mechanisms that seek to engage the interests of the agent through the identification of carrots and penalties that will influence behaviour, and the deployment of

---

52 M Busuioc and M Lodge, 'The Reputational Basis of Public Accountability' (2016) 29(2) *Governance* 247–263, 248.

53 K Strøm, 'Delegation and Accountability in Parliamentary Democracies' (2000) 37(3) *European Journal of Political Research* 261–290, 266. R Keohane, 'Global Governance and Democratic Accountability' in Held and Koenig-Archibugi (Eds) *Taming Globalization: Frontiers of Governance* (Cambridge University Press, 2003) 130.

54 B Holmstrom and P Milgrom, 'Multitask Principal-Agent Analyses: Incentive Contracts, Asset Ownership, and Job Design' (1991) 7 *Journal of Law, Economics, & Organization* 24–52.

55 SP Shapiro, 'Agency Theory' (2005) 31 *Annual Review of Sociology* 263–284, 275. T Schillemans, 'Moving Beyond the Clash of Interests: On Stewardship Theory and the Relationships Between Central Government Departments and Public Agencies' (2013) 15(4) *Public Management Review* 541–562, 542.

56 MW Dowdle, *Public Accountability: Designs, Dilemmas and Experiences* (Cambridge University Press, 2006) 119.

clear standards of conduct, and appropriate conduct monitoring instruments.[57] In domestic institutional administration, the need to find power management strategies for structures where incentives are not a prominent feature, legal rules are typically resorted to due to their obligatory or punitive character.[58]

A recent meta-analysis of contributions to the accountability literature carried out by Schillemans in 2013,[59] identifies the delegation accountability model as the most prevalent in institutional design, as a method of assessing and addressing undesirable deviations of conduct from institutionalised expectation.[60] Schilleman's review suggests that an understanding of accountability formulated upon the delegation model requires considerable caution,[61] as the aim of this literature had predominantly been to describe and evidence operational failures in existing institutions, rather than establish normative models.[62] Insight into some problematic areas of delegation is traceable to earlier influential authors, such as Strøm,[63] who suggests that delegation-based accountability contains inherent design weaknesses: it may increasingly malfunction through the number of links in the chain of delegation, or when the conduct expectations of the persons who occupy the authority role of principals cannot be established with clarity, as competing conduct compulsion may ensue.[64] Strøm,[65] Mulgan,[66] and others,[67] have pointed out that there is a dependency on understanding expectations of conduct, thus highlighting communication clarity as a concern.

The delegation model has been the subject of a focused critique by authors Schillemans and Busuioc in recent research involving accountability in

57 E Weisband and A Ebrahim, 'Introduction: Forging Global Accountabilities' in Ebrahim and Weisband (Eds) *Global Accountabilities: Participation, Pluralism and Public Ethics* (Cambridge University Press, 2007) 1.

58 R Mulgan, 'The Processes of Public Accountability' (1997) 56 *Australian Journal of Public Administration* 25–36, 30. R Mulgan, *Holding Power to Account: Accountability in Modern Democracies* (Palgrave Macmillan, 2003) 22.

59 Schillemans (2013) at 9 and 12, supra at 55.

60 Schillemans (2013) at 13 and 14, supra at 55.

61 Schillemans (2013) at 17, supra at 55.

62 Schillemans (2013) at 12 and 17, supra at 55.

63 See Strøm (2000) at 266, supra at 53.

64 Strøm (2000), at 284, supra at 53.

65 *Ibid.*

66 Mulgan (2000) at 556, supra at 18.

67 See M Bovens, P Hart, and T Schillemans, 'Does Accountability Work? An Assessment Tool' (2008) 86 *Public Administration* 225–42, 232.

international institutions.[68] The authors have pointed out the problematic nature of conduct anticipation by reference to what they have named as *principal drift*, a factor that undermines the assumptions made in principal-agent theory regarding the need for agent control by principals.[69] Among the studies reviewed by the authors, issues such as the lack of political will by principals to support a specific course of action,[70] inconsistency between accountability standards and pre-existing institutional rules,[71] and a lack of appropriate communication or performance of the applicable rules of conduct by principals,[72] may erode the functions and outcomes of accountability. Similarly, other authors have also pointed at lack of appropriate engagement by the principal as the possible cause of failure of accountability mechanisms.[73] Of course, these critiques do not render the rational basis of the delegation models inoperative. They merely serve as a reminder that this approach may be too limited to fully comprehend the full spectrum of accountability dimensions, particularly when arrangements result in the subversion, rather than the affirmation of the institutional or organizational order that the accountability measure was meant to protect. This problem calls for enhanced awareness of context as well as the need to ensure that the actor in authority is not isolated, and that he/she also gives account in respect of their function and conduct in the organizational context.

5.2.2 *Autonomy and Transparency in Conduct Disclosure*

The insight by Dubnick and Yang that accountability is the mechanism whereby individual autonomy is balanced with the needs of the contextual (social) order,[74] is relevant in this respect. As a social mechanism, the existence

68 T Schillemans and M Busuioc, 'Predicting Public Sector Accountability: From Agency Drift to Forum Drift' (2015) 25(1) *Journal of Public Administration Research and Theory* 191–215, 191.

69 *Ibid.*

70 LA Dicke and JS Ott, 'A Test: Can Stewardship Theory Serve as a Second Conceptual Foundation for Accountability Methods in Contracted Human Services?' (2002) 25(4) *International Journal of Public Administration* 463–487.

71 C Farrell and J Law, 'Changing Forms of Accountability in Education: A Case Study of LEAs in Wales' (1999) *Public Administration* 77(2) 293–310.

72 PH Jos and ME Tompkins, 'The Accountability Paradox in an Age of Reinvention' (2004) *Administration and Society* 36(3) 255–281.

73 U Morth, 'Public and Private Partnerships as Dilemmas Between Efficiency and Democratic Accountability: the Case of Galileo' (2007) 29(5) *European integration* 601–617. M Busuioc, *European Agencies: Law and Practices of Accountability* (Oxford University Press, 2013).

74 Dubnick and Yang (2011) at 180, supra at 51.

of accountability only makes sense when the actor who gives account has some degree of autonomy, and thus the ability to make choices in decision-making in the first place.[75] This consideration is also at the heart of the need for the actor in authority to give account him/herself: the possibility that individual actors disengage from the institutional mandate around which institutionalised accountability processes revolve, causing the mechanism to fail from the top down. Sinclair has highlighted accountability's impact as a 'trade-off' between freedom, and the duties of compliance and disclosure that are present as part of the participation of the actor in the specific institutional context to which the accountability process pertains.[76] Busuioc, Curtin and Groenleer have explored the relationship between accountability and autonomy in European agencies. They have illustrated how the process of accountability is appropriate when the actor giving account had some autonomy to act in the first place, albeit within a conduct mandate and restrictions established or implied within the relevant competence rules.[77] Indeed, it can be argued that accountability is conceptually independent from forms of coercive intervention, where the objective is to completely eliminate an actor's autonomy.[78] It may be inferred from these insights that, for an individual actor, there is a price to be paid for belonging to a certain social or institutional context, and accountability is the mechanism whereby that price is exacted.

In view of these factors, another element emerges as important: The integrity of the actors, whereby they make a commitment to disclosure their conduct without withholding the relevant information. In the words of Bovens:

> (…) the explanation should be directed at a specific forum (…) the actor must feel obliged to come forward, instead of being at liberty to provide any account whatsoever.[79]

Yet, certain types of accountability design may undermine this important requisite. As Gupta and van Asselt point out, certain contexts may unwittingly

---

75 WP Birkett, *Concepts of Accountability* (University of New South Wales, 1988) 5.

76 See Sinclair (1995) at 232, supra at 17.

77 M Busuioc, D Curtin and M Groenleer, "Agency Growth Between Autonomy and Accountability: The European Police Office as a 'Living Institution'" (2011) 18(6) *Journal of European Public Policy* 848–867, 850.

78 JL Holzgrefe and RO Keohane, *Humanitarian Intervention: Ethical, Legal and Political Dilemmas* (Cambridge University Press, 2003) 28.

79 M Bovens, 'New Forms of Accountability and EU Governance' (2007) 5(1) *Comparative European Politics* 104–120, 107.

undermine, rather than promote, conduct disclosure transparency.[80] One of the fundamental challenges is that transparency as to the actor's own conduct may carry a punitive implication in cases where disclosure carries negative consequences for the account-giver, such as a sanction or removal of privileges, or loss of reputation or social opprobrium. In these cases, transparency can be perceived as a sanction in itself.[81] This punitive potential gives transparency in conduct disclosure a double edge: it means that, on the one hand, conduct disclosure may operate in a similar manner to a sanction, namely as *ex ante* deterrent to deviant conduct under the expected conduct standards held by the authority and/or the community.[82] On the other hand, if associated to the imposition of sanctions it may also create avoidance responses, generating a loss of integrity and ultimately causing opacity.[83] Dubnick and Yang highlight in this respect the association of accountability with frustrated expectations in the delivery of 'truth'.[84] Hence, autonomy is not only at the heart of accountability: it is also a potentially distorting factor in relation to its basic function of ensuring the disclosure certain conducts or facts.[85] Where autonomy results in the delivery of untruths or partial truths, the resulting epistemic voids prevent accountability from performing its core function of ensuring the visibility of relevant information.[86] Thus, as Mulgan pointed out, the presence of sanctions in accountability procedures should not be taken lightly, and may not always be appropriate.[87]

In cases where assessment of conduct is backed by a form of sanction, a lack of appropriate conduct disclosure is likely to be detrimental from the

80 A Gupta and H van Asselt, 'Transparency in Multilateral Climate Politics: Furthering (or Distracting from) Accountability?' (2017) *Regulation and Governance* [online only – accessed on 20 March 2021 via https://doi.org/10.1111/rego.12159].

81 See Meijer (2007) at 169, supra at 34.

82 OR Young, 'The Effectiveness of International Institutions: Hard Cases and Critical Variables' in Rosenau and Czempiel (Eds) *Governance Without Government: Order and Change in World Politics* (Cambridge University Press, 1992) 176. A Chayes, and AH Chayes, *The New Sovereignty* (Harvard University Press, 1995) 151.

83 J Fox, 'The Uncertain Relationship Between Transparency and Accountability' (2007) 17(5) *Development in Practice* 663–671, 668.

84 Dubnick and Yang (2011) at 174, supra at 51.

85 MJ Dubnick and K Yang, 'The Pursuit of Accountability: Promises, Problems, and Prospects' in Menzel and White (Eds) *The State of Public Administration: Issues, Challenges and Opportunities* (ME Sharpe, 2010) 172.

86 M Mason, *The New Accountability: Environmental Responsibility Across Borders* (Earthscan, 2005) 4–5.

87 Mulgan (2000) at 555, supra at 18.

perspective of, both, conduct assessment and institutional learning.[88] In these cases, it may be appropriate to re-consider an emphasis on sanctions in favour of the establishment of clearer mandatory duties,[89] accompanied perhaps conduct disclosure incentives to foster compliance.[90] Further, the effectiveness of accountability may also depend on elements that are external to the will of the account-giving actor. The presence of actors with the right expertise and ability to identify, interpret and communicate the information being transmitted may be important,[91] as could be the ability to transmit to the account-giving actor the empirical, functional, or ontological rationale behind the need for an evaluation of his or her conduct, and thus the necessity of disclosure.[92]

5.3 Tabular Analysis

The above paragraphs unveil the complex individual and social elements that may be involved in an accountability process. Given this complexity, the value of accountability analysis may be profound, reaching beyond the predominantly ex-post and bilateral/reciprocal elements of damage to rights that are characteristic of the responsibility regime, as discussed in Chapter 4. In the words of Koenig-Archibugi:

> (...) accountability can be used as an analytical lens that may help observers capture certain relationships of communication and power better than other analytical concepts. In other words, conceptualizing a cluster of interactions as an accountability relationship may

88 Mason (2008) at 12, supra at 89. For a study on the difficulties in the calculation of liabilities as a result of epistemic uncertainty in the context of high seas fisheries, see Serdy (2016a) at 375, supra at 2.

89 L Pellizzoni, 'Responsibility and Environmental Governance' (2004) 13(3) Environmental Politics 541–565, 560. KH Whiteside, *Precautionary Politics: Principle and Practice in Confronting Environmental Risk* (MIT Press, 2006) 117.

90 MW Dowdle, *Public Accountability: Designs, Dilemmas and Experiences* (Cambridge University Press, 2006) 95. See also C Lindstedt and D Naurin 'Transparency is Not Enough: Making Transparency Effective in Reducing Corruption' (2010) 31 *International Political Science Review* 301–322.

91 Gupta and von Asselt at 14, supra at 80.

92 See A Bianchi, 'On Power and Illusion' in Bianchi and Peters (Eds) Transparency in International Law (Cambridge University Press, 2013) 10. See also TN Hale, 'Transparency, Accountability, and Global Governance' (2008) 14(1) *Global Governance* 73–94.

> illuminate, rather than obfuscate, their core features, dynamics and implications.[93]

The analysis contained in the preceding sections suggests that there are multiple variables of accountability, and indicates that, to simply view accountability from the minimalist lens of a 'core' concept, which enables its delimitation as a simple bilateral mechanism of conduct disclosure, may appear reductionist. Viewed through a broader, more nuanced lens that includes social interactions, accountability emerges in its full potential as an instrument of social and institutional power. The commonly held perspectives that associate accountability design to the presence of individual incentives and disincentives are important to explain conduct,[94] but care should be taken that they are sufficiently nuanced or flexible not obscure the impact on conduct of the social context, and the presence or absence of processes of socialisation.[95] Accountability also emerges as distinct from transparency.[96] These elements can be summarised as follows (Table 1).

The above concludes the section, with a set of elements and parameters through which certain processes may be analysed in order to identify whether they may classified as accountability, and whether they have been appropriately designed to address the complexities and tensions outlined in previous paragraphs.

It should be recalled that there is potential for accountability to take many shapes within the many forms of institutional arrangements that exist at the national, regional, and global levels. It is further recalled that accountability has an infamously protean quality, having been called chameleonic,[97] and janus-faced.[98] Throughout all its possible permutations, however, its conceptual core determines its key characteristic: the communication of and actor's conduct through disclose to another against a set of standards, rules and/or expectations. The effectiveness of accountability will depend on a range of internal and external elements: a feeling of compulsion must be generated, so

93 M Koenig-Archibugi, 'Accountbility in Transnational Relations: How Distinctive Is It?' (2010) 33(5) *West European Politics* 1142–1164, 1145.

94 M Bovens, T Schillemans, and RE Goodin, 'Public Accountability' in Bovens, Schillemans and Goodin (Eds) *The Oxford handbook of Public Accountability* (Oxford University Press, 2014) 12.

95 Dubnick (2002), at 407, supra at 41.

96 J Brunee and E Hey, 'Transparency and International Environmental Institutions' in A Bianchi and A Peters (Eds) *Transparency in International Law* (2013) 23.

97 Sinclair (1995) at 219, supra at 17.

98 Rached (2019) at 319, supra at 20.

TABLE 1 Conceptual – analytical framework. The columns in white contain the minimum or 'core' elements necessary for accountability to exist. Grey columns contain additional elements that contemporary accountability scholarship and practice hold as the most common. The dark grey columns contain the elements revealed from a social context perspective.

Who (actors)	**What (performance)**	**Why (functions)**	**How (methods)**	**Whom (relationship)**
Accountor (gives account)	Discloses information through narration or justification concerning own behaviour or performance, previously conducted under conditions of relative autonomy, against a backdrop of pre-established conduct rules, standards, or expectations.	To inform of conduct details and/or methods by reference to conduct rules and obtain feedback.	Responds to duty of disclosure and narration or justification and its functional and/or ontological rationale.	External or internal compulsion. (internal = voluntary, possible reputational gains; external = mediated by incentives, sanctions, or reputational elements)
		To permit conduct assessment / build cooperation/ trust and/ or enable learning or correction.	Responds to conduct rules and their rationale, and expertise/ authority of the accountee.	

TABLE 1 Conceptual – analytical framework (*cont.*)

Who (actors)	What (performance)	Why (functions)	How (methods)	Whom (relationship)
		To publically narrate/ justify/ perform an act of compliance or allegiance to a rule or norm.	Responds to community awareness of the norm and expertise/ social compulsion potential in community awareness.	
Accountee (calls for account)	Receives interprets conduct information and assesses conduct	To learn and/ or interpret /assess / evaluate conduct information.	Possesses social, moral, technical expertise, or a legal right, or other source of authority.	Internal or external compulsion. Relationship hierarchical or horizontal.
		To assess conduct & require explanation, rectification or sanction.	May delegate function on independent third party.	Relationship hierarchical or horizontal.
	Assesses conduct and can mandate rectification or sanction.	To give the conduct and the rules a social interaction context.	May be a principal in an agency relationship.	Relationship is hierarchical.

TABLE 1 Conceptual – analytical framework (*cont.*)

Who (actors)	What (performance)	Why (functions)	How (methods)	Whom (relationship)
Community (institution or other collective in the context of which the relationship is situated)	Witnesses and interprets the performance of the accountor and accountee. Can feedback on said performance.	To give the conduct a social context, amplify ex-ante interpretive pressure, sometimes through anticipation of ex-post consequences.	To contextualise the rules and the conduct to social awareness and expectations. Stronger reputational drivers.	Internal or external compulsion depending on objective. Relationship may be hierarchical or horizontal, depending on type of arrangement.

that participation in the process is done with integrity. Also, elements capable of undermining transparency in conduct disclosure should be assessed and, if appropriate, eliminated. Communication must be adequate, intelligible, and understandable by those in the community to which it is relevant. Further, as Bovens points out, it is those with the power to act who must give account.[99]

5.4 Re-conceptualisation of the IUU Fishing Compliance System as Accountability Mechanism

In order to contextualise accountability to the realities of IUU fishing, let us commence with a summary of the features of IUU fishing, as set out in previous chapters. Firstly, IUU fishing as a compliance system is comprised to two main elements: the IUU fishing interpretive lens, and the leverage and enforcement mechanisms whereby compliance with the understandings and expectations incorporated into the 'IUU' interpretive is ensured. The lens has been captured by Article 1(e) of the 2009 Agreement on Port State Measures

99 Bovens (2007) at 110 and 112, supra at 79.

to Prevent, Deter and Eliminate Illegal, Unreported and Unregulated Fishing PSMA, which indicates:

> (e) illegal, unreported and unregulated fishing refers to the activities set out in paragraph 3 of the 2001 FAO International Plan of Action to Prevent, Deter and Eliminate Illegal, Unreported and Unregulated Fishing, hereinafter referred to as 'IUU fishing'.

In turn, such 'activities' remain undefined, to be identified by reference to the groups of categories set out in paragraph 3 of the IPOA IUU, which in a unitary sense operates as a hybrid lens comprising legal and non-legal criteria. Through that lens, events that may or may not possess legal significance may be incorporated for analysis vis-à-vis the conduct of States. The previous chapter clarified that this hybridity refers to the potential of RFMO rules and measures to operate as conduct standards of sorts, agreed by some States and not others. Those rules and measures, however, are situated always under the umbrella of the international legal framework. As a compliance system, the IUU fishing interpretive lens is complemented by enforcement mechanisms that aim at ensuring that States comply with certain RFMO rules and measures. This ensures that the vessels flagged to those States have access to ports, and the seafood products they capture can enter international markets. Herein lies the key effectiveness mechanism of the IUU fishing compliance mechanism. It operates through the convergence of conduct rules and standards (adopted by law, or by RFMO s), incentives (port and markets services) and disincentives (suspension of those services).

5.4.1 *Core Accountability Re-construction in the IUU Fishing Context: Tabular Representation*

It is recalled that the core elements of accountability were described by Mulgan,[100] and have been set out in the white sections of Table 1. For ease of reference, the 'core' section of the table is reproduced, as follows (Table 2).

As illustrated in the table, the core concept elements are reflected in the IUU fishing compliance paradigm: The EU determines the rules of its market on IUU fishing control via EU legislation, namely the EU IUU Regulation, containing a definition of the IUU fishing interpretive lens.[101] In the context of market measures adopted by some RFMO s, the process of disclosure is carried

100 Mulgan (2000) at 555, supra at 18.

101 Council Regulation 1005/2008 Article 3.

TABLE 2 Core concept elements

Who (actors)	What (performance)	Why (functions)	How (methods)
Accountor (gives account) – Statessubjected to market measures	Discloses information through narration or justification concerning own behaviour or performance – *States submit information regarding their performance as regulators of vessels subsequently identified as engaging in IUU fishing operations*	To inform of conduct details and/or methods by reference to conduct rules and obtain feedback – *Includes conduct evaluation against the rules imported by the IUU fishing lens*	Responds to duty of disclosure and narration or justification and its functional and/ or ontological rationale–*Responds to verification requirement in order to ensure it can continue to trade national vessel captures*
Accountee (calls for account) – Market State arrangements via RFMOs or the EU	Receives and interprets conduct information and assesses conduct – *Receives information from third States to enable verification and evaluation of their regulatory activity and vessel compliance*	To learn and/ or interpret / assess conduct – *evaluates vessel activity information*	Possesses technical expertise, a legal right, or other source of authority – *Granted by the CDS inside an RFMO, or by the EU IUU Regulation*

out through the statistical data contained in the catch documentation scheme (CDS), designed to identify IUU fishing activity in the custody chain.[102] In both cases, flag State participation in the schemes implies their acceptance of IUU fishing as interpretive lens, and participation in market mechanisms implies participation in the IUU fishing compliance system. Both the IUU Regulation and the CDS establish mechanisms whereby the flag State must certify the accuracy of the information submitted by their vessels when they unload in a port of the EU or the RFMO aiming for first sale.[103] Such certification might be subject to verification by the relevant market State authorities and, in the case of the IUU Regulation, by the European Commission, if sufficient evidence has been obtained via member State ports to suspect IUU fishing activity.[104]

Verification procedures may lead to a suspension in importations until the Commission is able to conclude its checks, which may depend in whole or in part on the response it gets from the flag State.[105] It is straightforward to infer from the market-based character of the enforcement dimension of the IUU fishing compliance paradigm, that participation in the accountability process is incentivised by the opportunity to trade in the vast EU market.[106] The disclosure and verification requirements of the process enables assessment of the flag State's regulatory conduct by the European Commission, and may lead to reputation loss and other undesirable consequences. Furthermore, the nature of the disclosures is objective, and difficult to hide despite the likelihood of sanction: the flag States are required to open up to verification their system for regulation of fishing vessels, and are required to explain how it has implemented international law, as well as existing RFMO rules and measures in the areas where the vessels entitled to fly its flag operate.

5.4.2 *Broader Accountability Re-construction*

In addition to the above, it is also important to take into account the social drivers of accountability, as depicted in the remaining sections of Table 3, which are reproduced as follows (Table 3).

Procedurally, the IUU Regulation has a well-defined process of contestation and conduct justification, which is set out in Article 32. The provision in

102 See ISSF, 'RFMO Catch Documentation Scheme: A Summary' (WCPFC, 2016) WCPFC-2016-CDSIWG03-OP01.

103 *Ibid.* Also, Council Regulation 1005/2008 Chapter III, and Annex IV.

104 Council Regulation 1005/2008 Article 17.

105 Council Regulation 1005/2008 Articles 17.7 and 18.

106 MA Young, 'International trade law compatibility of market-related measures to combat illegal, unreported and unregulated (IUU) fishing' (2016) 69 *Marine Policy* 209–219, 209.

TABLE 3 Social / public accountability elements

Who (actors)	What (performance)	Why (functions)	How (methods)	Whom (relationship)
Accountor (gives account)				External or internal compulsion – *Main market driver is rational in nature, as participation in the CDS or IUU Regulation processes ensures access to market benefits*
		To permit conduct assessment / build cooperation/ trust and/ or enable learning – *participates to permit conduct assessment as required by the established process*	Responds to conduct rules and their rationale, and expertise/ authority of the accountee – *the processes of participation are compulsory to all participants in the market*	
		To publically narrate/ justify/ perform an act of compliance or allegiance to a norm – *participation is public and has a reputational dimension*	Responds to community awareness of the norm and expertise/social compulsion potential in community awareness–*aligned with increasing public narratives recognising undesirable nature of IUU fishing*	

TABLE 3 Social / public accountability elements (*cont.*)

Who (actors)	What (performance)	Why (functions)	How (methods)	Whom (relationship)
Accountee (calls for account)				Internal or external compulsion – *International Organisations exerting regulatory authority over participants*
		To assess conduct & require rectification or sanction	May delegate function on independent third party – *European Commission partly delegates IUU fishing risk assessment processes onto member States in which ports the IUU vessels unload*	Relationship hierarchical or horizontal - *Relationship is theoretically horizontal, but mediated by economic drivers that may be difficult for poorer States to resist*
	Assesses conduct and can mandate rectification or sanction – *Can demand conduct rectification, and determine suspension of market access benefits*	To give the conduct and the rules a social interaction context – *Processes are public, and market suspension carries a reputational penalty and related public opprobrium*	May be a principal in an agency relationship – *No, relationships are theoretically horizontal, but determined by conduct drivers, locked by legal obligation on participants*	Relationship is hierarchical – *rights and obligations exist for participants, once legally locked in*

TABLE 3 Social / public accountability elements (*cont.*)

Who (actors)	What (performance)	Why (functions)	How (methods)	Whom (relationship)
Community (institution or other collective in the context of which the relationship is situated)	Witnesses and interprets the performance of the accountor and accountee – *other States, organisations & NGOs witness IUU designations (reputational dimension)*	As above.	To contextualise the rules and the conduct to social awareness and expectations. Stronger reputational drivers – *relevance of increasing dominance of anti-IUU narratives and growth in treaties*	Internal or external compulsion depending on objective – *objective is conduct assessment, as IUU conducts are, if not corrected, extirpated from the market sphere*

sub-paragraphs (a) and (d) respectively obligate the European Commission to give reasons justifying the identification of the flag State as a candidate for the IUU list, and to clearly set out the consequences of the identification. In addition, sub-paragraph (b) establishes a duty to give the flag State in question an opportunity to respond to the allegations. Article 32.2 requires the Commission to include in the notification a request for the flag State to take measures for the cessation of the IUU fishing activities and to prevent future activities. Article 32.4 also requires the Commission to give the flag State time to answer. Should the corrective action by the flag State not be forthcoming or be deemed insufficient, the consequences in the notice may ensue, and the sanctioning procedures of the IUU Regulation are set out in Articles 44 and 45. The public naming as non-cooperating State element of the notification and sanctioning processes is particularly marked with the IUU Regulation, given its global and very visible nature. It is recalled that the processes of verification, warning and sanction of the IUU Regulation are not only performed publically, but States that undergo a public warning, therefore are likely to suffer reputation loss by association to the IUU fishing label,[107] prior to suffering the

107 Council Regulation 1005/2007 Articles 32 and 33.

removal of market access by way of sanction.[108] The public scenario demarcated by the IUU Regulation confers onto the processes a performance value, which serves to affirm a certain kind of *status quo* and expectations of compliance for all fishing States that trade with the EU.

It follows from the above that for the purposes of accountability analysis, the IUU fishing compliance system responds remarkably well to an accountability conceptualisation, as it replicates all the key elements of the core accountability mechanism, and most of the elements in the broader model. It is clear from the features depicted in the table that the CDS and IUU Regulation processes contain a rational conduct driver in the shape of market access. This driver ensures participation, and the public removal of the opportunity to participate and 'non-cooperating' designation act as sanction. These are preceded by a warning about deviation from conduct expectations, which can also be read as a notice capable of triggering reputational loss. Thus, the public ritual of accountability is accomplished.

5.4.3 *Application of Critiques to Rational Models and Sanctions*

The presence of sanctions and rational drivers suggests that the critiques highlighted in section 2 of this chapter may be relevant, and should be considered. With regard to sanction, the market enforcement mechanisms of the IUU fishing compliance paradigm do not appear vulnerable to distortion concerning a lack of integrity in the information-giving narrative of the accountor. The reason for this is that the autonomy of participants in market processes is quite constrained, once their participation is locked in. The account-giving flag State retains autonomy only insofar as they are not forced to participate. As already explained, once they participate they are locked in a formal process, which is established by each RFMO in respect of the CDS, and by Article 17 and Annex IV of the IUU Regulation. Being a part of these mechanisms implies the need to make systematic disclosures of key capture data, without which participation would not be possible. The systematic nature of these processes means that sanctions do not really have the potential for causing a lack of integrity in the disclosures, because the nature of the process does not have sufficient flexibility to allow for this. The limited autonomy of participants suggests these are strong models of accountability. Nevertheless, a softer accountability mechanism may not be more desirable, given that those processes directly counter opacity, which is a persistent characteristic in IUU fishing.[109] An

108 Council Regulation 1005/2007 Article 38.

109 See Chapter 1, Section 1.1.2.

empirical illustration of this can be seen in some of the past procedures of the International Commission for the Conservation of Atlantic Tunas (ICCAT), where sanctions have been documented to have had the undesirable effect of conditioning conduct disclosure, as States chose not to disclose incriminating information to ICCAT in order to avoid negative rolling quota consequences.[110]

The lack of autonomy in the CDS and EU IUU Regulation disclosure processes means that the actors in authority (respectively RFMO port States and European Commission) should be particularly sensitive to their own position as authority actors within a strong accountability procedure. In order to avoid an undesirable disconnection from the contextual rules in which they operate, they should implement processes whereby they, as 'accountees', become also 'accountors'. This caveat is important in particular for the EU, as its procedures for the operationalisation of market measures operate by reference to conduct rules, and their interpretation is not open to scrutiny for the purposes of public comment or review. The process is therefore in principle vulnerable to a potential problem capable of undermining effectiveness: the potential for the accountee to deviate from the purpose of the rules that the market mechanisms are purported to enforce, and in the midst of which they operate. In addition, it is recalled from prior discussion that the IUU fishing interpretive lens is problematic for a similar reason: the fact that it is blind to the possibility that the RFMO rules that it incorporates into the analysis of undesirable activity may be tainted by legitimacy flaws. That same uncritical approach is then susceptible of being incorporated into enforcement mechanisms, such as the IUU Regulation.

5.5 Limitations of the Conceptual Accountability Model

As market regulator in respect of IUU fishing activities, the EU in principle ensures that market decisions involving trade suspensions against third States are sufficiently objective that they do not fall foul of WTO rules on bias.[111] However, as already explained, the IUU fishing compliance paradigm is vulnerable to blindness in respect of bias in RFMO rules. This critique is significant, for two reasons. Firstly, the legality of the market measures depends on

110 See HR Koehler, 'Promoting Compliance in Tuna RFMOs: a Comprehensive Baseline Survey of the Current Mechanics of Reviewing, Assessing and Addressing Compliance with RFMO Obligations and Measures' (International Seafood Sustainability Foundation, 2013) 6–16.

111 See Young (2016) at 209, supra at 106.

their compliance with a number of conditions established in Article XX of the GATT, which are relevant to legitimacy. Secondly, the bias issue taints the very claim to effectiveness upon which the functionality of the IUU fishing lens rests, as previously explained. The conceptual accountability model constructed in this chapter above, and re-constructed in the empirical and regulatory context of IUU fishing paradigm has highlighted some weaknesses in the paradigm's market mechanisms, which in particular cautions against a lack of oversight or review process, specially in respect of actors who are in a position of authority, and who receive account from others. Yet, at the same time the mechanism set out in this chapter lacks appropriate tools through which any legitimacy shortfalls may be identified within the accountability process. It is recalled that in the case of the IUU Regulation those legitimacy flaws may come into the IUU accountability mechanism 'ready made' within the RFMO rules. This realisation means that some modifications are desirable so that any flaws may be corrected, but the pathway that may lead to such correction cannot be found in the accountability model articulated here. Indeed, the concept of accountability only requires that the process of conduct evaluation be made against certain standards, expectations, or rules of conduct. Without a normative framework against which the validity of the rules being applied can be contrasted or verified, the mechanism is blind to the quality, status, or integrity of those rules. Without such tool, the IUU fishing compliance system continues to be blind to those rules, and re-conceptualisation is of little value. To overcome this limitation, accountability needs to be imbedded in a particular context that incorporates sources and standards of normativity. As Rached explains:

> In spite of its rather high currency, accountability does not partake in the select group of first-order political ideals: democracy, human rights, constitutionalism and rule of law (…). Rather than radiating a comprehensive legal or political vision, accountability supplies a power-constraining toolbox that allows for a variety of more or less attractive permutations. (…) The concept of accountability remains unstable because, among other things, its descriptive and normative aspects lack a clearer articulation. [112]

Thus, it is clear that a characterisation of the IUU fishing paradigm as a mere procedural accountability machine, whilst indeed quite straightforward, and

---

112 Rached (2016) at 317, supra at 20.

not altogether lacking in value, is nevertheless incomplete. A possible solution is set forth in the following chapter.

5.6 Conclusion

Accountability is distinguished from other concepts due to a minimum number of core features: firstly, it is a relational mechanism, whereby actors engage in a process of communication; secondly, it is characterised by the conduct disclosure of one actor, the accountor, to another, the accountee, by reference to norms, rules and expectations that the actors share. Additionally, the actions to which conduct disclosure refers, and the act of disclosure itself, may be conditioned by incentives, and by the potential for sanctions and penalties. Sanctions may have the detrimental effect of undermining transparency. The function of accountability gravitates to a great extent around the presence of conduct rules, norms or understandings that are not only shared by the individual actors, but also reflect expectations of the communities in the context of which the accountability process takes place. The ultimate function of accountability has been defined as the modulation of individual conduct to collective expectations, revealing the importance of the social, institutional or other collective context that defines the community at any one time. A reconstruction of the IUU fishing compliance system around this conceptual blueprint has evidenced that it indeed performs the function of a flag State accountability mechanism.

Beyond analytical effectiveness concerns, the accountability model presented in this study, and relied on to re-conceptualise the IUU fishing compliance system suggests that, despite the ease with which the paradigm can be reframed, the usefulness and capacity of this exercise is limited. This is because the elements for normative analysis that are required to identify potential legitimacy flaws that could be present in the RFMO rules and measures are lacking. It is recalled that the potential for such flaws to be present was identified as the key weakness in the system, and is traceable to the inability of the IUU fishing lens to enquire as to the objectivity of RFMO rules and measures. Although such problems may be rare, they are not irrelevant, as they constitute a systemic weakness that undermines the very effectiveness objective of the IUU fishing lens. The problem does not totally originate in the IUU lens itself, despite its lack of parsimony. It lies also in the lack of institutional strength in RFMOs and the excessive power of individual States (and other actors) to disrupt objectivity and effectiveness in decision-making.

The re-conceptualisation carried out here, though limited in its effects, can nevertheless be considered to be valuable as an analytic exercise through which to ensure that the procedure can be appropriately recognised, and distinguished from other mechanisms. The IUU fishing compliance paradigm can also be enhanced through this lens with some additional oversight and review safeguards concerning the relevant decision-making authorities (namely in some instances RFMOs and their port States, and in particular the European Commission). These changes may avoid mistakes in the decision-making process, and may address an important problem identified as an obstacle to accountability, and also as a factor for concern in the broader environmental law literature: that powerful actors performing functions though which they exert authority over others on behalf of a community of interests, such as States that form part of a treaty regime, may be cable of disengaging from their representative and interpretive role, and they eventually pursue individual rather than collective interests. Finally, in order to find a more comprehensive solution for the adaptation and development of the IUU fishing compliance paradigm, the conceptual accountability mechanism presented in this chapter must be given a normative dimension. This challenge is addressed in the next chapter.

CHAPTER 6

IUU Fishing as Flag State Accountability Paradigm

Introduction

The conceptual analysis has revealed accountability as a procedural apparatus with considerable analytical value for the purposes of the re-conceptualisation of the IUU fishing compliance system. Yet, it lacks a normative dimension. Addressing this limitation implies a need to take into consideration the criteria and values associated with the rules and standards that are needed for the conduct evaluation processes that characterise accountability frameworks. Building on this premise, this chapter has the objective to furnish the conceptual blueprint of accountability previously articulated with adequate normative parameters, upon which an IUU fishing accountability paradigm may be underpinned. These parameters should, on the one hand, not interfere with the effectiveness features of IUU fishing as a compliance paradigm, yet it should also be capable of addressing the concerns around the legitimacy safeguards that it currently lacks, and ensure that it sustains the objectivity that is required for its appropriate co-existence and interaction with the international legal framework.

The legal analysis carried out in the first part of this book is useful as a reminder that the IUU fishing compliance system principally gravitates around RFMO rules and measures, and can obscure international law. Transformed into an accountability paradigm, however, IUU fishing will need to incorporate rules and standards that are shared by all the the parties taking part in the accountability mechanism. This includes the contextual group or 'community' in which the mechanism in question may be situated. From the accountability perspective, this implies a need to pay attention to broader rules. Common or overlapping treaty frameworks, and general international obligations, become contextually relevant. The enquiry contained in this chapter illuminates the mechanisms through which they should be brought into the paradigm, and delves deeper into the reasons why this should be so.

6.1 The IUU Fishing Accountability Paradigm and Effectiveness

The validity of IUU fishing as a compliance paradigm is based on the accurate premise that a system of rules, expectations, and/or standards, may possess

 | DOI:10.1163/9789004463219_008

effectiveness, even if it has no legal status. The effectiveness of the IUU fishing compliance model depends on two factors. Firstly, effectiveness depends on rules are appropriate to address the relevant conducts. This aspect of effectiveness was explored in chapter 2, where it was found that treaty and many RFMO rules are fit for purpose. Secondly, it also depends on the fact that it enables international organisations to suspend the benefits of international trading against certain flag States, in circumstances that are not clearly provided for by treaty or general international law. Attempting to strip the IUU fishing compliance system of this extra-legal dimension would emasculate it, depriving it from an element that is essential to its effectiveness. However, effectiveness also depends on additional factors. The analysis conducted in chapters 3 and 4 has also shown that effectiveness is closely connected to the legitimacy conditions that influence the processes whereby a rule is made, and its resulting objectivity. It was also seen that, problematically, the IUU fishing compliance system has not been furnished with adequate safeguards to ensure that the rules it seeks to enforce have been adopted in a way that guarantees their objectivity.

These considerations are relevant in any context where the effectiveness of a rule or rule system is important. In particular, procedural safeguards resulting in rule objectivity are considered paramount in contexts where *general* compliance is expected.[1] This is a key consideration for the IUU fishing compliance system, given that a lack of objectivity could be implicit in some RFMO rules, whilst compliance with them is expected from all that come into contact with the areas or stocks under their governance. The accountability re-construction conducted in the previous chapter has resulted in useful analytical insights as to accountability's value to ensure that decision-making in international organisations is furnished with procedural disclosures and conduct oversight. Yet, beyond a requirement that such disclosures be made against conduct rules that are held in common, there is little insight into the reasons why this should be so, and how to attain it. These objectives are addressed in this final chapter.

6.2 The IUU Fishing Accountability Paradigm and Normativity

RFMO rules operate under, and co-exist with, a range of inter-locking and over-arching global and regional treaty rules, as well as as norms of international

1 See M Fitzmaurice, 'Legitimacy of International Environmental Law. The Sovereign States Overwhelmed by Obligations: Responsibility to React to Problems Beyond National Jurisdiction?' (2017) *Max-Planck-Institut für ausländisches öffentliches Recht und Völkerrecht* 339–370.

legal custom. This last category is particularly important in contexts where no other rules are held in common by the actors that are involved in an accountability mechanism. They are the only legal rules, or *norms*, that carry an expectation of general compliance. The *pacta tertiis* principle is not relevant against these rules, because they do not emanate from treaty. Hence, normativity in the IUU fishing accountability paradigm may revolve around articulating a methodology whereby the apparent 'void' filled by RFMO rules and measures is instead understood as a sometimes thinly but nevertheless *fully* legalised space. This is so because general norms are legally binding on all States. Yet, they can depend on either treaty rules or GAIRS for their implementation, as well as jurisprudence and authoritative interpretations, due to their open texture. The appropriate development of legal frameworks depends on these additional rules, and on related interpretive processes. In the high seas, fragmentation characterises the fabric of international fisheries law. Its emphasis on regionalism, and the absence of recognised GAIRS means that there are significant voids where norms are difficult to implement. As seen in Chapter 3, treaty is essential to facilitate implementation, and to establish the appropriate standards for responsibility assessments and determinations. As argued by Oral in her commentary of the South China Sea case, different overlapping and converging treaties may be relevant for the interpretation of general obligations, such as the duty to protect the marine environment set out in Article 192 of the LOSC.[2] Without defined rules such as those contained in treaty, the meaning and impact of such obligations may be very thin, and State responsibility may be rendered blunt and largely ineffective other than in very limited circumstances.

Leading scholars have acknowledged that the effectiveness of international law – namely its ability to successfully establish a legal order that is accepted by States, is likely to be associated with factors that often transcend 'made' law.[3] Typically, legal as well as political factors can have an influence in effectiveness.[4] Franck has highlighted that an excessive focus on positive law can obscure factors of an extra-legal nature that may be significant to ensuring the

2 See N Oral, 'The South China Sea Arbitral Award: A Triumph for Part XII of UNCLOS and the Protection and Preservation of the Marine Environment' in Jayakumar, Koh, Beckman, Davenport and Phan (Eds) The South China Sea Arbitration: The Legal Dimension (Elgar, 2018) 223.

3 See for example HJ Morgenthau, 'Positivism, Functionalism, and International Law' (1940) 34 *American Journal of International Law* 260–284, 267 and 269.

4 JG Ruggie, 'Continuity and Transformation in the World Polity: Toward a Neorealist Synthesis' (1983) 35(2) *World Politics* 261–285, 277. R Keohane, *After Hegemony* (Princeton University Press, 1984) 88.

effectiveness of law and, ultimately, its normativity.[5] In the context of the IUU fishing accountability there is no need to discuss 'sources' of normativity in the sense of the 'creation' of brand new legal rules. The function of accountability is to enhance and perpetuate an expectation of compliance with rules and measures that exist already. The problem principally concerns how the IUU fishing interpretive lens, and specifically its unregulated fishing filter, can be applied in contexts where the conduct rules are not contained or endorsed by a fisheries treaty to which the accountability actors are a party. In those circumstances, the rules either have to be common to both actors in other ways, or be obviously objective and therefore free of potential biases, and capable of generating compliance. Normativity is, therefore, not a simple matter of relying on RFMO rules and measures in order to fill the gaps left by the fragmentation of the international legal system. Those rules and measures should be considered as part of the broader legal rule and norm context.

6.3 The IUU Fishing Paradigm and Regime Complexes

Serdy, who has evaluated the IUU fishing compliance system from a legal perspective, found that international organisations and RFMOs in particular, unconstrained by clear legal standards, can take biased decisions against some States.[6] Serdy's critique reflects profound and widely shared concerns regarding the status of international law in respect of global governance. This concern is particularly relevant to governance spaces that exist outside of specific treaty regimes. Such regimes are complex rule frameworks governed by a treaty. Regimes do not exist in a void: they co-exist in a broad legal context populated by other treaties, as well as customary norms.[7] Rule interactions can also occur across regimes, and around their margins. Certain rules, such as GAIRS, have a derivative legal force born of their function and ability to enable the implementation of legal obligations. Others yet have no actual legal force, but may be *lex ferenda*, which is a legal rule 'in the making' that has therefore not yet been established as part of the body of positive law.[8]

---

5 TM Franck, *The Power of Legitimacy Among Nations* (Oxford University Press, 1990) 706.

6 A Serdy, The New Entrants Problem in International Fisheries Law (Cambridge University Press, 2016a) 153.

7 See E Benvenisti and GW Downs, 'The Empire's New Clothes: Political Economy and the Fragmentation of International Law' (2007) 60(2) *Stanford Law Review* 595–632, 597.

8 H Thirlway, 'Reflections on Lex Ferenda' (2001) 32 *Netherlands Yearbook of International Law* 3–26.

Whether operating regionally or globally via coordinated State agencies, international organisations such as RFMOs operate through bodies such as committees, secretariats, and commissions.[9] Generally, a constitutive treaty underpins this type of international arrangement, demarcating their function and objectives. Upon the treaty platform, there may be secondary rules binding upon the treaty parties, as well as other rules of a political nature elaborated in order to assist the aims of the regime, and to support the operation of the institutional elements entrusted with the enterprise functions.[10] Taken as a unit, these institutional and instrumental complexes integrate the regime.[11] The proliferation of regimes, as mechanisms to achieve the objectives of a group of States, has been associated to benefits such as facilitating cooperation in situations of potential friction, relieving uncertainty in situations where coordinated or joint approaches are required, and adding stability and predictability to shared State enterprises in an increasingly complex and globalised world.[12] Various regimes can converge, and overlap, for example in order to operate in pursuit of a shared objective. This can be optimum where all or most States parties belong to the same regimes.

It is useful to proceed to an overview of the regime complexity that is identifiable in some of the incarnations of the IUU fishing regulatory model. In the case of the market mechanisms applied by individual RFMOs, the traceability procedure of the Catch Documentation Scheme (CDS) comprises a statistical tool able to record captures in the regulated area through to volumes unloaded in port. The CDS is usually applied to a single high value species, ensuring traceability and incentivising the vessels flagged to States that participate in the scheme.[13] The objectivity and relative simplicity of the scheme contrasts with the more ambitious, but considerably more complex and less parsimonious mechanism of the EU.[14] It is recalled from Chapter 4 that the EU mechanism has been articulated on the legal bases established by the EU

9 J Brunnée, 'COPing With Consent: Law-Making under Multilateral Environmental Agreements' (2002) 15(1) *Leiden Journal of International Law* 1–52, 7 and 15.

10 J Brunnee, 'International Environmental Law and Community Interests: Procedural Aspects' in Benvenisti and Nolte (Eds) *Community Interests Across International Law* (Oxford University Press, 2018) 166.

11 SD Krasner, 'Structural Causes and Regime Consequences: Regimes as Intervening Variables' in Krasner (Ed) *International Regimes* (Cornell University Press, 1983) 2.

12 Keohane (1984) at 34, 62, and 158, supra at 4. E Weisband and A Ebrahim, 'Introduction: Forging Global Accountabilities' in Ebrahim and Weisband (Eds) *Global Accountabilities: Participation, Pluralism and Public Ethics* (Cambridge University Press, 2007) 7.

13 See G Hosch, 'Trade Measures to Combat IUU Fishing: Comparative Analysis of Unilateral and Multilateral Approaches' (2016) Issue Paper 6 of the International Centre for Trade and Sustainable Development, 1.

14 See Chapter 5, Section 5.2.2.

IUU Regulation. The key regime features of the market mechanism established by the IUU Regulation are as follows: The basic procedure that underpins the IUU Regulation is the 'catch certification scheme' (CCS),[15] a certificate where vessel operators enter vessel, operator, and catch data that must be validated by their flag States, to be inspected upon landing at an EU member State port.[16] The nature of the infringements is set out in Article 3 of the Regulation, which in essence replicates the serious infringements list contained in Article 21.11 of the 1995 Fish Stocks Agreement (UNFSA),[17] albeit without explicit reference to the UNFSA, to which *inter alia* unauthorised transhipment has been added. References to the international legal obligations of the flag State are contained in several provisions of the IUU Regulation, many of which have the function of implementing the UNFSA regime. Paragraph 15 of its Preamble, for example, indicates that the CCS contains evidence of the legality of the products, meaning that the flag State must ensure that the activities of its vessels are in accordance with international conservation and management measures. This reference, which can be understood as a requirement to comply with the rules and measures of RFMOs, in essence replicates the basic cooperation requirement of Articles 8 and 17 of the UNFSA, whereby State parties of this agreement must comply with the rules of RFMOs, irrespective of membership status. This is reinforced by Article 2 of the IUU Regulation, which reflects in essence the definition of IUU fishing contained in paragraph 3 of the IPOA IUU.

In addition, Article 31.3 of the IUU Regulation indicates that a State may be identified as a non-cooperating third country 'if it fails to discharge the duties incumbent upon it under international law as flag, port, coastal or market State, to take action to prevent, deter and eliminate IUU fishing'. Hence, notwithstanding its participation in the market regime of the IUU Regulation as a flag State that oversees the legality of the activities of its fishing vessels, once investigations are under way, breaches of international law in respect of its regulatory conduct in other capacities may be taken into consideration by the European Commission under the scope of the IUU Regulation. In addition, Article 31.5 establishes a series of factual guidelines for the flag State to observe as elements that the European Commission will take into account, such as severity of enforcement measures, and gravity of the IUU fishing

15 A model of the CCS is set out at EC 1005/2008, Annex II.

16 IUU Regulation, Article 17.

17 1995 United Nations Agreement for the Implementation of the Provisions of the United Nations Convention on the Law of the Sea of 10 December 1982 relating to the Conservation and Management of Straddling Fish Stocks and Highly Migratory Fish Stocks, 2167 UNTS 88.

manifestations, albeit disembodied from legal context. Further, Article 31.6 of the IUU Regulation indicates as follows:

> For the purposes of paragraph 3, the Commission shall also consider the following elements:
>
> (a) the ratification of, or accession of their countries concerned to, international fisheries instruments, and in particular the Unclos, the UN Fish Stocks Agreement and the FAO Compliance Agreement;
> (b) the status of the third country concerned as a contracting party to regional fisheries management organisations, or its agreement to apply the conservation and management measures adopted by them;
> (c) any act or omission by the third country concerned that may have diminished the effectiveness of applicable laws, regulation or international conservation and management measures.

These rather broad parameters serve to identify the concurrent, and often overlapping, regimes under which a flag State may be evaluated. If found to be in non-compliance, another procedure is engaged under Article 31 of the IUU Regulation, which may result in a trade suspension. In the implementation of such an event, the Commission would be subject to the parameters of Article XX exemptions contained in the GATT. Prior to this step, the Commission proceeds to the public identification of the flag State as 'non-cooperating'.[18]

The above outlines the complex nature of IUU fishing as a flag State accountability paradigm, whereby diverse regimes can converge at any one time. Various regime rules interlock and/or may be resorted to in order to interpret the conduct of the flag State that must give account. In the context of the IUU Regulation, the European Commission is the only interlocutor with authority to interpret the acts or omissions of third States, and the degree to which they have contravened or undermined any rules. From the perspective of a conceptual accountability analysis, this aspect of the IUU Regulation can arguably be said to lack safeguards in respect of rule selection and interpretation. Such safeguards should be established to ensure, firstly, that the meaning ascribed to a rule is consistent and non-biased. Further,

---

18 IUU Regulation Article 35.

the accountability framework articulated in the previous chapter suggests that it is also advisable to take into account the 'shared understandings' of the rules and standards that other members of the 'community' possess. Whilst the meaning of community here might be confusing, in principle any State to whom a decision under the EU IUU Regulation applies, could be said to form part of such community at the time of the decision. The State will share and therefore have to interpret and deal with any international treaties or non-treaty rules to which the decision refers in its assessment of the flag State's conduct. Consequently, the interpretations that those States give to the provisions contained in such international instruments should in principle be taken into consideration by the Commission too, for the purposes of informing the decision-making process. Particularly important is the identification of rule interpretations or standard setting that, through replication across different RFMO s or other regional practices, may become apparent to have become the practice of that State. In addition, special attention should be paid to practices that either have become generalised, or are close to doing so. A small number of examples of standards that may well be developing towards GAIRS status, such as the assignation of IMO vessel identification numbers, VMS standards, or the quantum of fines, were discussed in Chapter 3.

6.4 Shared Rules and Norms in Regime Complexes

Regimes are defined by collective objectives, but their alignment to incentives and interests of the participants can add stability by fixing strategic positions.[19] This insight captures one of the main mechanisms of the IUU Regulation: the regime is underpinned by market participation incentives and a series of potential sanctions associated to misconduct. The alignment between incentives on the one hand, and norms and/or rules on the other is important, because compliance is vulnerable to economic power. This is a factor that some scholars associate to the 'thin' normativity of international legal norms.[20] For

19 JL Dunoff, SR Ratner and D Wippman, *International Law Norms, Actors, Process: A Problem-Oriented Aproach* (Aspen Publishers, 2010) 993. See also A Chayes, and AH Chayes, *The New Sovereignty* (Harvard University Press, 1995) 26 and 27.

20 See J Brunnee and SJ Toope, *Legitimacy and Legality in International Law* (Cambridge University Press, 2010) 12. KW Abbott, RO Keohane, A Moravcsik, AM Slaughter and D Snidal, 'The Concept of Legalization' (2000) 54 *International Organization* 401–419. Regarding the impossibility to locate the ultimate triggers of obligation within the legal

accountability purposes, any misalignments between the priorities of powerful international actors and legal normativity may cause a loss of effectiveness in the accountability mechanism. This implies an assumption that powerful interests may ultimately be able to determine the content or understanding of rules and/or norms, and shape the resulting regime to their preferences.[21] These assumptions are supported by some legal scholars,[22] with some authors having argued that ambiguity in international law may be the result of strategic use of power by some powerful States,[23] and indeterminate rules having been described as the 'handmaiden' of power.[24] Interpreting legal rules so that their meaning is well understood and operationalised inside regimes may, by contrast, facilitate the balancing of collective normative objectives against existing dominant interests, affording the possibility of 'contingent' compromises. This may enable communities to avoid decisions that are rooted predominantly on the preferences of powerful actors, and therefore more likely to be tainted with bias.[25]

Full engagement with the interlocking and overarching rule frameworks of a regime complex is a key factor in addressing those problematic areas. In the context of the IUU fishing accountability paradigm, the task at hand is not only one of assessing instances of international responsibility. For that purpose, systemic interpretation of applicable rules of international law is appropriate, and to be expected.[26] The IUU scenario also implies a need to interpret measures that are not legally binding, as well as the broader context of international law. This requires that international actors consciously 'undo' the blurring effect of the IUU fishing lens, with the aim of giving visibility to the legal

---

nature of rules, see R Higgins, *Problems and Process: International Law and How We Use It* (Clarendon Press, 1994)16. For a discussion on the lineage of this position within legal scholarship to Hobbes and Puffendorf, see SG Sreejith, 'Public International Law and the WTO: A Reckoning of Legal Positivism and Neoliberalism' (2007) 9 *San Diego International Law Journal* 5–79, 9.

21 See Morgenthau (1940) at 260, supra at 3. Sreejith (2007) at 77, supra at 20.

22 See M Koskenniemi, *The Gentle civilizer of Nations: The Rise and Fall of International Law 1870–1960* (Cambridge University Press, 2001) 461.

23 JL Goldsmith, and E Posner, *The Limits of International Law* (Oxford University Press, 2005) 13.

24 N Krisch, 'International Law in Times of Hegemony: Unequal Power and the Shaping of the International Legal Order' (2005) 16(3) *European Journal of International Law* 369–409, 371.

25 J Dill, *Legitimate Targets? Social Construction, International Law and US Bombing* (Cambridge University Press, 2014) 58.

26 See C McLachlan, 'The Principle of Systemic Intergration and Article 31(3)(c) of the Vienna Convention' (2005) 54 International Community Law Quarterly 279–320.

framework, including customary norms. The task thus requires that a methodology be found whereby rules that are not legally binding may be interpreted in a manner that can evaluate their legitimacy and objectivity, *and* that ensures that they are coherent with their international legal context.

According to Finnemore, part of the normative power of international rules may be the result of the complex interactions to which actors are subjected as part of their participation in regimes.[27] In synergy with this insight, Chayes and Chayes indicate that a 'discursive process of explanation, justification, and persuasion is a central attribute of international affairs' in the routine context of regime interactions – a more prevalent scenario to the extraordinary instances in which the interpretation of international rules is conducted by international courts.[28] Thus, processes of decision contestation, such as those articulated through mechanisms of accountability, can have a role to play in achieving not only better rule definition,[29] but also in ensuring decisions are interpreted in a manner that is coherent with the relevant aspects of the international legal framework. Several accountability scholars have called for special attention to be paid to the processes of interaction between regime actors and rules in order to understand the potential of such interactions to reinforce accountability processes.[30]

These processes are likely to be particularly fruitful in cases where States participate in several regimes. The EU, as authority in charge of the implementation of the IUU Regulation, is also a member of all major RFMOs, as well as the conference of the parties of all global fisheries and many environmental treaties. There is the implementation of the IUU Regulation significant potential for interpretive cross-fertilisation, likely to enhance coherence across regimes, and across them and general international obligations. In the context of treaty interpretation McLachlan argues that part of the work involved in the process of interpreting legal rules revolves around the production of a shared

27 This assertion is supported by empirical research in the context of international organisations: See M Finnemore, 'International Organizations as Teachers of Norms: The United Nations Education, Scientific and Cultural Organization and Science Policy' (1993) 47 *International Organization* 565–598, 594 & 596.

28 Chayes and Chayes (1995), at 122, supra at 19.

29 See JL Mashaw 'Accountability and Institutional Design: Some Thoughts on the Grammar of Governance' *Public Law Working Paper* 116 (2006) 115.

30 In particular K Yang, 'Further Understanding Accountability in Public Organizations: Actionable Knowledge and the Structure-Agency Duality' (2012) 44(3) *Administration and Society* 255–284, 272. See also M Dubnick, 'Accountability and the Promise of Performance: in Search of the Mechanisms (2005) *Public Performance & Management Review* 28(3) 376–417.

lexicon that can support and guide not only the instant treaty negotiation, but also inform subsequent iterative processes, with the result that future international activity shares normative elements of prior treaties.[31] In regimes where legal and non-legal rules co-exist, there is no reason why many aspects of the legal lexicon could not be shared. In this regard, the IUU Regulation places the European Commission in a unique position to survey shared lexicons with which to inform the IUU Regulation decision-making processes.

6.4.1 *Norms and Practice in Regime Complexes*

Accountability has a performative social function demarcating and showcasing desirable conducts to others in the community. These same or similar premises have been rehearsed by social theorists. The sociologist Wenger developed the idea based on the notion that order in a social community depends on the opportunities for collective learning generated by community interactions, in which actors routinely engage with their norms.[32] Similarly, the 'structurationist' theoretical view of government in society, advanced by sociologist Anthony Giddens,[33] and later developed by other scholars in the social sciences,[34] also pays attention to the influence of actor interaction with rules, in the perpetuation of socially relevant norms. From these perspectives, accountability relates to systemic practices whose effect is to consolidate and crystallise social rule and norm frameworks.[35]

Fuller's own account of the force of legal norms through interaction between rules and social forces is synergistic with this vision, as interaction for Fuller transcends the activities of legal and judicial institutions, and is mirrored by broader informal social understandings and practices.[36] Thus, from these

---

31 Mc Lachlan at 284, supra at 26.

32 E Wenger, *Communities of Practice: Learning, Meaning, and Identity* (Cambridge University Press, 1998) 7 and 75.

33 A Giddens, *Central Problems in Social Theory: Action, Structure, and Contradiction in Social Analysis* (University of California Press, 1992).

34 A Langley, 'Strategies for Theorising on Process Data.' (1999) *Academy of Management Review*, 24(4) 691–710. C Argyris, 'Actionable Knowledge', in H Tsoukas and C Knudsen (Eds) *The Oxford Handbook of Organisation Theory* (Oxford University Press 2003, New York) 423–452. M Pozzebon and A Pinsonneault, 'Challenges in Conducting Empirical Work Using Structuration Theory' (2005) *Organization Studies*, 26(9) 1353–1376. MJ Dubnick and K Yang, 'The Pursuit of Accountability: Promise, Problems, and Prospects' in White and Menzel (Eds) The State of Public Administration: Issue, Challenges, Opportunities (Routledge, 2011) 171.

35 Giddens (1992) at 56–58, supra at 33. A Wendt, 'The Agent-Structure Problem in International Relations Theory' (1987) 41 *International Organization* 335–370, 359.

36 L Fuller, 'Human Interaction and the Law' in Winston (Ed) *The Principles of Social Order: Selected Essays of Lon L Fuller* (Duke University Press, 1981) 212.

relational perspectives, the clarification, consolidation, and evolution of rules and norms is shaped by social interaction and performance patterns of mutual rule-actor interpretation and understanding.[37] The central idea of socially and publically *practiced* rules being at the heart of the active maintenance and progressive evolution of the legal order has also reached international relations scholarship. Onuf, Ruggie and Kratochvil, the early developers of the 'constructivist' school of international relations, conceive legal and other norms as having the potential to produce interaction across actor identities within an institutionalised arrangement or community.[38] This is achieved through cognitive frameworks made by rules, in which actors engage via their participation, interpretation, and exercise.[39] The emphasis of this perspective is on the ability of the rule-actor interaction in shaping the interests, preferences, and therefore the conducts, of the actors.[40] Common subjective views then percolate to the collective sphere to progressive forge common expectations.[41] As Wendt explains (emphasis added):

> An institution is a relatively stable set or 'structure' of identities and interests. Such structures are often codified in formal rules and norms, *but these have motivational force only in virtue of actors' socialization to and participation in collective knowledge.*[42]

The above is directly relevant to all accountability mechanisms and, indeed, to the IUU fishing paradigm as a particular incarnation of accountability. Indeed, in order to realise is function to consolidate the social order via the evaluation of individual conducts, accountability requires interaction not only between each of the actors and their community, but also highlights *the need for engagement with the norms and rules.*

---

37 Postema (1994), at 364, supra at 93.

38 NG Onuf, *'World of Our Making: Rules and Rule in Social Theory'* (Routledge, 1989) 148. JG Ruggie, 'What Makes the World Hang Together? Neo-Utilitarianism and the Social Constructivist Challenge' (1998) 52 *International Organization* 855–885, 871 and 876.

39 EB Haas and JG Ruggie, 'What Message in the Medium of Information Systems?' (1982) 26 *International Studies Quarterly* 190–219, 190.

40 F Kratochwil and JG Ruggie, 'International Organization: a State of the Art on an Art of the State' (1986) 40(4) *International Organization* 753–775, 764.

41 F Kratochwil, *Rules, Norms and Decisions: On the Conditions of Practical and Legal Reasoning in International Relations and Domestic Affairs* (Cambridge University Press, 1989) 31. A Wendt, 'Collective Identity Formation and the International State' (1994) 88(2) *American Political Science Review* 384–396, 390.

42 A Wendt, 'Anarchy is What States Make of It: The Social Construction of Power Politics' (1992) 46 *International Organization* 391–425, 399.

6.4.2 *Accountability as an 'Interactional' Site of Rule Socialisation*

Legal scholars Brunnee and Toope have studied constructivism closely, and share its fundamental principle that the force of normativity is rooted in the ability of norm-bearing rules to influence actors in tight social contexts.[43] Under this perspective, State actors are considered porous to the 'structure' provided by interaction with the rules that integrate the regimes in which the interactions occur.[44] This is, essentially, a re-formulation of Fuller's social understanding of obligation,[45] the State actor's individual strategic interests do not percolate to the regime context intact, and are modified over time, as State actor identities are progressively shaped through interaction with the other actors and rules.[46] There is a significant implication of this insight for accountability in the context of IUU fishing: namely, that mechanisms of actor-rule interaction, have a role to play not only in promoting compliance with rules: they can also influence the interpretation of norms, contribute to their progressive clarification and, arguably, the incremental evolution of their meaning over time.

Much of the theoretical debate has gravitated around the question of whether the source of compulsion of legal rules is or not a reflection of legal form alone.[47] Yet, for the purposes of accountability, the debate can be limited to insight into the consolidation and implementation of existing legal norms. Actual compulsion (the essential factor that underpins the effectiveness of a norm or rule) may be seen as emanating from an ongoing process, in which the clarification and crystallisation of a rule of conduct is at least partially dependent on the interactive processes through which it is interpreted in a community context.[48] Those interactive processes can involve the progressive identification and clarification of standards of conduct able to facilitate

43 Brunnee and Toope (2010) at 14, supra at 60.

44 This ultimately practical, social community context separates the constructivist perspective from deontological positions whereby certain normative concepts exist *a priori*, based on universal conceptions of normativity. See J Rawls in *A Theory of Justice* (Harvard University Press, 1971), and P Allott, 'Mare Nostrum' (1992) *American Journal of international Law* 86(4) 764–787. These are traceable to Kant. See I Kant, *Critique of Pure Reason* (St Martin's Press, 1965).

45 See Fuller (1969) at 20, supra at 92.

46 F Kratochwil, 'On the Notion of Interest in International Relations (1982) 36 *International Organization* 1–30, 27.

47 Finnemore and Toope (2001) at 766, supra at 111. Brunnee and Toope (2010) at 8, 24, and 354, supra at 60. See also C Chinkin, 'The Challenge of Soft Law: Development and change in International Law' (1989) 38 International and Comparative Law Quarterly 850–866, 866.

48 G Teubner, 'Substantive and Reflexive Elements in Modern Law' (1983) 17(2) Law & Society Review 239–285, 248. Brunnee and Toope (2010) at 7, supra at 60.

the implementation of open textured obligations. Those processes may even involve the participation of non-State actors.[49] In regard to the type of interactions that is needed, Brunee and Toope argue that:

> (...) agents must reason further with the norms to apply them in specific contexts, characteristically relying on analogy to argue a point. It is therefore essential that relatively stable patterns of expectation emerge both amongst the governed and between the governed and the governing. *But relatively stable expectations or, to adopt constructivist language, shared understandings, are only likely to arise from repeated social practice.*[50] (emphasis added)

The above suggests that the IUU fishing paradigm, if understood as an accountability framework, could reinforce the effectiveness of legal norms and rules in two distinct, but interrelated ways: One of them relates to the role of its compliance function under treaty law and binding RFMO rules and measures, as they may have been infringed in cases of *illegal fishing*. The other way, however, could be understood to exist at the margins of treaty law, but not unconnected from general obligations. This requires engaging in arguments concerning their interpretation and application in cases of *unregulated fishing*, including engaging in reasoning by reference to other relevant rules and conduct standards as may be relevant.

6.4.2.1 A Methodology for the Norm-Rule-Conduct Evaluation Space

Postema has argued that the ability of a rule to facilitate comprehension of its practical import to the members of a community is key to the maintenance of its shared meaning, and its effectiveness via a compulsion effect and ability to generate compliance.[51] The action of reason-giving in respect of norm-application, is the practical substratum that generates confidence that the interpretation of a rule is comparable to that of other members of the group.[52] If comparable, that signals that it is therefore the right meaning of the norm. Practical reason-giving is a critical element in what maintains the understanding of a rule, its acceptance as binding, and therefore its effectiveness. According to Postema, the *practical import* of a rule, namely the reason why it is imperative to act in a certain manner, should be *common*

49 See Brunnee and Toope (2010) at 79, supra at 60.
50 Brunnee and Toope (2010) at 24, supra at 60.
51 Postema (1994) at 365, supra at 93.
52 Postema (1994), at 365 and 377, supra at 93.

and public.[53] This can only be ensured through the participation of community actors with the appropriate knowledge, and for their opinions to be known. This insight supports the vision of the accountability process as agora: a space whereby the meaning of a rule can be discussed by community members with expertise in the meaning of the rules, as well as expertise in the nature and impact of the activities being evaluated, but open to the community too. This is necessary to fully open up the practical import of the rule, and to ensure that the meaning of the rule is consistent with its understanding by all actors to whom it is relevant. In this debate, the relationship between the rule and any applicable general obligations, and any relevant analogy examples, should also be made known. This level of rule and norm engagement ensures that an accountability mechanism becomes a site for the appraisal of the interpretation of rules as well as conducts.

In the context of the IUU fishing paradigm, the implications are important. Firstly, without this kind of engagement it is not possible to address the legitimacy flaws that might have affected the individual RFMO rules at the moment of their inception, and therefore it would not be possible to assess and confirm their objectivity, their coherence with the international legal framework, or their equivalence with other RFMO rules or decisions to which the flag State may also be a party.

6.4.2.2 Interpretive Reciprocity and Analogy

From the interactional perspective, the idea of generality is not only based on objectivity, but also on congruence between law and practice. For Postema, the premise of generality, which he discusses in the context of custom, is always situated inside a social context mediated by norms and rules: 'What qualifies a norm as a normatively significant custom, (...) is its integration in a discursive, deed-based system of norms'.[54] This social form of interpretive reciprocity is essential for interpreting expectations of coherence or generality. This means general norms acquire significance inductively, as a consequence of constant interpretation and re-interpretation of the many rules that have the potential to underpin them and give then practical context. In this sense, the IUU Regulation and the RFMO frameworks ought to be seen as tools in a broad system of implementation of general obligations, that spans across and throughout different regime contexts. To avoid excessive fragmentation through practice within specific decision-making fora, interpretive practice

53 Postema (1994), at 371, supra at 93.
54 Postema (2012), at 735, supra at 132.

should consciously reference global treaty, customary obligations, and general international law, as well as establish analogies with other similar institutional fora.

In particular, recourse to interpretation of treaty and general obligations should guide the decision-making processes applied in the implementation of the IUU Regulation, given the privileged position of the European Commission as conduct and rule arbiter. This opens an opportunity for ex-post analysis of RFMO rules and measures, and their application to non-member States. As Brunee and Toope explain: regime rules may concern actors outside the regime as a result of plurality and diversity.[55] This is palpable in the IUU Regulation, where multiple RFMO and other treaty regimes are brought to convergence as part of its enforcement machinery. The IUU Regulation is allocating onto the European Commission an evaluative and interpretive lynchpin role, as it confers the power to bring forth all kinds of rules, and the potential to place them under assessment alongside the actions of State actors.

6.4.3 *IUU Fishing as Flag State Accountability Paradigm*

The interpretive reciprocity and analogy approach, though feasible in principle, can be easily undermined simply by lack of engagement with the relevant legal rules and norms. Indeed, RFMO management discussions and negotiations are often undertaken as part of processes where enquiry on the scope of international rights and obligations rarely features, and where the information needed to make such assessments may not even be available for evaluation and comment.[56] Further under the implementation mechanisms of Article 31 of the IUU Regulation, the European Commission can segregate the RFMO rules from the international legal framework, as if they pertained to different and unconnected regimes. Firstly, the IUU Regulation in its Article 31.6, it establishes a mandatory process of conduct evaluation whereby the performance of the flag State is to be assessed by the European Commission under the LOSC, the Compliance Agreement, and the UNFSA.[57] The ratification or accession by the flag State to the treaties is, in principle, taken into account. These provisions identify the applicable legal rules to the relationship between the EU and the respondent flag State, and define the 'community' or regime, for accountability purposes. Yet, subparagraphs (b) and (c) of Article 31.6 establish a different position in respect of RFMO rules. Indeed, under paragraph (b) the

55 Brunnee and Toope (2010) at 18 and 21, supra at 60.

56 MT Petersson, 'Transparency in global fisheries governance: The role of non-governmental organizations' (2020) Marine Policy 104128.

57 Pursuant to the notification of the flag State under Article 20 of the Regulation.

flag State may be a member, but also a cooperating non-member of an RFMO. It is recalled that the degree of formality and closeness and participation of non-cooperating non-members in RFMOs can vary, and be very different to that of members. Moreover, under Article 31.6(c), non-member States are also caught by RFMO rules for the purposes of the IUU Regulation, insofar as acts by their vessels than undermine those rules are also to be taken into consideration by the European Commission in determining whether the flag State is a non-cooperating State. Hence, in respect of RFMO rules, there does not need to be evidence of formal acceptance by the flag State of the rules of that particular RFMO. The requirement that the rules have to be 'shared' does not have a formal dimension.

This is a key feature of IUU fishing as a compliance paradigm, and can be observed for example in the Cambodia decision, as it was made public by the European Commission.[58] Similarly, more recent decisions of the Commission follow a similar trend. In a recent decision vis-à-vis Liberia, the Commission establishes an expectation of compliance with RFMO rules practically without reference to the international legal obligations of Liberia.[59] A similar rationale is visible in the previous decision regarding Comoros.[60] There is no adequate evaluation or assessment of any legal obligations that might be relevant. This includes not only obligations that may imply a State's acceptance of RFMO rules, such as the cooperation provisions under the UNFSA, but also general obligations generically binding a flag State to cooperation for the purposes of preserving the marine environment and conserving its fishery resources. The establishment of a mutual exclusion between formal and informal rules in the operation of the same regime complex deprives accountability of an important element in effectiveness: the potential to expose norms to appropriate actor interaction, limiting both its compliance function, and its potential to foster clarity, and either consolidate or permit the evolution of meaning through ongoing interpretation.

---

58 Commission Decision of 15 November 2012 on notifying the third countries that the Commission considers as possible of being identified as non-cooperating third countries pursuant to Council Regulation (EC) No 1005/2008 establishing a Community system to prevent, deter and eliminate illegal, unreported and unregulated fishing (2012) OJEU 55 C 354/13.

59 See Paragraphs 27 to 33 of the Commission Decision of 23 may 2017 notifying the Republic of Liberia of the possibility of being identified as a non-cooperating third country in fighting illegal, unreported and unregulated fishing (2017) OJEU C 169/11.

60 Commission Implementing Decision (EU) 2017/889 of 23 May 2017 identifying the Union of Comoros as a non-cooperating third country in fighting in illegal, unreported and unregulated fishing (2017) OJEU L 135/35.

Further, there is in the implementation of the IUU Regulation little attempt to identify the RFMO rules, processes and programmes that are alleged to have been undermined. Similarly, discussion on practical import of other legal rules is not consistent. Later decisions do not appear to necessarily have taken into account obligations derived from treaties to which the flag State is a party, or general duties in respect of which the State is legally bound. Reference to such rules is important for the flag State to justify how it is meeting its cooperation and conservation obligations in the ocean areas where their vessels are routinely operating. As Young has argued, a regime rule interpreted in a certain way within a regime, then applied to actors who have not participated in the creation or interpretation/evaluation of that rule, typically actors outside of the regime, may give rise to legality as well as legitimacy concerns.[61] Divergent interpretive practices resulting in the adoption of particular regime rules and norms may serve localised communities well, but may at the same time weaken the legal force of broader norms, such as those of a customary nature, under the strain of differing interpretations.[62] It is in this context of interpretive plurality where an accountability approach to implementing the IUU Regulation has the potential to promote congruence, and work towards a more coherent legal and governance landscape. This is a task whose effectiveness depends on willingness by international organisations such as the EU that engage with the routine evaluation of State conducts. For those organisations to actively engage in supporting the congruence of their regimes with relevant aspects of international law could be more powerful than the occasional, exceptional intervention of international courts and tribunals.

6.4.3.1 Addressing the Legality Critique

As jurisprudence on matters of international fisheries law has been advancing in recent years, the European Commission has the opportunity to incorporate legal argumentations set out by international courts and tribunals, and of leading scholars in respect of the interpretation of general obligations that are relevant to the conservation and management of living marine sources. As

61 See M Young, 'Regime Interaction in Creating, Implementing and Enforcing International Law' in Young (Ed) *Regime Interaction in International Law: Facing Fragmentation* (Cambridge University Press, 2012) 10 and 85. JL Dunoff, 'A New Approach to Regime Interaction' in Young (Ed) *Regime Interaction in International Law: Facing Fragmentation'* (Cambridge University Press, 2012) 163.

62 See in this regard J Crawford and P Nevill, 'Relations Between International Courts and Tribunals: The Regime Problem' in Young (Ed) *Regime Interaction in International Law: Facing Fragmentation* (Cambridge University Press, 2012) 257. Also, Black (2017) at 4, supra at 147.

discussed in previous chapters, Tanaka argues that that the general obligation in LOSC Article 192 concerns the destruction of ecosystems, which may occur via environmentally harmful fishing to be assessed by experts, and this damage may be caused by IUU fishing.[63] Another dimension of this norm is the potential for the destruction of the commercial viability of a high seas species, which as discussed in Chapter 3 could in effect eliminate the freedom of fishing for the purposes of exploitation, and thus enable the invocation of responsibility. In this regard, it should be born in mind that a significant number of species are either targeted or systematically captured as bycatch without adequate protections and that some may be nearing commercial extinction.[64] Further, endangering an already vulnerable species can also potentially contravene Article 194(5) of the LOSC. Although it is unclear if this provision benefits from customary legal status, the LOSC is nevertheless a widely ratified global treaty. Treaty rules and standards, specially in respect of well ratified treaties, perform an important role in facilitating the implementation of general legal obligations, particularly when similar provisions can be identified across diverse treaty regimes, to which a flag State whose conduct is under evaluation is a party.[65] In addition, there is also a general duty to cooperate, which for the purposes of the conservation of high seas fisheries resources involves a requirement for meaningful engagement in multilateral management efforts. Given that fishery management is not viable without catch data, it can be assumed that the facilitation to RFMO s that request it of capture information available to the flag State may be the minimum standard for international cooperation in the management of high seas fisheries.[66] Insofar as catch data production in accessible formats can be interpreted as objective criteria, this should apply irrespective of membership status, specially where the flag State under evaluation is collecting high seas catch data for the purposes of other RFMOs or similar arrangements. At least from the perspective of the minimum conduct criteria established by these general obligations, and in the context of convergent

63 Y Tanaka, 'Reflections on the Implications of Environmental Norms for Fishing: The Link between the Regulation of Fishing and the Protection of Marine Biological Diversity' (2020) 22 *International Community Law Review* 389–409, 398 & 400.

64 LA Robertson, RA Watson, and CJ Kein, 'Over 90 Endangered Fish and Invertabrates are Caught in Industrial Fisheries' (2020) 11(4764) *Nature Communications* 1–11.

65 Tanaka (2020) at 398–400, supra at 102. See also N Oral, 'The south China Sea Arbitral Award: A Triumph for Part XII of UNCLOS and the Protection and Preservation of the Marine Environment' in Jayakumar, Koh, Beckman, Davenport and Phan (Eds) *The South China Sea Arbitration: The Legal Dimension* (Elgar, 2018) 223.

66 See A Serdy, *The New Entrants Problem in International Fisheries Law* (Cambridge University Press, 2016a) 264.

treaty rules to which the EU and the flag State are parties, the effect of the *pacta tertiis* principle is unlikely to be problematic.

Lastly, the implementation of the IUU Regulation also provides an ideal platform to identify areas of practice consensus in respect of implementation standards, through comparative examinations of State commitments across different RFMOs and similar regional fora, as well as emerging trends that may support the establishment of GAIRS.[67] As discussed in Chapter 2, a number of general practice standards, such as rules banning large-scale driftnetting, or assigning a minimum penalty quantum to illegal fishing infractions already exist. In addition, commonalities across RFMO rules can be identified in order to consider and even foster the formation of GAIRS. It is recalled, for example, that the requirement for a unique vessel identification number (UVI) in the form of a number assigned freely by the International Maritime Organization (IMO), in respect of vessels of 100 gross tonnes or more, might be argued to either have become such a standard or be in the process of consolidating as such. Its adoption by the FAO Global Record of Fishing Vessels, Refrigerated Transport Vessels and Supply vessels (Global Record),[68] as one of its five public data fields may finally support its crystallisation.[69] In turn, this may serve to define some aspects of interpretation and application of the duties enshrined in LOSC Article 94 and 119 for exercising jurisdiction over vessels in the high seas. The requirement for an UVI should therefore be promoted to a *coherent* rule that can be applied objectively across different but equivalent RFMO contexts, and reconstituted into a single regulatory conduct standard via the contestation processes of the EU IUU Regulation.

By consciously fostering the progressive development of GAIRS, the Commission could significantly enhance the functionality of IUU fishing as a flag State accountability paradigm, beyond the mere uncritical facilitation of RFMO measure enforcement. It could work towards a more discerning regime complex aimed at reinforcing and supporting the development of the

67 It should be noted that the consensus method of interpretation is accepted in other areas of European legal practice. For insight, see D Kagiaros, and VP Tzevelekos, 'The Importance of State Practice in the Shaping of International Standards Pertaining to the Clash between Free Speech and the Banning of Negationism' (2020) Open Research Exeter [accessed on 21 March 2021 via https://ore.exeter.ac.uk/repository/handle/10871/39737].

68 See FAO, 'The Global Record of Fishing Vessels, Refrigerated Transport Vessels and Supply Vessels: Providing a Single Access Point for Information on Vessels Used for Fishing and Fishing Related Activities to Combat Illegal, Unreported and Unregulated Fishing' (2016) 2, C-2017/23 [GRWG].

69 See GRWG, pages 2 and 7.

international legal framework for the high seas, as well ensuring that RFMO rules are free from bias. Even if it reserves the ultimate position of authority to itself, as corresponds to its role as EU market gatekeeper, the Commission should nevertheless carry out a transparent evaluation not only of the conducts under assessment, but also of the rules being applied, and allow independent expert insight into their meaning, and ideally also an opportunity of contestation by third States. This approach would also ensure that the findings of the previous chapter concerning 'principal drift' are taken into account, and that decisions are taken in accordance with a shared rule framework.[70] The progressive development and consolidation of these techniques would incrementally clarify and develop the international legal framework, and limit the significance of the *pacta tertiis* critique for the purpose of applying RFMO rules.[71] A well-developed set of treaty derived rules, equivalent standards across RFMOs, and GAIRS, may eventually narrow the 'unregulated' element in the IUU fishing lens and, in time, perhaps even eliminate it altogether.

6.4.3.2 Addressing the Legitimacy Critique

The legitimacy flaws that have been identified in this study of the IUU fishing paradigm are not exclusive to RFMOs, but reflect a problem that occurs more broadly across international organisations, and in respect of which there is a recognised need to put in place safeguards. Much of the emphasis in the implementation of the IUU Regulation should be focused on safeguarding the objectivity of RFMO rules and, in cases where legitimacy is found lacking, identify those rules so that they are not enforced, and that their flaws are not replicated in the future.

Additionally, the legitimacy critique levelled against IUU fishing is also relevant in this context. It should be noted that legal scholars generally understand legitimacy by reference to Franck,[72] for whom legitimacy is the result of the convergence of certain factors in the process that precedes the final adoption of a rule,[73] as already discussed in Chapter 5. He defines legitimacy as follows:

---

70 See T Schillemans and M Busuioc, 'Predicting Public Sector Accountability: From Agency Drift to Forum Drift' (2015) 25(1) *Journal of Public Administration Research and Theory* 191–215.

71 E Franckx, *Vessel-source Pollution and Coastal State Jurisdiction: The Work of the ILA Committee on Coastal State Jurisdiction Relating to Marine Pollution* (Kluwer Law, 2001) 110.

72 TM Franck, 'Legitimacy in the International System' (1988) 82 *American Journal of International Law* 705–759. Franck (1990), supra at 5. TM Franck, *Fairness in International Law and Institutions* (Oxford University Press, 1995).

73 Fitzmaurice (2017) 367, supra at 1.

> Legitimacy is used here to mean that quality of a rule which derives from a perception on the part of those to whom it is addressed that it has come into being in accordance with right process. Right process includes the notion of valid sources but also encompasses literary, socio-anthropological and philosophical insights.[74]

Frank predominantly conceives the elements of legitimacy as external factors that converge, prior to the rule's final formalisation.[75] This type of 'input' legitimacy guards against the conditions that can result in a rule, measure, or decision being biased, which may occur when decision-making processes are not appropriately designed to ensure objectivity. As discussed in previous chapters, decision-making problems with comparable legitimacy flaws have been documented in relation to RFMO rules and measures.[76] To avoid this problem in the context of decisions under the IUU Regulation, the Commission could underpin decision-making in third country assessments with the interpretive and analogy safeguards described in section 6.4.2.2. By working towards the enhancement of those safeguards, the Commission would be fostering the development of an adequate accountability system, and counter criticisms of opacity.

Additionally, from the interactional perspective, legitimacy is not limited to a set of prior conditions culminating in static rules: legitimacy is required on an ongoing basis for the maintenance of authority and therefore effectiveness, and is nurtured through repeated processes of interpretation, implementation, and other social engagement.[77] Legitimacy can, from this perspective, be strengthened by ongoing participation in processes of argumentation, provided that appropriate engagement with the rules is enabled, and takes place.[78] This is a particularly important function when it comes to the application of rules and measures that could be biased as a result of flawed decision-making

74 Franck (1988) at 706, supra at 141.

75 See JG Postema, 'Implicit Law' (1994) 13(3) *Law and Philosophy*, 361–387, 363.

76 See A Serdy, 'Pacta Tertiis and Regional Fisheries Management Mechanisms: The IUU Fishing Concept as an Illegitimate Short-Cut to a Legitimate Goal' (2017) 48(3) *Ocean Development and International Law* 345–364, 345.

77 See the critique made by Finnemore and Toope (2001) at 750, supra at 111. For contextual scholarship, see EL Lutz and K Sikkink, 'International Human Rights Law and Practice in Latin America' (2000) 54(3) *International Organization* 633–659.

78 Legitimacy can in some literatures be associated to considerations of efficiency. See J Black, 'Says who? Liquid Authority and Interpretive Control in Transnational Regulatory Regimes' (2017) 9(2) *International Theory* 286–310, 295. See also J Black and D Rouch, 'The Development of the Global Markets as Rule-Makers: Engagement and Legitimacy' (2008) 2(3) *Law and Financial Markets Review* 218–233.

procedures. An ongoing process of accountability, whereby those rules are subjected to additional evaluation and interpretation by reference to relevant legal norms, generally applicable standards, or treaty rules whose relevance may de discerned by analogy, may be able to counterbalance the effect of an implicit flaw, enhance rule coherence, and foster effectiveness.

6.5 Conclusion

This chapter has argued that, by re-framing the concept of accountability under certain aspects of interactional legal theory, accountability can be reinterpreted and contextualised in an international legal setting. This re-framing enables insight into how international legal rules can operate for the purposes of accountability, and into the interactive processes that bring those rules into focus in particular contexts. Those processes help maintain the relevance and vigour of those rules in the international communities to which they apply. Through the interactional frame, accountability becomes not only a mechanism to promote compliance, but can also be seen as capable of performing a more nuanced role: that of enhancing the effectiveness of the international rules-based order, whilst protecting the legitimacy of rules, and by extension the autonomy of States as ultimate subject of international law. This balancing function is especially important when it comes to decision-making processes, and processes whereby those decisions are subjected to evaluation and challenge. This is because practical processes whereby actors engage openly with rules help keep the rules meaningful to their community, and shape their refinement, and interpretive evolution. By re-constituting the idea of IUU fishing into a flag State accountability paradigm in this way, the implementation of the IUU Regulation can be seen in a new light. This mechanism has been singled out as a case study, firstly, because of the significant and well-documented impact that the IUU Regulation has had, and keeps having, on third States. Secondly, but of equal importance, is the potential of this high-profile instrument to shape the evolution of the international legal framework of high seas fisheries through ongoing interpretative practice. Such practice can occur in the context of carding and market suspension decisions, which are taken after evaluating the conduct of States against a series of criteria, as part of the implementation of the Regulation.

If understood as a flag State accountability paradigm, the implementation of the IUU Regulation should include efforts to identify rules that are shared by all participants. This should include RFMO rules where possible. This will have the effect of protecting the rules and measures legitimately adopted by

RFMOs, whilst also affording mechanisms for the identification of rules and measures that fail to meet minimum legitimacy standards, preventing any bias to be amplified via their enforcement. Other rules that it may be appropriate to bring to the conduct evaluation process are relevant treaties to which the States under evaluation are parties alongside the EU, and customary law obligations. Interpretation of the relevant provisions should be discussed, and their coherence with the treaty and custom obligations that are contextually relevant ascertained. Argumentations should be made public, so that actors concerned can have an opportunity to express their agreement, or to contest the interpretations in question. In addition, efforts should be made towards the identification of GAIRS, and to promote their consolidation. In this way, the suggested re-construction serves to give the IUU fishing paradigm a functionality that, far from obscuring international law in matters of high seas fisheries, in fact promotes its refinement, maintenance, and progressive development. Lastly, the accountability analysis carried out in this study has also highlighted the need for powerful actors that seek to make others accountable to be subjected to the same system of rules. By strengthening the visibility and functionality of objective rules upon which to base carding and market suspension decisions, the flag State accountability paradigm presented here also helps in attaining that objective.

Conclusion

IUU fishing, understood as a single interpretive lens, has emerged in this study as an instrument that should only be used to address undesirable fishing activities in the high seas. The unregulated fishing 'filter' of the IUU lens is the key element that gives functional meaning to the 'IUU fishing' umbrella. It is, however, a less than ideal interpretive device for evaluating fishing activities that take place in waters under the jurisdiction of coastal States. There, assessments of domestic illegality or international responsibility are more appropriate. In the high seas, however, it is a different matter. Whereas destructive fishing activities have been on the increase, international law has been weak and inadequate to offer effective solutions. In response, the advent of IUU fishing as a governance tool has transformed how flag States are perceived, and how they are held to account. IUU fishing categorisations and their associated market measures have placed renewed emphasis on compliance with the rules and measures established by RFMO s. There is widespread agreement that flag States should cooperate with these organisations, and participate in RFMO fora when their vessels target the fisheries they regulate. RFMO s have become important centres for governance cooperation, and are rightly considered essential in the ongoing combat against IUU fishing activities.

The success of IUU fishing as a governance idea has come hand in hand with a trend for holding flag States accountable when the activities of their vessels have the effect of undermining RFMO rules and conservation and management and other related measures. As part of this trend, flag States are seen as legitimate subjects and recipients of the governance output of RFMOs. Backed by measures capable of curtailing access to markets and services, the IUU fishing compliance mechanism has helped counteract the problem of evasion of RFMO measures. It has served to ensure that these governance organisations gain more support and momentum, enhancing their effectiveness through additional adherence by flag States. As a compliance system, the IUU fishing lens and its backing mechanisms have had the effect of buttressing the role of RFMO s as sources of rules, and of expectations with regard to the conduct of flag States as regulators of fishing activities. Simultaneously, however, the notion of IUU fishing as currently formulated cannot guarantee that the rules and measures adopted by RFMO s are optimally conceived, or applied objectively. Neither can it ensure that those rules and measures are sufficient or effective in eliminating undesirable conducts, or attaining desirable conservation and management outcomes.

 | DOI:10.1163/9789004463219_009

Additionally, the IUU fishing lens is not entirely conducive to clarifying the international legal obligations of States in matters of high seas fisheries. The lens can conflate matters of domestic legality and international responsibility, for example. It can also obscure international legal rights and obligations, and sideline interpretive and argumentation processes capable of producing objective rules and standards in favour of broad but unclear labels. Those are also the processes that can support the implementation of international obligations, as well as foster the development of the existing international legal framework in matters of high seas fisheries into a clear, comprehensive, and effective rule system. Some actors invested in high seas fishery conservation and management may believe this is a price worth paying, given the perception of the legal framework established by the LOSC for the management of high seas resources as ineffectual. Yet, the analysis presented here indicates that such belief may be misplaced.

Like other contributions to the international fisheries law literature, this study highlights that the key elements of the international legal framework for the regulation of high seas fisheries, namely the relevant international customary duties and the obligations contained in the LOSC and its implementing treaties are insufficient to ensure that fishing activities in the high seas are appropriately managed and controlled. Weakness also stems from the reciprocal structure of State responsibility, and the requirement of an injury to a State right to prompt its activation. Another obstacle is the due diligence nature of many obligations associated to the protection of the marine environment and its living resources. Not being obligations of result, even cases of egregious illegal fishing may, depending on the circumstances, be insufficient to establish a breach. Further, the framework of treaty law established in the fisheries treaties that define and help implement the LOSC does contain certain flaws and inadequacies, some of which are significant.

Despite this, the importance of the fisheries treaties, and the Fist Stocks Agreement in particular, to facilitate cooperation in matters of high seas conservation and management, cannot be overstated. The Fish Stocks Agreement has been instrumental in consolidating the RFMO model of cooperation in matters concerning the management of straddling and highly migratory stocks, many of which occur at least in part in the high seas. This treaty, the Compliance Agreement, and the Port State Measures Agreement have also served to clarify important obligations contained in the LOSC, developing them in some cases. Further, it should be pointed out that the law of international State responsibility is not entirely devoid of value, as is often argued. The discussion in Chapter 3 indicates how a breach in the due diligence obligation to protect the marine environment and conserve its living resources that results in the commercial extinction of a marine species might serve as a basis for invoking State responsibility. Yet, the is no real management potential in this option: its value lies in being a last resort to avoid a final or long-term collapse of a high seas species, and rescue alongside it the right of States to set the conditions for its exploitation. This may yet be the last line of defence available to some intensively fished pelagic sharks from commercial extinction.[1]

Nevertheless, the protections offered by general international law are far from sufficient. It can be difficult to determine what specific conducts can be expected of States under customary obligations without recourse to treaty law or GAIRS. These effectiveness limitations reflect the lack of development that characterises a substantial part of the legal framework for fisheries purposes, given the lack of binding force of the better defined and more apposite FAO voluntary instruments. Further, the legal framework is far from comprehensive, and there are still areas and species that fall outside the remit of fisheries treaties and of RFMOs management areas. Importantly, the absence of well-defined GAIRS for the purposes of high seas fisheries management and the authorisation and control of fishing vessels means that there is a lack of homogeneous conduct standards able to support the implementation of general obligations. In short, the international legal framework of the high seas is short of clarity and refinement, is fragmented and underdeveloped, and lacks the effectiveness to rectify State conducts that fall short of a desirable level of diligence.[2]

When these difficulties are considered, the shift towards an apparently progressive reliance on the IUU fishing interpretive lens may seem understandable and appropriate. Yet, this shift has been seen here to be potentially problematic. International law is implemented, refined and developed through the practice of States and other international actors, and this involves interpretive and argumentation processes that engage with existing international legal rules. Because the IUU fishing lens can obscure existing rights and obligations, it does not always support these practices, and indeed has in practice often sidelined them. The IUU fishing lens, specially in respect of its unregulated fishing component, should not be seen *as an end in itself*, but rather as a prompt to work towards better and more comprehensive regulation taking existing international duties as an explicit frame of reference. This implies the need for practices that identify such obligations, and assume the effort needed

1 See N Queiroz et al, 'Global Spatial Risk Assessment of Sharks under the Footprint of Fisheries' (2019) 572 *Nature* 7770.

2 For example, under the auspices of RFMOs, critically endangered species have continued being targeted without appropriate controls. See *ibid.*

for the development of secondary rules and standards as may be necessary to facilitate their implementation. It is one of the main arguments in this book that the concept of accountability, appropriately interpreted through certain aspects of interactional legal theory, can serve as a blueprint through which to reinterpret the idea of IUU fishing, so that it is able to achieve this objective. Further, if correctly put into practice, IUU fishing as a flag State accountability model or 'paradigm' could also serve to counterbalance certain flaws in the RFMO governance system, in a way that it at present cannot do.

As discussed, market practices, particularly in the context of the implementation of the EU IUU Regulation, rely heavily on arguments of compliance with RFMO decisions. Yet, some of the decision-making approaches established in RFMOs have been criticised for objectivity and effectiveness failures and a relative lack of transparency. Whilst it is unquestionable that RFMOs have made an effort to evolve and improve, and have made important contributions to high seas fishery management, conservation outcomes have been suboptimal. A lack of objectivity and/or transparency in decision-making can directly and indirectly compromise the effectiveness of these organisations. Bias in membership and decision-making processes can also be problematic from the perspective of legitimacy, particularly as the IUU fishing compliance system implies an expectation of compliance from members and non-members alike. The transformation of the market-based IUU fishing compliance mechanisms into a flag State accountability paradigm has the potential to counterbalance those legitimacy limitations if appropriately articulated.

Such transformation would need to incorporate the core features of accountability and be conscious of known risks. It should facilitate the disclosure of an actor's conduct against a set of standards, rules and/or expectations. The legitimacy and participation factors that ensure a feeling of compulsion should be protected. Obstacles capable of undermining transparency in conduct disclosure should be eliminated, and disincentives to disclosure removed or balanced. The information disclosed must be meaningful and accessible by all members of the community to which it is relevant. Critically, actors with power must also give account and permit and address counter-arguments. Most importantly, identifiable rules and conduct standards should become the backbone and benchmark of State conduct evaluation processes.

The accountability framework presented here could guide the implementation of the IUU Regulation, and of other market mechanisms established by other international organisations or States in future. The clear identification of RFMO rules enables their open examination, so that if a suspicion of bias exists it can be identified and counterbalanced where possible. This approach should reinforce confidence in the legitimacy of most rules, which are generally not tainted. Secondly, for accountability to be meaningful, it is not sufficient to base conduct evaluations on rules: those rules must also be shared by all participants. This requirement implies a need to reflect upon the role of RFMO rules and measures in implementing international legal duties, including treaty and customary law obligations. As recent jurisprudence has indicated, the interpretation of obligations can be supported by reference to treaties to which all States concerned are a party. There is no reason why such references cannot extend to treaties that are not fisheries-specific, such as those established for the protection of migratory species, biodiversity, or marine habitats.

Similarly, the carding and market suspension processes of the IUU Regulation should also strive to identify conduct standards that could form the basis for GAIRS. It is possible that the IUU Regulation processes could serve to catalyse the harmonisation of regional standards, by establishing co-relations across different RFMOs, and other regional fora, on a case by case basis. Such work has the potential to support the progressive establishment of GAIRS, fostering their eventual consolidation.[3] Embedding this consciousness into the carding and market suspension processes of the IUU Regulation would enhance the transparency and objectivity of procedures, reinforcing the authority of resulting EU Commission decisions vis-à-vis third States. Further, if appropriately implemented, this system would serve to re-valorise and strengthen international law, and to contribute to its implementation and development via the identification and promotion of rules, measures, and practices that have the potential to grow into GAIRS. This would be a result fully aligned with the values and objectives upon which the EU is founded.

Ongoing and open engagement with international obligations will serve to maintain their visibility, and to clarify their meaning and purpose. This is particularly important in contexts where decision-making has been criticised for lacking clarity or objectivity, as some of the literature reviewed for the purpose of this study indicates in respect of the implementation of the IUU Regulation, and some of the decision-making procedures of RFMOs and their outcomes. These should be legal rule and norm engagement processes where open expert interpretations of international obligations, and GAIRS assessments where relevant, are set out, so that they can be understood and, where appropriate, questioned or challenged. This should progressively clarify what practices are to be expected from States and other international actors in response to

3 Caution must be had, of course, in ensuring that GAIRS are used by reference to the relevant legal obligations, from which they derive legal force that they otherwise lack on their own.

existing obligations, and foster their integration into established practices addressing unregulated fishing.

Nevertheless, the flag State accountability paradigm presented here cannot address all the problems and limitations that this study has highlighted. For example, the lack of definition of 'real interest' in the Fish Stocks Agreement, which is too weak to ensure objectivity in RFMO new membership conditions, cannot be satisfactorily remedied in this way. Yet, the proposed reconfiguration of the IUU fishing paradigm can offer some additional legitimacy safeguards, prevent the enforcement of biased rules, and support a governance system upon which both States and international organisations can be held to account on the basis of clear and objective rules and standards. The value of the proposed transformation also lies in the approximation of international legal norms, rules and standards to practices of argumentation and decision-making that are currently essentially managerial. This metamorphosis cannot address all existing flaws, but it can help address limitations associated to lack of clarity in the legal framework, and its underdevelopment.

This transformation can be accomplished only through an awareness that the State conduct evaluation and compliance processes that underpin IUU fishing market suspension procedures are practices that have the potential to impact on international law. They can obscure legal obligations, or they can give them visibility, help clarify their meaning, facilitate their implementation, and support their dynamic interpretation. The effectiveness of international law does not depend exclusively on the creation of new treaties, but also – primarily – on the successful assimilation of existing rules into routine and systemic processes of oversight, assessment, and compliance. Assimilation into the EU IUU Regulation is important, because this instrument occupies a prominent position as a mechanism of global governance. Its accountability potential is therefore powerful and far-reaching. Of course, in future, other eventual systems for the imposition of market measures to combat undesirable fishing activities could also incorporate the accountability features described here to ensure a coherent approach to rule and norm engagement.

In the high seas, marine living resources are under increasing pressure from legal, illegal, and unregulated fishing. Those resources are, however thinly and imperfectly, covered by international legal regimes that are insufficiently developed, and at risk from marginalisation. The proposal in this study, if adopted, should help address this unsatisfactory situation. Yet, there is also a paradox in this offering, as the transformation of the IUU fishing interpretive lens into a fully-fledged flag State accountability paradigm may also herald its ultimate demise. If reconstructed along the lines set out here, the need for an 'unregulated' fishing component in the IUU fishing interpretive lens should diminish over time. Progressively, the IUU fishing lens may cease to be useful, as a clearer and more comprehensive international legal and regulatory framework begins to emerge, supported by processes of accountability.

Bibliography

Books

Allott P, *Eunomia: New Order for a New World* (Oxford University Press, 1990).

Anand RP, *Origin and Development Of the Law of the Sea: History of International Law Revisited* (Cambridge University Press, 1983).

Barnes RA, *Property Rights and Natural Resources* (Hart, 2009).

Barrett S, *Why Cooperate? The Incentive to Supply Global Public Goods* (Oxford University Press, 2007).

Becker-Lorca A, *Mestizo International Law: A Global Intellectual History 1842–1933* (Cambridge University Press, 2014).

Birkett WP, *Concepts of Accountability* (University of New South Wales, 1988).

Birnie PW and Boyle AE, *International Law and the Environment* (Oxford University Press, 1994).

Birnie PW, Boyle AE, and Redgwell C, *International Law and the Environment* (Oxford University Press, 2009).

Boczek BA, *Flags of Convenience* (Harvard University Press, 1962).

Bovens M, '*The Quest for Responsibility: Accountability and Citizenship in Complex Organisations*' (Cambridge University Press, 1998).

Brunnee J and Toope S, *Legitimacy and Legality in International Law: An Interactional Account* (Cambridge University Press, 2010).

Bull H, *The Anarchical Society: A Study of Order in World Politics* (Palgrave Macmillan, 2012).

Burke WT, *The New International Law of Fisheries: UNCLOS 1982 and Beyond* (Clarendon Press, 1994).

Busuioc M, *European Agencies: Law and Practices of Accountability* (Oxford University Press, 2013).

Calley D, *Market Denial and International Fisheries Regulation: The Targeted and Effective Use of Trade Measures Against the Flag of Convenience Fishing Industry* (Martinus Nijhoff, 2011).

Chayes A and Chayes AH, *The New Sovereignty* (Harvard University Press, 1998).

Cheng B, *General Principles of Law as Applied by International Courts and Tribunals* (Cambridge University Press, 1953).

Churchill RR and Lowe AV, *The Law of the Sea* (Manchester University Press, 1999).

Collier D and Gerring J, *Concepts and Method in Social Science: The Tradition of Giovanni Sartori* (Routledge, 2006).

Collins R, *The Institutional Problem in Modern International Law* (Bloomsbury Publishing, 2016).

Crawford J, *Brownlie's Principles of Public International Law* (Oxford University Press, 2012).

Crawford J, and Koskenniemi M, *The Cambridge Companion to International Law* (Cambridge University Press, 2012).

Curtin D, *Executive Power of the European Union: Law, Practices, and the Living Constitution* (Oxford University Press, 2009).

Davis G, Weller P and Lewis C, *Corporate Management in Australian Government: Reconciling Accountability and Efficiency* (Macmillan, 1989).

Day P and Klein R, *Accountabilities: Five Public Services* (Tavistock, 1987).

De Arechaga EJ, *International Law in the Past Third of a Century* (Martinus Nijhoff, 1978).

Dill J, *Legitimate Targets? Social Construction, International Law and US Bombing* (Cambridge University Press, 2014).

Dowdle MW, *Public Accountability: Designs, Dilemmas and Experiences* (Cambridge University Press, 2006).

Dubnick MJ, *Accountability as a Cultural Keyword* (The Oxford Handbook of Public Accountability 2014).

Dunoff JL, Ratner SR and Wippman D, *International Law Norms, Actors, Process: A Problem-Oriented Aproach* (Aspen Publishers, 2010).

Dworkin R, *Law's Empire* (Harvard University Press, 1986).

Erkkilä T, *Government Transparency: Impacts and Unintended Consequences* (Palgrave Macmillan, 2012).

Fitzmaurice MA, *Whaling and International Law* (Cambridge University Press, 2015).

Franck TM, *The Power of Legitimacy Among Nations* (Oxford University Press, 1990).

Fuller LL, *The Morality of Law* (Yale University Press, 1969).

Giddens A, *Central Problems in Social Theory: Action, Structure, and Contradiction in Social Analysis* (University of California Press, 1992).

Goldsmith JL and Posner EA, *The Limits of International Law* (Oxford University Press, 2005).

Grafton RQ et al, *Handbook of Marine Fisheries Conservation and Management* (Oxford University Press, 2010).

Guilfoyle D, *Shipping Interdiction and the Law of the Sea* (Cambridge University Press, 2009).

Guzman AT, *'How International Law Works: A Rational Choice Theory'* (Oxford University Press, 2008).

Hantrais L, *International Comparative Research: Theory, Methods and Practice* (Palgrave Macmillan, 2008).

Harrison J, *Making the Law of the Sea: A Study in the Development of International Law* (Cambridge University Press, 2011).

Hart HLA, *Essays in Jurisprudence and Philosophy* (Clarendon Press, 1983).

Held D and Koenig-Achbugi M, (Eds) *Taming Globalization: Frontiers of Governance* (Cambridge University Press, 2003).

Henkin L, *How Nations Behave* (Columbia University Press, 1979).

Higgins R, *Problems and Process: International Law and How We Use It* (Oxford University Press, 1995).

Holzgrefe JL and Keohane RO, *Humanitarian Intervention: Ethical, Legal and Political Dilemmas* (Cambridge University Press, 2003).

Kant I, *Critique of Pure Reason* (St Martin's Press, 1965).

Keohane RO, *After Hegemony: Cooperation and Discord in the World Political Economy* (Princeton University Press, 1984).

Klabbers J, *International Law* (Cambridge University Press, 2013).

Klabbers J, *An Introduction to International Organization* (Cambridge University Press, 2015).

Koontz H and O'Donnell C, *Principles of Management 5th* (McGraw-Hill, 1972).

Koskenniemi M, *The Gentle Civilizer Of Nations: The Rise and Fall of International Law 1870–1960*, (Cambridge University Press, 2001).

Koskenniemi M, *From Apology to Utopia: The Structure of International Legal Argument* (Cambridge University Press, 2005).

Koskenniemi M, 'A History of International Law Histories' in Fassbender and Peters (Eds) *The Oxford Handbook of International Law* (Oxford University Press, 2012).

Kratochwil F, *Rules, Norms and Decisions: On the Conditions of Practical and Legal Reasoning in International Relations and Domestic Affairs* (Cambridge University Press, 1989).

Lobach T, *Law, Technology and Science for Oceans in Globalisation* (Martinus Nijhoff, 2010).

Malanczuk P, *Akehurst's Modern Introduction to International Law* (Routledge, 1997).

Marr S, *The Precautionary Principle in the Law of the Sea* (Martinus Nijhoff, 2003).

Mason M, *The New Accountability: Environmental Responsibility Across Borders* (Earthscan, 2005).

May L, *Sharing Responsibility* (University of Chicago Press, 1992).

Mulgan R, *Holding Power to Account: Accountability in Modern Democracies* (Palgrave Macmillan,2003).

Nollkaemper A, *Issues of Shared Responsibility before the International Court of Justice* (Amsterdam Center for International Law, 2011).

O'Connell D, *The International Law of the Sea Vol. 2* (Oxford University Press, 1984).

Okowa PN, *State Responsibility for Transboundary Air Pollution in International Law* (Oxford University Press).

Onuf NG, *World of Our Making: Rules and Rule in Social Theory* (1989).

Onuf NG, *World of Our Making: Rules and Rule in Social Theory and International Relations* (Routledge, 2012).

Palma M, Tsamenyi M and William RE, *Promoting Sustainable Fisheries: the International Legal and Policy Framework to Combat Illegal, Unreported and Unregulated Fishing* (2010).

Rawls J, *A Theory of Justice* (Harvard University Press, 1971).

Raz J, *The Authority of Law: Essays on law and Morality* (Clarendon Press, 1979).

Reus-Smit C, *The Politics of International Law* (Cambridge University Press, 2004).

Rosenau JN and Czempiel EO, *Governance Without Government: Order and Change in World Politics* (Cambridge University Press, 1992).

Ruggie JG, *Constructing the World Polity: Essays on International Institutionalization* (Routledge, 2002).

Sands P, *Principles of International Environmental Law I: Frameworks, Standards and Implementation* (Manchester University Press, 1995).

Sartori G, *Social Science Concepts: A Systematic Analysis* (Sage Publications, 1984).

Scelle G, *Manuel de Droit International Public* (Domat Montchrestien, 1948).

Serdy A, *The New Entrants Problem in International Fisheries Law* (Cambridge University Press, 2016a).

Shaw NM, *International Law* (Cambridge University Press, 2008).

Stone, 'Defending the Global Commons' in Sands (Ed) *Greening International Law* (Earthscan, 1993).

Sutinen JG et al, *A Handbook on Governance and Socioeconomics of Large Marine Ecosystems* (University of Rhode Island Press, 2006).

Tams CJ, *Enforcing Obligations Erga Omnes in International Law* (Cambridge University Press, 2005).

Tanaka Y, *The International Law of the Sea* (Cambridge University Press 2012).

Tanaka Y, *A Dual Approach to Ocean Governance: the Cases of Zonal and Integrated Management in International Law of the Sea* (Routledge, 2016).

Takei Y, *Filling Regulatory Gaps in High Seas Fisheries: Discrete high Seas Fish Stocks, Deep-sea Fisheries and Vulnerable Marine Ecosystems* (Martinus Nijhoff, 2013).

Thynne I, and Goldring J, *Accountability and Control: Government Officials and the Exercise of Power* (LBC Information Services, 1987).

Von Glahn G and Taulbee JL, *Law Among Nations: An Introduction to Public International Law* (Routledge, 2016).

Wakefield J, *Reforming the Common Fisheries Policy* (Elgar, 2016).

Warner R, *Protecting the Oceans Beyond National Jurisdiction: Strengthening the International Legal Framework* (Martinus Nijhoff, 2009).

Wenger E, *Communities of Practice: Learning, Meaning, and Identity* (Cambridge University Press, 1998).

Wheaton H, *Elements of International Law* (Sampson Low, 1866).

Whiteside KH, *Precautionary Politics: Principle and Practice in Confronting Environmental Risk* (MIT Press, 2006).

Yarwood L, *State Accountability under International Law: Holding States Accountable for a Breach of Ius Cogens Norms* (Routledge, 2011).
Young M, *Trading Fish, Saving Fish: The Interaction between Regimes in International Law* (Cambridge University Press, 2011).
Young O and Osherenko G, *Polar Politics: Creating International Environmental Regimes* (Cornell University Press, 1993).

Book Chapters

Argyris C, 'Actionable Knowledge', in Tsoukas H and Knudsen C (Eds) *The Oxford Handbook of Organisation Theory* (Oxford University Press, 2003).
Barnes R, 'Entitlement to Marine Living Resources in Areas beyond National Jurisdiction' *The International Legal Regime of Areas beyond National Jurisdiction* (Martinus Nijhoff, 2010).
Barnes R, 'Fisheries and Marine Biodiversity' in Fitzmaurice, Ong and Merkouris (Eds) *Research Handbook on International Environmental Law* (Edward Elgar Publishing, 2010).
Barnes RA, 'The Law of the Sea 1850–2010' in Starkey and Heidbrink (Eds) *A History of the North Atlantic Fisheries, Volume 2* (German Maritime Museum, 2012).
Barnes RA and Massarella C, 'High Seas fisheries' in Morgera and Kulovesi (Eds) *Research Handbook on International Law and Natural Resources* (Elgar, 2016).
Barrett J, 'The UN Convention on the Law of the Sea: A "Living" Treaty?' in Barrett and Barnes (Eds) *Law of the Sea: UNCLOS as a Living Treaty* (British Institute of International and Comparative Law, 2016).
Bekkers V et al, 'Governance and the Democratic Deficit: An Evaluation' in Bekkers, Dijkstra, Edwards and Fenger (Eds) *Governance and the Democratic Deficit* (Aldershot, 2007).
Bianchi A, 'On Power and Illusion' in Bianchi and Peters (Eds) *Transparency in International Law* (Cambridge University Press, 2013).
Black J, 'Transparent Policy Measures' in Black, Hashimzade, and Myles (Eds) *Oxford Dictionary of Economics* (Oxford University Press, 1997).
Bovens M, 'The Concept of Public Accountability' in Ferlie, Lynn and Pollitt (Eds) *The Oxford Handbook of Public Management* (Oxford University Press, 2005).
Bovens M, 'Public Accountability' in Ferlie, Lynn, and Pollitt (Eds) *The Oxford Handbook of Public Management* (Oxford University Press, 2005).
Boyle A, 'Remedying Harm to International Common Spaces and Resources: Compensation and Other Approaches' in Wetterstein (Ed) *Harm to the Environment: The Right to Compensation and the Assessment of Damages* (Clarendon, 1997).

Boyle A, 'Further Development of the 1982 Convention on the Law of the Sea: Mechanisms for Change' in Freestone, Barnes, and Ong (Eds) *The Law of the Sea: Progress and Prospects* (Oxford University Press, 2006).

Boyle A and Freestone D, 'Introduction', in Boyle and Freestone (Eds) *International Law and Sustainable Development* (Oxford University Press, 1999).

Brunnee J, 'Multilateral Environmental Agreements and the Compliance Continuum' in Winter (Ed) *Multilevel Governance of Global Environmental Change* (Cambridge University Press, 2006).

Brunnee J, 'International Environmental Law and Community Interests: Procedural Aspects' in Benvenisti, Nolte and Yalin-Mor (Eds) *Community Interests Across International Law* (Oxford University Press, 2018).

Brunee J and Hey E, 'Transparency and International Environmental institutions' in Bianchi A and Peters A (Eds) *Transparency in International Law* (2013).

Brunnee J and Toope S, 'Interactional Legal Theory, the International Rule of Law and Global Constitutionalism' in Lang and Wiener (Eds) *Handbook on Global Constitutionalism* (Edward Elgar Publishing, 2017).

Caiden GE, 'The Problem of Ensuring the Public Accountability of Public Officials' in Jabbra and Dwivedi (Eds) *Public Service Accountability* (Kumarian, 1988).

Chinkin C, 'Dispute Resolution and the Law of the Sea: Regional Problems and Prospects: in Crawford and Rothwell (Eds) *The Law of the Sea in the Asian Pacific Region* (Martinus Nijhoff, 1995).

Cot JP, 'The Law of the Sea and the Margin of Appreciation' in Ndiaye and Wolfrum (Eds) *Law of the Sea, Environmental Law and Settlement of disputes: Liber Amicorum Judge Thomas A Mensah* (Martinus Nijhoff, 2007).

Crawford J, 'Responsibility for Breaches of Communitarian Norms: An Appraisal of Article 48 of the ilc Articles on Responsibility of States for Wrongful Acts', in Ulrich Fastenrath et al (Eds) *From Bilateralism to Community Interest: Essays in Honour of Bruno Simma* (Oxford University Press, 2011).

Crawford J and Nevill P, 'Relations Between International Courts and Tribunals: The Regime Problem' in Young (Ed) *Regime Interaction in International Law: Facing Fragmentation* (Cambridge University Press, 2012).

Crawford J and Watkins J, 'International Responsibility' in Besson and Tassioulas (Eds) *The Philosophy of International Law* (Oxford University Press, 2010).

Dann P and von Engelhardt M, 'Legal Approaches to Global Governance and Accountability: Informal Lawmaking, International Public Authority, and Global Administrative Law Compared' in Pauwelyn, Wessel and Wouters (Eds) *Informal International Lawmaking* (Oxford University Press, 2012).

DeConing E, 'Fisheries Crime' in Elliott and Schaedla (Eds) *Handbook of Transnational Environmental Crime* (Elgar, 2016).

De Sombre E, 'Flags of Convenience and Property Rights in the High Seas' in R Allen, J Joseph and D Squires (Eds) *Conservation and Management of Transnational Tuna Fisheries* (Wiley-Blackwell, 2010).

Dubnick MJ, 'Clarifying Accountability: an Ethical Theory Framework' in Sampford and Preston (Eds) *Public Sector Ethics* (Routledge, 1998).

Dubnick MJ and Frederickson HG, 'Introduction: The Promises of Accountability Research' in Dubnick and Frederickson (Eds) *Accountable Governance: Problems and Promises* (Sharpe, 2011).

Dubnick MJ and Yang K, 'The Pursuit of Accountability: Promises, Problems, and Prospects' in Menzel and White (Eds) *The State of Public Administration: Issues, Challenges and Opportunities* (Sharpe, 2010).

Dunoff JL, 'A New Approach to Regime Interaction' in Young (Ed) *Regime Interaction in International Law: Facing Fragmentation*' (Cambridge University Press, 2012).

Freestone D, 'Problems of High Seas Governance' in Vidas D and Schei PJ (Eds) *The World Ocean in Globalization: Climate Change, Sustainable Fisheries, Biodiversity, Shipping, Regional Issues* (2011).

Fuller L, 'Human Interaction and the Law' in Winston (Ed) *The Principles of Social Order: Selected Essays of Lon L Fuller* (Duke University Press, 1981).

Gjerde K, 'High Seas Fisheries Governance: Prospects and Challenges in the 21st Century' in Vidas and Schei (Eds) *The World Ocean in Globalisation: Challenges and Responses* (Martinus Nijhoff, 2011).

Goodwin-Gill GS, 'State Responsibility and Good Faith Obligation in International Law' in Fitzmaurice and Sarooshi (Eds) *Issues of State Responsibility Before International Judicial Institutions* (Hart Publishing, 2004).

Guilfoyle D, 'The High Seas' in Rothwell et al (Eds) *The Oxford Handbook of the Law of the Sea* (Oxford University Press, 2015).

Harlow C, 'Accountability and Constitutional Law' in Bovens, Goodin and Schillemans (Eds) *The Oxford Handbook of Public Accountability* (Oxford University Press, 2014).

Harrison J, 'Safeguards Against Excessive Enforcement Measures in the Exclusive Economic Zone – Law and Practice' in Ringbom (Ed) *Jurisdiction over Ships: Post UNCLOS Developments in the Law of the Sea* (Brill Nijhoff, 2015).

Hart HLA, 'The Concept of Law' in Raz and Bullock (Eds) *The Concept of Law* (Clarendon Press, 1994).

Hart HLA, 'Positivism and the Separation of Law and Morals' in Kavanagh and Oberdiek (Eds) *Arguing About Law* (Routledge, 2009).

Jones GW, 'The Search for Local Accountability' in Leach (Ed) *Strengthening Local Government in the 1990s* (Longman, 1992).

Keohane R, 'Global Governance and Democratic Accountability' in Held D and Koenig-Achbugi M, (Eds) *Taming Globalization: Frontiers of Governance* (Cambridge University Press, 2003).

Kingsbury B and Donaldson E, 'From Bilateralism to Publicness' in Fastenrath et al (Eds) *From Bilateralism to Community Interests: Essays in Honour of Bruno Simma* (Oxford University Press, 2011).

Kingsbury B, 'Global Environmental Governance as Administration: Implications for International Law' in Bodansky, Brunnee and Hey (Eds) *Oxford Handbook of International Environmental Law* (Oxford University Press, 2007).

Koppell J, 'Accountable Global Governance Organizations' in Bovens, Gooding and Schillemas (Eds) *The Oxford Handbook of Public Accountability* (Oxford University Press, 2014).

Koskenniemi M, 'A History of international Law Histories' in Fassbender and Peters (Eds) *The Oxford Handbook of International Law* (Oxford University Press, 2012).

Krasner, 'Structural Causes and Regime Consequences: Regimes as Intervening Variables' in Krasner (Ed) *International Regimes* (Cornell University Press, 1983).

Lobach T, 'Combatting iuu Fishing: Interaction of Global and Regional Initiatives' in Vidas (Ed) *Law, Technology and Science for Oceans in Globalisation: iuu Fishing, Oil Pollution, Bioprospecting, Outer Continental Shelf* (Cambridge University Press, 2010).

McDougal M and Lasswell H, 'The Identification and Appraisal of Diverse Systems of Public Order' in Falk and Mendlowitz (Eds) *The Strategy of World Order: International Law* (World Law Fund, 1966).

Okowa P, 'Environmental Dispute Settlement: Some Reflections on Recent Developments' in Evans (Ed) *Remedies in International Law* (Hart, 1998).

Oral N, 'The south China Sea Arbitral Award: A Triumph for Part XII of UNCLOS and the Protection and Preservation of the Marine Environment' in Jayakumar, Koh, Beckman, Davenport and Phan (Eds) *The South China Sea Arbitration: The Legal Dimension* (Elgar, 2018).

Oude Elferink AG, 'The Genuine Link Concept: Time for a Post Mortem?' in Dekker and Post (Eds) *On the Foundations and Sources of International Law* (TCM Asser Press, 2003).

Pauwelyn J, 'Is it International Law or Not, and Does It Even Matter?' in Pauwelyn, Wessel and Wouters (Eds) *Informal International Lawmaking* (Oxford University Press, 2012).

Pauwelyn J, Wessel RA, and Wouters J, 'An Introduction to Informal International Lawmaking' in Pauwelyn, Wessel and Wouters (Eds) *Informal International Lawmaking* (Oxford University Press, 2012).

Postema GJ, Custom in International Law: A Normative Practice Account' in Perreau-Saussine and Murphy (Eds) *The Nature of Customary Law: Legal, Historical and Philosophical Perspectives* (Cambridge University Press, 2007).

Rayfuse R, 'Regional Fisheries Management Organizations' in Rothwell et al (Eds) *The Oxford Handbook of the Law of the Sea* (Oxford University Press, 2015).

Raz J, 'Legal Positivism and the Sources of Law' in Kavanagh and Oberdiek (Eds) *Arguing About Law* (Routledge, 2009).

Redgwell C, 'The Never Ending Story: The Role of gairs in UNCLOS Implementation in the Offshore Energy Sector' in Barrett and Barnes (Eds) *Law of the Sea: UNCLOS as a Living Treaty* (British Institute of International and Comparative Law, 2016).

Scelle G, 'Le Phénomène Juridique du Dédoublement Fonctionnel' in Schatzel (Ed) *Rechtsfragen der Internationalen Organisation*, Festschrift für Hans Wehberg zu Seinem Gebrutstag (1956).

Simma B, 'Reciprocity' in Bernhardt (Ed) *Encyclopaedia of Public International Law Vol IV* (North Holland Publishing, 2009).

Stein E, 'Bruno Simma, The Positivist?' in Fastenrath, et al (Eds) *From Bilateralism to Community Interests: Essays in Honour of Bruno Simma* (Oxford University Press, 2011).

Stern B, 'A Plea for Reconstruction of International Responsibility Based on the Notion of Legal Injury' in Ragazzi (Ed) *International Responsibility Today: Essays in Memory of Oscar Schachter* (Martinus Nijhoff, 2005).

Stokke OS, Management Options for High Seas Fisheries: Making Regime Complexes More Effective, in Caddell and Molenaar (Eds) *Strengthening International Fisheries Law in an Era of Changing Oceans* (Hart, 2019).

Tams CJ, 'Individual States as Guardians of Community interests' in Fastenrath et al (Eds) *From Bilateralism to Community interests: Essays in Honour of Bruno Simma* (Oxford University Press, 2011).

Tanaka Y, 'Protection of Community Interests in international Law: The Case of the Law of the Sea' in Von Bogdandy and Wolfrum (Eds) *Max Planck Yearbook of United Nations Law* (Koninklijk, 2011).

Toope S, 'Interactional Legal Theory, the International Rule of Law and Global Constitutionalism' in Lang and Wiener (Eds) *Handbook on Global Constitutionalism* (Elgar, 2017).

Tsamenyi M and Palma MA, 'Long-Range Identification and Tracking Systems for Vessels: Legal and Technical Issues' in *Lloyd's MIU Handbook of Maritime Security* (Lloyd's, 2008).

Van der Marel ER, 'An Opaque Blacklist: the Lack of Transparency in Identifying Non Cooperating Countries under the EU iuu Regulation' in Martin, Salonidis and Hioueras (Eds) *Natural Resources and the Law of the Sea* (Juris, 2017).

Van Der Marel ER, 'Problems and Progress in Combating iuu Fishing', in Caddell and Molenaar (Eds) *Strengthening International Fisheries Law in an Era of Changing Oceans* (Hart, 2019).

Vidas D, 'iuu Fishing or iuu Operations? Some Observations on Diagnosis and Current Treatment' in Caron DD and Scheiber HN (Eds) *Bringing New Law to Ocean Waters* (2004).

Von Bogdandy A, 'General Principles of International Public Authority: Sketching a Research Field' in Von Bogdandy (Ed) *The Exercise of Public Authority by International Institutions* (Springer, 2010).

Von Bogdandy A, Dann P and Goldmann M, 'Developing the Publicness of Public International Law: Towards a Legal Framework for Global Governance Activities' in von Bogdandy, Wolfrum, von Bernstorff et al (Eds) *The Exercise of Public Authority by International Institutions* (Springer, 2010).

Vukas B and Vidas D, 'Flags of Convenience and High Seas Fishing: The Emergence of a Legal Framework' in Stokke OS (Ed) *Governing High Seas Fisheries* (Oxford University Press, 2001).

Weisband E and Ebrahim A, 'Introduction: Forging Global Accountabilities' in Ebrahim and Weisband (Eds) *Global Accountabilities: Participation, Pluralism and Public Ethics* (Cambridge University Press, 2007).

Wiswall FL, 'Flags of Convenience' in William Lovett (Ed) *US Shipping Policies and the World Market* (Quorum, 1996).

Young M, 'Introduction' in Young (Ed) *Regime Interaction in International Law: Facing Fragmentation* (Cambridge University Press, 2012).

Young M, 'Regime Interaction in Creating, Implementing and Enforcing International Law' in Young (Ed) *Regime Interaction in International Law: Facing Fragmentation* (Cambridge University Press, 2012).

Young OR, 'The Effectiveness of International Institutions: Hard Cases and Critical Variables' in Rosenau and Czempiel (Eds) *Governance Without Government: Order and Change in World Politics* (Cambridge University Press, 1992).

Journal Articles

Abbott KW, Keohane RO, Moravcsik A, Slaughter AM and Snidal D, 'The Concept of Legalization' (2000) 54 *International Organization* 401.

Abraham A, 'The Ombudsman and Individual Rights' (2008) 61(2) *Parliamentary Affairs* 370.

Ago R, Second Report on State Responsibility (1970) 2(1) *Yearbook of the International Law Commission* 192.

Alland D, 'Countermeasures of General Interest' (2002) 13 *European Journal of International Law* 1221.

Allison EH, 'Big Laws, Small Catches: Global Ocean Governance and The Fisheries Crisis' (2001) 13 *Journal of international Development* 933.

Allott P, 'Mare Nostrum' (1992) 86(4) *American Journal of international Law* 764.

Alvarez JE, 'International Organizations: Then and Now' (2006) 100 *American Journal of International Law* 324.

Bache I and Chapman R, 'Democracy Through Multilevel Governance? The Implementation of the Structural Funds in South Yorkshire' (2008) 21 *Governance: An international Journal of Policy, Administration and Institutions* 397.

Baird R, 'ccamlr Initiatives to Counter Flag State Non-Enforcement in Southern Ocean Fisheries' (2005) 36(4) *Victoria University of Wellington Law Review* 733.

Baird R, 'Illegal, Unreported and Unregulated Fishing: an Analysis of the Legal, Economic and Historical Factors Relevant to its Development and Persistence' (2004) 5 *Melbourne Journal of International Law* 299.

Balton DA, 'Strengthening the Law of the Sea: The New Agreement on Straddling fish Stocks and Highly Migratory Fish Stocks' (1996) 27 *Ocean Development & International Law* 125.

Balton DA, and Koehler HR, 'Reviewing the United Nations Fish Stocks Treaty' (2006) 7(1) *Sustainable Development Law & Policy* 4.

Barnes RA, 'Consolidating Governance Principles for Areas Beyond National Jurisdiction' (2012) 27 *international Journal of Marine and Coastal Law* 261.

Barnes R, 'Objective Regimes Revisited' (2004) 9 *Asian Yearbook of International Law* 95.

Barnett MN and Finnemore M, 'The Politics, Power and Pathologies of International Organizations' (1999) 53 *International Organization* 699.

Barr MS and Miller GP, 'Global Administrative Law: The View from Basel' (2006) 17 *European Journal of international Law* 15.

Belhabib D et al, 'Fisheries Catch Misreporting and its Implications: The Case of Senegal' (2014) 151 *Fisheries Research* 1.

Benvenisti E, 'Sovereigns as Trustees of Humanity: on the Accountability of States to Foreign Stakeholders' (2013) 107(2) *American Journal of International Law* 295.

Benvenisti E and Downs GW, The Empire's New Clothes: Political Economy and the Fragmentation of International Law' (2007) 60(2) *Stanford Law Review* 595.

Becker MA, 'The Shifting Public Order of the Oceans: Freedom of Navigation and the Interdiction of Ships at Sea' (2005) 46(1) *Harvard International Law Journal* 131.

Berman PS, 'A Pluralist Approach to International Law' (2007) 32 *Yale Journal of International Law* 301.

Biermann F and Gupta A, 'Accountability and Legitimacy in Earth System Governance: A Research Framework' (2011) 70 *Ecological Economics* 1856.

Biermann F et al, 'The Fragmentation of Global Governance Architectures: A Framework for analysis' (2009) 9(4) *Global Environmental Politics* 14.

Birkinshaw PJ, 'Freedom of Information and Openness: Fundamental Human Rights' (2006) 58 *Administrative Law Review* 177.

Black J and Rouch D, 'The Development of the Global Markets as Rule-Makers: Engagement and Legitimacy' (2008) 2(3) *Law and Financial Markets Review* 218.

Black J, 'Says who? Liquid Authority and Interpretive Control in Transnational Regulatory Regimes' (2017) 9(2) *International Theory* 286.

Bleckmann A, 'The Subjective Right in Public International Law', (1985) 28 *German Yearbook of International Law* 144.

Bodansky B, 'The Legitimacy of International Governance: a Coming Challenge for International Environmental Law' (1999) 93(3) *American Journal of International Law* 596.

Bodin J, les Six Livres de La Republique (Iacques du Puys, 1483) as cited by S Beaulac, 'Emer de Vattel and the Externalization of Sovereignty' (2003) 5 *Journal of the History of International Law* 237.

Borit M and Olsen P, 'Evaluation Framework for Regulatory Requirements Related to Data Recording and Traceability Designed to Prevent Illegal, Unreported and Unregulated Fishing' (2012) 36 *Marine Policy* 96.

Bovens M, 'New Forms of Accountability and EU Governance' (2007) 5(1) *Comparative European Politics* 104.

Bovens M, 'Two Concepts of Accountability: Accountability as a Virtue and as a Mechanism' (2010) 33(5) *West European Politics* 946.

Bovens M, Schillemans T and Hart P, 'Does Public Accountability Work? An Assessment Tool in Public Administration' (2008) 86(1) *Public Administration* 225.

Boyle A, 'Problems of Compulsory Jurisdiction and the Settlement of Disputes Relating to Straddling Fish Stocks' (1999) 14(1) *International Journal of Marine and Coastal Law* 14.

Boyle AE, 'Some Reflections on the Relationship of Treaties and Soft Law' (1999) 48 *International and Comparative Law Quarterly* 901.

Boyle AE, 'Further Development of the Law of the Sea Convention: Mechanisms for Change' (2005) 54(3) *International and Comparative Law Quarterly* 563.

Boyle AE, 'Globalising Environmental Liability: The Interplay of National and International Law' (2005) 17 *Journal of Environmental Law* 3.

Boyle AE, 'The Environmental Jurisprudence of the International Tribunal for the law of the Sea' (2007) 22(3) *International Journal of Marine and Coastal Law* 369.

Boyle A, 'UNCLOS Dispute Settlement and the Uses and Abuses of Part XV' (2014) 47(1) *Revue Belge de Droit International Belgian Review of International Law* 182.

Bratspies R, 'Finessing King Neptune: Fisheries Management and the Limits of International Law' (2001) 25 *Harvard Environmental Law Review* 213.

Brown Weiss E, 'Invoking State Responsibility in the Twenty First Century' (2002) 96 *American Journal of International Law* 798.

Brownlie I, 'The Relations of Nationality in Public International Law' (1963) 39 *British Year Book of International Law* 284.

Brunnée J, 'COPing With Consent: Law-Making under Multilateral Environmental Agreements' (2002) 15(1) *Leiden Journal of International Law* 1.

Brunnee J, 'International Legal Accountability through the Lens of the Law of State Responsibility' (2005) 36 *Netherlands Yearbook of International Law* 3.

Brunnee J and Toope SJ, 'International Law and Constructivism: Elements of an Interactional Theory of International Law' (2000) 39(19) *Columbia Journal of Transnational Law* 19.

Buchanan A and Keohane RO, 'The Legitimacy of Global Governance Institutions' (2006) 20(4) *Ethics and International Affairs* 405.

Busuioc M, Curtin D and Groenleer M, "Agency Growth Between Autonomy and Accountability: The European Police Office as a 'Living Institution'" (2011) 18(6) *Journal of European Public Policy* 848.

Busuioc M, and Lodge M, 'The Reputational Basis of Public Accountability' (2016) 29(2) *Governance* 247.

Caddell R, 'Caught in the net: Driftnet Fishing Restrictions and the European Court of Justice' (2010) 22(2) *Journal of environmental Law* 301.

Caminos H and Molitor MR, 'Progressive Development of International Law and the Package Deal' (1985) 79(4) *American Journal of International Law* 871.

Cançado Trindade AA, 'International Law for Humankind: Towards a New Ius Gentium' (2005) 9 *Recueil des Cours* 316.

Cantrell R, 'Finding Nemo ... and Eating Him: The Failure of the United Nations to Force Internalization of the Negative Social Costs That Result from Overfishing' (2006) 5 *Washington Universities Global Studies Law Review* 38.

Carr C, '*Recent Developments in Compliance and Enforcement for International Fisheries*' (1997) 24 *Ecology Law Quarterly* 847.

Carroz JE and Savini MJ, 'The New International Law Of Fisheries Emerging From Bilateral Agreements' (1979) 3(2) *Marine Policy* 79.

Chayes A, and Chayes AH, 'On Compliance' (1993) 47(2) *International Organization* 175.

Checkel JT, 'The Constructivist Turn in International Relations Theory (1998) 50 *World Politics* 324.

Chesterman S, 'Globalization Rules: Accountability, Power, and the Prospects for Global Administrative Law' (2008) 14(1) *Global Governance: A Review of Multilateralism and International Organizations* 39.

Chinkin C, 'The Challenge of Soft Law: Development and Change in International Law' (1989) 38(4) *International and Comparative Law Quarterly* 850.

Cho Y, 'The Concept of "Developing Countries" in the Context of the wto Fisheries Subsidies Negotiation' (2018) 9(2) *Beijing Law Review* 137.

Churchill, 'The Barents Sea Loophole Agreement: a "Coastal State" Solution to a Straddling Stock Problem' (1999) 14(4) *International Journal of Marine and Coastal Law* 467.

Churchill R, 'The Persisting Problem of Non-Compliance with the Law of the Sea Convention: Disorder in the Oceans' (2012) 27(4) *International Journal of Marine and Coastal Law* 813.

Clark NA, Ardron JA, and Pendleton LH, 'Evaluating the Basic Elements of Transparency of Regional Fisheries Management Organizations' (2015) 15 *Marine Policy* 158.

Coglianti-Bantz VP, 'Disentangling the Genuine Link: Enquiries in Sea, Air and Space Law' (2010) 79(3) *Nordic Journal of International Law* 383.

Collier D and Levitsky S, Democracy with Adjectives: Conceptual Innovation in Comparative Research (1997) 49(3) *World Politics* 430.

Collier D and Mahon JE, 'Conceptual "Stretching" Revisited: Adapting Categories in Comparative Analysis' (1993) 87(4) *American Political Science Review* 845.

Conway T et al, 'Rights and Livelihoods Approaches: Exploring Policy Dimensions' (2002) *Natural Resource Perspectives* 1.

Cox A, 'An economic Analysis of Illegal, Unreported and Unregulated (IUU) Fishing: Key Drivers and Possible Solutions' (2006) 30(6) *Marine Policy* 689.

Crawford J, Peel J and Olleson S, 'The ilc's Articles on Responsibility of States for Internationally Wrongful Acts: Completion of the Second Reading' (2001) 12(5) *European Journal of International Law* 43.

Crothers GT and Nelson L, 'High Seas Fisheries Governance: a Framework for the Future?' (2006) 1 *Marine Resource Economics* 341.

Cullis-Suzuki S and Pauly D, 'Failing the High Seas: A Global Evaluation of Regional Fisheries Management Organizations' (2010) 34(5) *Marine Policy* 1036.

Curtin D and Nollkaemper A, 'Conceptualizing Accountability in International and European Law' (2006) 36 *Netherlands Yearbook of International Law* 6.

D'Aspremont J, 'Contemporary International Rulemaking and the Public Character of International Law' (2006) 12 *Working Papers of the Institute for International Law and Justice* 23.

De Bruyn P, Murua H and Aranda M, 'The Precautionary Approach to Fisheries Management: how This Is Taken into Account by Tuna Regional Fisheries Management Organisations (RFMOs)' (2013) 38 *Marine Policy* 397.

De Coning E, and Witbooi E, 'Towards a New 'Fisheries Crime' Paradigm: Africa as an Illustrative Example' (2015) 60 *Marine Policy*, 208.

De Coning E, 'Why Are Some Flag States Unable or Unwilling to Address IUU Fishing?' (2020) 22 *International Community Law Review* 487.

DeSombre ER, 'Fishing Under Flags of Convenience: Using Market Power to Increase Participation in International Regulation' (2005) 5(4) *Global Environmental Politics* 73.

DeSombre ER, 'Globalization, Competition, and Convergence: Shipping and the Race to the Middle' (2008) 14(2) *Global Governance: A Review of Multilateralism and International Organizations* 179.

Detsis E et al, 'Project Catch: A Space Based Solution to Combat Illegal, Unreported and Unregulated Fishing. Part I: Vessel Monitoring Systems' (2012) 80 *Acta Astronautica* 114.

De Yturriaga JA, 'Fishing in the High Seas: From the 1982 UN Convention on the Law of the Sea to the 1995 Agreement on Straddling and Highly Migratory Fish Stocks' (1995) 3 *African Yearbook of International Law* 151.

Dicke LA and Ott JS, 'A Test: Can Stewardship Theory Serve as a Second Conceptual Foundation for Accountability Methods in Contracted Human Services?' (2002) 25(4) *International Journal of Public Administration* 463.

Djalal H, 'The Emergence of the Concept of Fishing Entities: A Note' (2006) 37(2) *Ocean Development and International Law* 117.

Doumboya A et al, 'Assessing the Effectiveness of Monitoring Control and Surveillance of Illegal Fishing: The Case of West Africa' (2017) 50(4) *Frontiers in Marine Policy* 1.

Dubnick MJ, 'Seeking Salvation for Accountability' (2002) *Annual Meeting of the American Political Science Association* 7.

Dubnick MJ, 'Accountability and the Promise of Performance: in Search of the Mechanisms (2005) 28(3) *Public Performance & Management Review* 376.

Dubnick MJ, 'Move Over Daniel We Need Some "Accountability Space"' (2011) 43(6) *Administration & Society* 704.

Dunbabin J, 'Review: The Holy Bureaucrat: Eudes Rigaud and Religious Reform in Thirteenth-Century Normandy' (2007) 122 *English Historical Review* 1385.

Dunn DC et al, 'Empowering High Seas Governance with Satellite Vessel Tracking Data' (2018) *Fish and Fisheries* 1.

Dulvy NK, Sadovy Y and Reynolds JD, 'Extinction Vulnerability in Marine Populations' (2003) 4(1) *Fish and Fisheries* 25.

Dupuy PM, 'Soft Law and the International Law of the Environment' (1990) 12 *Michigan Journal of International Law* 420.

Dyzenhaus D, 'Accountability and the Concept of Global Administrative Law' (2009) 3 *Acta Juridica* 3.

Dzidzornu DM, 'Marine Environment Protection under Regional Conventions: Limits to the Contribution of Procedural Norms' (2002) *Ocean Development and International Law* 291.

Edeson W, 'The International Plan of Action on Illegal Unreported and Unregulated Fishing: the Legal Context of a Non-Legally Binding Instrument' (2001) 16(4) *International Journal of Marine and Coastal Law* 603.

Eliantonio M, 'The Role of NGOs in Environmental Implementation Conflicts: 'Stuck in the Middle' Between Infringement Proceedings and Preliminary Rulings?' (2018) 40(6) *Journal of European Integration* 753.

Elvestad C and Kvalvik I, 'Implementing the EU IUU Regulation: Enhancing Flag State Performance through Trade Measures' (2015) 46(3) *Ocean Development and International Law* 241.

Erikstein K and Swan J, 'Voluntary Guidelines for Flag State Performance: A New Tool to Conquer IUU Fishing' (2014) 29 *International Journal of Marine and Coastal Law* 116.

Erkkilä T, 'Governance and Accountability: A Shift in Conceptualization' (2007) 31(1) *Public Administration Quarterly* 1.

Ewell C et al, 'Potential Ecological and social Benefits of a Moratorium on Transhhipment on the High Seas' (2017) 81 *Marine Policy* 293.

Ezzamel M, 'Accounting, Control and Accountability: Preliminary Evidence from Ancient Egypt' (1997) 8(6) *Critical Perspectives on Accounting* 563.

Fabra A, Gascon V and Werner R, as cited in Agoes ER, 'Development Toward the Adoption of the fao Agreement on Port State Measures to Prevent, Deter and Eliminate Illegal, Unreported and Unregulated Fishing' (2010) 8 *Indonesian Journal of International Law* 202.

Farrell C and Law J, 'Changing Forms of Accountability in Education: A Case Study of LEAs in Wales' (1999) 77(2) *Public Administration* 293.

Fife RE, 'Elements of Nordic Practice 2006: Norwegian Measures Taken against Stateless Vessel Conducting Unauthorized Fishing on the High Seas' (2007) 76(2–3) *Nordic Journal of International Law* 301.

Finnemore M and Sikkink K, 'International Norm Dynamics and Political Change' (1998) 52 *International Organization* 887.

Finnemore M and Toope S, 'Alternatives to Legalization: Richer Views of Law and Politics' (2001) 55(3) *International Organization* 743.

Finnemore M, 'International Organizations as Teachers of Norms: The United Nations Education, Scientific and Cultural Organization and Science Policy' (1993) 47 *International Organization* 565.

Fitzmaurice G, Second Report: Draft Article 19(1)(iv) (1957) *II Year Book of the International Law Commission* 16.

Fitzmaurice M, 'Some Reflections on Public Participation in Environmental Matters as a Human Right in International Law' (2002) 2 *Non-State Actors and International Law* 1.

Fitzmaurice M, 'Third Parties and the Law of Treaties' (2002b) 37(6) *Max Planck Yearbook of United Nations Law* 137.

Fitzmaurice M, 'Legitimacy of International Environmental Law. The Sovereign States Overwhelmed by Obligations: Responsibility to React to Problems Beyond National Jurisdiction?' (2017) 77 *Zeitschrift für ausländisches öffentliches Recht und Völkerrecht* 339.

Fitzmaurice M and C Redgwell C, 'Environmental Non-Compliance Procedures and International Law' (2000) 31 *Netherlands Yearbook of International Law* 35.

Flothman S et al, 'Closing Loopholes: Getting Illegal Fishing Under Control' (2010) 328(5983), *Science* 1235.

Fox J, 'The Uncertain Relationship Between Transparency and Accountability' (2007) 17(5) *Development in Practice* 663.

Franck TM, 'Legitimacy in the International System' (1988) 82 *American Journal of International Law* 705.

Franckx E, 'Pacta Tertiis and the Agreement for the Implementation of the Straddling and Highly Migratory Fish Stocks Provisions of the United Nations Convention on the Law of the Sea' (2000) 8(49) *Tulane Journal of International and Comparative Law* 62.

Freestone D and Makuch Z, 'The New International Environmental Law of Fisheries: the 1995 United Nations Straddling Stocks Agreement' (1997) 7(1) *Yearbook of International Environmental Law* 3.

Freestone D, 'International Governance, Responsibility and Management of Areas Beyond National Jurisdiction' (2012) 27 *International Journal of Marine and Coastal Law* 191.

Freestone D, 'Modern Principles of High Seas Governance: The Legal Underpinnings' (2009) 39(1) *International Environmental Policy and Law* 44.

Furlong WJ, 'The Deterrent Effect of Regulatory Enforcement in the Fishery' (1991) 67(1) *Land Economics* 116.

George M, 'Fisheries Protections in the Context of the Geo-Political Tensions in the South China Sea' (2012) 43(1) *Journal of Maritime Law and Commerce* 85.

Gilman E and Kingma E, 'Standard for Assessing Transparency in information on Compliance with Obligations of Regional Fisheries Management Organizations: Validation through Assessment of the Western and Central Pacific Fisheries Commission' (2013) 84 *Ocean & Coastal Management* 31.

Gilman E, Passfield K and Nakamura K, 'Performance of Regional Fisheries Management Organizations: Ecosystem-Based Governance of Bycatch and Discards' (2013) 15(2) *Fish and Fisheries* 327.

Goldstein J and Martin L, 'Legalization, Trade Liberalization, and Domestic Politics: a Cautionary Note' (2000) 54(3) *International Organization* 603.

Goodhart M, 'Democratic Accountability in Global Politics: Norms, Not Agents' (2011) 73(1) *The Journal of Politics* 45.

Goodman C, 'The Regime for Flag State Responsibility in International Fisheries Law – Effective Fact, Creative Fiction, or Further Work Required' (2009) 23(2) *Australian and New Zealand Maritime Law Journal* 157.

Grant RW and Keohane RO, 'Accountability and Abuses of Power in World Politics' (2005) 99 *American Political Science Review* 29.

Gray R, 'Accounting And Environmentalism: An Exploration Of The Challenge Of Gently Accounting For Accountability, Transparency And Sustainability' (1992) 17(5) *Accounting, Organizations and Society* 399.

Guilfoyle D, 'Interdicting Vessels to Enforce the Common Interest: Maritime Countermeasures and the Use of Force' (2007) 56(1) *International and Comparative Law Quarterly* 69.

Gupta A and van Asselt H, 'Transparency in Multilateral Climate Politics: Furthering (or Distracting from) Accountability?' (2017) *Regulation and Governance* (forthcoming).

Gupta A, 'Transparency Under Scrutiny: Information disclosure in Global Environmental Governance' (2008) 8(2) *Global Environmental Policy* 1.

Guruswamy L, 'The Promise of the United Nations Convention on the Law of the Sea (UNCLOS): Justice in Trade and Environment Disputes' (1998) 25 *Ecology Law Quarterly* 189.

Guzman AT and Meyer TL, 'International Common Law: The Soft Law of International Tribunals' (2009) 9 *Chicago Journal of International Law* 515.

Haas EB and Ruggie JG, 'What Message in the Medium of Information Systems?' (1982) *International Studies Quarterly* 26.

Haas P, 'Do Regimes Matter? Epistemic Communities and Mediterranean Pollution Control' (1989) 43 International Organization 377.

Hale TN, 'Transparency, Accountability, and Global Governance' (2008) 14(1) *Global Governance* 73.

Handl G, 'Compliance Control Mechanisms and International Environmental Obligations, (1995) 5 *Tulane Journal of International Law* 29.

Handl G, 'State Responsibility for Illegal, Unreported and Unregulated Fishing in Foreign EEZs' (2014) 44(1–2) *Environmental Policy and Law* 158.

Hardin G, 'The Tragedy of the Commons' (2009) 1(3) *Journal of Natural Resources Policy Research* 243.

Haque MS, 'Significance of Accountability under the New Approach to Public Governance' (2000) 66(4) *International Review of Administrative Sciences* 599.

Hayashi, 'The Management of Transboundary Fish Stocks under the LOS Convention' (1993) 8(2) *International Journal of Marine and Coastal Law* 245.

Hayashi M, 'The 1995 Agreement on the Conservation and Management of Straddling and Highly Migratory Fish Stocks: Significance for the Law of the Sea Convention' (1996) 29(1–3) *Ocean and Coastal Management* 51.

Hayashi M, 'Global Governance of Deep-Sea Fisheries' (2004) 19(3) *International Journal of Marine and Coastal Law* 289.

Hayashi M, 'International Measures to Combat Illegal, Unreported and Unregulated (iuu) Fishing and Japan' (2008) 51 *Japanese Yearbook of International Law* 57.

He J, 'The EU Illegal, Unreported, and Unregulated Fishing Regulation Based on Trade and Market-Related Measures: Unilateralism or a Model Law?' (2017) 20(2) *Journal of International Wildlife Law & Policy* 168.

Henriksen T and Hoel AH, 'Determining Allocation: From Paper to Practice in the Distribution of Fishing Rights Between Countries' (2011) 1(2) *Ocean Development & international Law* 66.

Henriksen T, 'Revisiting the Freedom of Fishing and Legal Obligations on States Not Party to Regional Fisheries Management Organizations' (2009) 40(1) *Ocean Development and International Law* 80.

Hernandez GI, 'A Reluctant Guardian: The International Court of Justice and the Concept of 'International Community' (2013) *British Yearbook of International Law* 13.

Hey E, 'Global Fisheries Regulations in the First Half of the 1990s' (1996) 11(4) *International Journal of Marine and Coastal Law* 459.

Holmstrom B and Milgrom P, 'Multitask Principal-Agent Analyses: Incentive Contracts, Asset Ownership, and Job Design' (1991) 7 *Journal of Law, Economics, & Organization* 24.

Honniball AN, 'Unilateral Trade measures and the Importance of Defining iuu Fishing' (2020) 7(2) *The Journal of Territorial and Maritime Studies* 7.

Hood C, 'What Happens When Transparency Meets Blame Avoidance?' (2007) 9 *Public Management Review* 191.

Hosch G, 'Trade Measures to Combat iuu Fishing: Comparative Analysis of Unilateral and Multilateral Approaches' (2016) 6(1) *International Centre Trade and Sustainable Development* 1.

Hüpkes E, Quintyn M, and Taylor MW, 'The Accountability of Financial Sector Supervisors–Principles and Practice' (2005) 16(6) *European Business Law Review* 1575.

Jos PH and Tompkins ME, 'The Accountability Paraqdox in an Age of Reinvention' (2004) 36(3) *Administration and Society* 225.

Juda L, 'The 1995 United Nations Agreement on Straddling Fish Stocks and Highly Migratory Fish Stocks: A Critique' (1997) 28(2) *Ocean Development and International Law* 147.

Kahn PW, 'American Hegemony and International Law – Speaking Law to Power: Popular Sovereignty, Human Rights, and the New International Order' (2000) 1(1) *Chicago Journal of International Law* 1.

Keohane R, 'Multilateralism: An Agenda for Research' (1990) 45(4) *Journal of Global Policy Analysis* 731.

Keohane R, 'International Relations and International Law: Two Optics' (1997) 38 *Harvard International Law Journal* 487.

Kim HJ, 'The Return to a Mare Clausum Through Regional Fisheries Management Organizations? (2013) 44 *Ocean Development and International Law* 205.

Kingsbury B, 'The Concept of Compliance as a Function of Competing Conceptions of International Law' (1998) 19(2) *Michigan Journal of International Law* 345.

Kingsbury B, 'The Concept of Law in Global Administrative Law' (2009) 20(1) *European Journal of International Law* 25.

Kingsbury B and Donaldson MC, 'From Bilateralism to Publicness in International Law' (2011) 256 *New York University Public Law and Legal Theory Working Paper* 80.

Kingsbury B, Krisch N and Stewart R, 'The Emergence of Global Administrative Law' (2005) 68(15) *Law and Contemporary Problems* 14.

Klabbers J, 'The Redundancy of Soft Law' (1996) 65 *Nordic Journal of International Law* 167.

Klabbers J, 'The Undesirability of Soft Law' (1998) 67(4) *Nordic Journal of International Law* 381.

Koenig-Archibugi M, 'Accountability in Transnational Relations: How Distinctive Is it?' (2010) 33 *West European Politics* 1142.

Koh HH, 'Why Do Nations Obey International Law?' (1997) 106(8) *Yale Law Journal* 2599.

Koh TB, 'A Constitution for the Oceans' (2012) *Revista de Drept Maritim* 23.

Kojima C, 'Implementing Community Interests in the Law of the Sea: the Conservation and Management of Marine Living Resources' (2009) 116 *The Chuo Law Review* 1.

Kooiman J, 'Social-Political Governance: Overview, Reflections and Design' (1999) 1(1) *Public Management: an International Journal of Research and Theory* 67.

Kornblau EM, 'United States v. Marino-Garcia: Criminal Jurisdiction over Stateless Vessels on the High Seas' (1983) 9(1) *Brooklyn Journal of International Law* 141.

Koskenniemi M, 'Governance and Public International Law' (2004) 37(3) *Kritische Justiz* 244.

Koskenniemi M, 'International law and Hegemony: A Reconfiguration' (2004) 17(2) *Cambridge Review of International Affairs* 197.

Kratochwil F and Ruggie JG, 'International Organization: A State of the Art on an Art of the State' (1986) 40(4) *International Organization* 755.

Kratochwil F, 'On the Notion of Interest in International Relations (1982) 36 *International Organization* 1.

Krisch N and Kingsbury B, 'Introduction: Global Governance and Global Administrative Law in the International Legal Order' (2006) 17(1) *European Journal of International Law* 1.

Krisch N, 'Liquid Authority in Global Governance' (2017) 9(2) *International Theory* 237.

Kunz J, 'The Meaning and the Range of the Norm Pacta Sunt Servanda' (1945) 39(2) *American Journal of International Law* 180.

Langley A, 'Strategies for Theorising on Process Data.' (1999) 24(4) *Academy of Management Review* 691.

Leach M, Mearns R and Schoones I, 'Environmental Entitlements: Dynamics and Institutions in Community-Based Natural Resource Management' (1999) 27 2 *World Development* 225.

Lee M and Abbott C, 'The Usual Suspects? Public Participation Under the Aarhus Convention' (2003) 66(1) *Modern Law Review* 80.

Le Gallic B and Cox A, 'An Economic Analysis of Illegal, Unreported and Unregulated (iuu) Fishing: Key Drivers and Possible Solutions' (2006) 30(6) *Marine Policy* 689.

Lindberg S, 'Mapping Accountability: Core Concept and Subtypes' (2013) 79(2) *International Review of Administrative Sciences* 202.

Lindstedt C and Naurin D 'Transparency is Not Enough: making Transparency Effective in Reducing Corruption' (2010) 31 *International Political Science Review* 301.

Lodge MW and Nandan SN, 'Some Suggestions Towards Better Implementation of the United Nations Agreement on Straddling fish Stocks and Highly Migratory Fish Stocks of 1995' (2005) 20(3) *International Journal of Marine and Coastal Law* 545.

Luhmann N, 'The Autopoiesis of Social Systems' (1986) 6(2) *Sociocybernetic Paradoxes* 172.

Lukashuk I, 'The Principle Pacta Sunt Servanda and the Nature of Obligation Under International Law' (1989) 83(3) *American Journal of International Law* 513.

Lutz EL and Sikkink K, 'International Human Rights Law and Practice in Latin America' (2000) 54(3) *International Organization* 633.

Mansfield B, 'Letter to the Editor: The Southern Bluefin Tuna Arbitration' (2002) 3 *Melbourne Journal of International Law* 53.

Mashaw JL 'Accountability and institutional Design: Some Thoughts on the Grammar of Governance' (2006) *Public Law Working Paper* 116.

Mason M, 'Information Disclosure and environmental Rights: The Aarhus Convention' (2010) 10(3) *Global Environmental Politics* 10.

Mc Connell ML, 'Darkening Confusion Mounted Upon Darkening Confusion: The Search for the Elusive Genuine Link' (1985) 16 *Journal of Maritime Law and Commerce* 365.

McCorquodale R and Simons P, 'Responsibility Beyond Borders: State Responsibility for Extraterritorial Violations by Corporations of International Human Rights Law' (2007) 70(4) *Modern Law Review* 598.

McDorman TL, 'Implementing Existing Tools: Turning Words into Actions–Decision-Making Processes of Regional Fisheries Management Organisations (RFMOs)' (2005) 20(3) *International Journal of Marine and Coastal Law* 423.

McDorman TL, 'Stateless Fishing Vessels, International Law and the UN High Seas Fisheries Conference' (1994) 25(4) *Journal of Maritime Law and Commerce* 531.

McDougal MS, Burke WT, and Vlasic IA, 'The Maintenance of Public Order at Sea and the Nationality of Ships' (1960) 54(1) *American Journal of International Law* 25.

McLachlan C, 'The Principle of Systemic Intergration and Article 31(3)(c) of the Vienna Convention' (2005) 54 *International Community Law Quarterly* 279.

Meijer AJ, Curtin D and Hillebrandt M, 'Open Government: Connecting Vision and Voice' (2012) 78 *International Review of Administrative Sciences* 10.

Meijer AJ, 'Publishing Public Performance Results On The Internet: Do Stakeholders Use The Internet To Hold Dutch Public Service Organizations To Account?' (2007) 24(1) *Government information Quarterly* 165.

Meijer AJ, 'Understanding Modern Transparency' (2009) 75 *International Review of the Administrative Sciences* 255.

Miller AMM, Bush SR, and Mol APJ, 'Power Europe: EU and the Illegal, Unreported and Unregulated Tuna Fisheries Regulation in the West and Central Pacific ocean' (2014) 45 *Marine Policy* 138.

Miller DD and Sumaila UR, 'Flag Use Behavior and iuu Activity within the International Fishing Fleet: Refining Definitions and Identifying Areas of Concern' (2014) 44 *Marine Policy* 204.

Molenaar EJ, 'Non-Participation in the Fish Stocks Agreement: Status and Reasons (2011) 26(2) *International Journal of Marine and Coastal Law* 195.

Molenaar EJ, 'Participation, Allocation and Unregulated Fishing: The Practice of Regional Fisheries Management Organisations' (2003) 18(4) *International Journal of Marine and Coastal Law* 457.

Molenaar EJ, 'Port State Jurisdiction: Toward Comprehensive, Mandatory and Global Coverage' (2006) 38(1–2) *Ocean Development and International Law* 225.

Molenaar EJ, 'The Concept of Real Interest and Other Aspects of Co-operation Through Regional Fisheries Management Mechanisms' (2000) 15 *International Journal of Marine and Coastal Law* 475.

Morgera E, 'An Update on the Aarhus Convention and its Continued Global Relevance' (2005) 14(2) *Review of European Community and International Environmental Law* 138.

Morgenthau HJ, 'Positivism, Functionalism, and International Law' (1940) 34 *American Journal of International Law* 260.

Morth U, 'Public and Private partnerships as Dilemmas Between Efficiency and Democratic Accountability: the Case of Galileo' (2007) 29(5) *European Integration* 601.

Mulgan R, 'Accountability: An Ever-Expanding Concept?' (2000) 78(3) *Public Administration* 555.

Mulgan R, 'Contracting out and Accountability' (1997) 56 *Australian Journal of Public Administration* 106.

Mulgan R, 'One Cheer for Hierarchy-Accountability in Disjointed Governance' (2003) 55(2) *Political Science* 6.

Mulgan R, 'The Processes of Public Accountability' (1997) 56 *Australian Journal of Public Administration* 25.

Munro GR, 'The United Nations Fish Stocks Agreement of 1995: History and Problems of Implementation' (2001) 15 *Marine Resources Economics* 265.

Nissenbaum H, Accountability in a Computerised Society' (1996) 2(25) *Science and Engineering Ethics* 29.

Nollkaemper A, 'Constitutionalization and the Unity of the Law of International Responsibility' (2009) 16(2) *Indiana Journal of Global Legal Studies* 535.

Nollkaemper A, The Problem of Many Hands in International Law (*Amsterdam Center for International Law*, 2015).

Nollkaemper A and Fabbricotti A, 'Political Economy and the Responsibility of States: The Problem of Many Hands in International Law' (2016) *The Political Economy of International Law: a European Perspective* 278.

Nye JS, 'Globalization's Democratic Deficit: How to Make International Institutions More Democratic' (2001) 80(4) *Foreign Affairs* 2.

Ørebech P and Sigurjonsson K, 'The 1995 United Nations Straddling and Highly Migratory Fish Stocks Agreement: Management, Enforcement and Dispute Settlement' (1998) 13(2) *International Journal of Marine and Coastal Law* 119.

Ørebech P, Sigurjonsson K and McDorman TL, 'The 1995 United Nations Straddling and Highly Migratory Fish Stocks Agreement: Management, Enforcement and Dispute Settlement' (1998) 13(2) *International Journal of Marine and Coastal Law* 119.

Oda S, 'Fisheries Under the United Nations Convention on the Law of the Sea' (1983) 77 *American Journal of International Law* 739.

Oral N, 'Reflections on the Past, Present, and Future of iuu Fishing under International Law' (2020) 22 *International Community Law Review* 368.

Orrego Vicuña F, 'Responsibility and Liability for Environmental Damage Under International Law: Issues and Trends' (1997) 10 *Georgia International Environmental Law Review* 279.

Österblom H, Sumaila UR, Bodin Ö, Sundberg JH and Press AJ, Adapting to Regional Enforcement: Fishing Down the Governance Index (2010) 5(9), *PloS one* 12832.

Pastor Ridruejo JA, 'Los Efectos de los Acuerdos Internacionales Respecto a los Terceros' (1960) 13(3) *Revista Espanola de Derecho Internacional* 387.

Pegram T and Acuto M, 'Introduction: Global Governance in the Interregnum' (2015) 43(2) *Millennium-Journal of Int'l Studies* 584.

Pellizzoni L, 'Responsibility and Environmental Governance' (2004) 13(3) *Environmental Politics* 541.

Petersson MT, 'Transparency in global fisheries governance: The role of non-governmental organizations' (2020) *Marine Policy* 104128.

Petrossian GA, Marteache N and Viollaz J, 'Where Do "Undocumented" Fish Land? An Empirical Assessment Of Port Characteristics For iuu Fishing' (2015) 21(3) *European Journal on Criminal Policy and Research* 337.

Petrossian GA, 'Preventing Illegal, Unreported And Unregulated (IUU) Fishing: A Situational Approach' (2015) 189 *Biological Conservation* 39.

Pitcher T et al, 'Not Honouring the Code' (2009) 457(7230) *Nature* 658.

Polacheck T, 'Politics and Independent Scientific Advice in rfmo Processes: A Case Study of Crossing Boundaries' (2012) 36(1) *Marine Policy* 132.

Pollitt C, 'Justification by Works or by Faith? Evaluating the New Public Management' (1995) 1(2) *Evaluation* 134.

Posner EA, 'Cost-Benefit Analysis as a Solution to a Principal-Agent Problem' (2001) *Administrative Law Review* 289.

Postema GJ, 'Implicit Law' (1994) 13 *Law and Philosophy* 361.

Pozzebon M and Pinsonneault A, 'Challenges in Conducting Empirical Work Using Structuration Theory' (2005) 26(9) *Organization Studies* 1353.

Queiroz N, et al, 'Global Spatial Risk Assessment of Sharks under the Footprint of Fisheries' (2019) 572 *Nature* 7770.

Rached DH, 'The Concepts of Accountability: Form in Search of Substance' (2016) 29 *Leiden Journal of International Law* 317.

Ratner BD, Asgard B and Allison EH, 'Fishing for Justice: Human Rights, Development, and Fisheries Sector Reform' (2014) 27 *Global Environmental Change* 120.

Rayfuse R, 'United Nations Agreement on Straddling and Highly Migratory Fish Stocks as an Objective Regime: A Case of Wishful Thinking?' (1999) 20 *Australian Yearbook of International Law* 253.

Rayfuse R, 'International Fisheries and Sustainability: Dealing with Uncertainty' (2000) 14 *Ocean Yearbook* 114.

Rayfuse R, 'Countermeasures and High Seas Fisheries Enforcement' (2004) 51 *Netherlands International Law Review* 41.

Rayfuse R, 'Regulation and Enforcement in the Law of the Sea: Emerging Assertions of a Right to Non-flag State Enforcement in the High Seas Fisheries and Disarmament Contexts' (2005) 24 *Australian Year Book of International Law* 181.

Rayfuse R and Warner R, 'Securing a Sustainable Furture for the Oceans Beyond National Jurisdiction: The Legal Basis for an Integrated Cross-Sectoral Regime for High Seas Governance for the 21st Century' (2008) *Int'l Journal of Marine and Coastal Law* 399.

Rayfuse R, and Wilder M, 'International Fisheries and Sustainability: Dealing with Uncertainty' (2000) 14 *Ocean Yearbook* 114.

Redgwell C, 'Mind the Gap in the gairs: The Role of other instruments in UNCLOS Regime Implementation in the Offshore Energy Sector' (2014) 29 *International Journal of Marine and Coastal Law* 600.

Reus-Smit C, 'Obligation Through Practice' (2011) 3(2) *International Theory* 339.

Roach JA, 'Today's Customary International Law of the Sea' (2014) 45(3) *Ocean Development & International Law* 239.

Robards MD et al, 'Conservation Science and Policy Applications of the Marine Vessel Automatic Identification System (AIS): A Review' (2016) 92(1) *Bulletin of Marine Science* 75.

Robertson LA, Watson RA, and Kein CJ, 'Over 90 Endangered Fish and Invertabrates are Caught in Industrial Fisheries' (2020) 11(4764) *Nature Communications* 1.

Rodenhoff V, 'The Aarhus Convention and its Implications for the Institutions of the European Community' (2002) 11(3) *Review of Environmental Comparative, International and European Law* 343.

Roeben V, 'Responsibility in International Law' (2012) 16 *Max Planck Yearbook of United Nations Law* 99.

Romzek BS and Dubnick MJ, 'Accountability in the Public Sector: Lessons from the Challenger Tragedy', (1987) 47(3) *Public Administration Review* 227.

Rose-Ackerman S and Halpaap AA, 'The Aarhus Convention and the Politics of Process: The Political Economy of Procedural Environmental Rights' (2002) *Research in Law and Economics* 20 27.

Rosello M, 'Cooperation and Unregulated Fishing: Interactions Between Customary International Law, and the European Union IUU Fishing Regulation' (2017) 84 *Marine Policy* 306.

Rosenau JN, 'Governing the Ungovernable: The Challenge of a Global Disaggregation of Authority' (2007) 1 *Regulation and Governance* 88.

Roth-Isigkeit D, 'The Blinkered Discipline? Martti Koskenniemi and Interdisciplinary Approaches to International Law' (2017) 9(3) *International Theory* 410.

Ruggie JG, 'International Responses to Technology: Concepts and Trends' (1975) 10 *International Organization* 29.

Ruggie JG, 'Continuity and Transformation in the World Polity: Toward a Neorealist Synthesis' (1983) 35(2) *World Politics* 261.

Ruggie JG, 'What Makes the World Hang Together? Neo-Utilitarianism and the Social Constructivist Challenge' (1998) 52 *International Organization* 855.

Sala E et al, 'The Economics of Fishing the High Seas' (2018) 4 *Science Advances* 1.

Sartori G, 'Concept Misformation in Comparative Politics' (1970) 64(04) *American Political Science Review* 1033.

Sato T, 'Legitimacy of International Organizations and Their Decisions: challenges that International Organizations Face in the 21st Century' (2009) 37(15) *Hitotsubashi Journal of Law and Politics* 11.

Schachter O, 'United Nations Law' (1994) 88 *American Journal of International Law* 1.

Shapiro SP, 'Agency Theory' (2005) 31 *Annual Review of Sociology* 263.

Schatz V, 'Combatting Illegal Fishing in the Exclusive Economic Zone – Flag State Obligations in the Context of the Primary Responsibility of the Coastal State' (2015) 7(2) *Goettingen Journal of International Law* 1.

Schiffman HS, 'The Dispute Settlement Mechanism of UNCLOS: A Potentially Important Framework for Marine Wildlife Management' (1998) 1(2) *Journal of International Wildlife Law & Policy* 293.

Schiffman HS, 'The Evolution of Fisheries Conservation and Management: A Look at the New South Pacific Regional Fisheries Management Organization in Law and Policy' (2011) 28(2) *Thomas L Cooley Law Review* 181.

Schillemans T, 'Accountability in the Shadow of Hierarchy: The Horizontal Accountability of Agencies' (2008) 8 *Public Organization Review* 175.

Schillemans T and Busuioc M, Predicting Public Sector Accountability: from Agency Drift to Forum Drift (2015) 25(1) *Journal of Public Administration Research and Theory* 191.

Schillemans T, Moving Beyond the Clash of Interests: On Stewardship Theory and the Relationships Between Central Government Departments and Public Agencies (2013) 15(4) *Public Management Review* 541.

Schillemans T, 'Remedies for the Accountability Deficit of Agencies: Does Horizontal Accountability Work?' (2011) 43 *Administration and Society* 387.

Schiller L et al, 'High Seas Fisheries Play a Negligible Role in Addressing Global Food Security' (2018) 4(8) *Environmental Studies* e8351.

Schmidt C, 'Economic Drivers of Illegal, Unreported and Unregulated (iuu) Fishing' (2005) 20(3) *International Journal of Marine and Coastal Law* 479.

Scobbie I, 'The Invocation of Responsibility for the Breach of Obligations under Peremptory Norms of General International Law' (2002) 13(5) *European Journal of International Law* 1201.

Seidman G,"The Origins of Accountability: Everything I Know about the Sovereign's Immunity, I Learned from King Henry III" (2004) 49 *Louisiana University Law Journal* 393.

Serdy A, 'Accounting for Catch in Internationally Managed Fisheries: What Role for State Responsibility' (2010) 15 *Ocean & Coastal Law Journal* 23.

Serdy A, 'Pacta Tertiis and Regional Fisheries Management Mechanisms: The IUU fishing Concept as an Illegitimate Short-Cut to a Legitimate Goal' (2017) 48 *Ocean Development & International Law* 345.

Serdy A, 'The Shaky Foundations of the fao Port State Measures Agreement: How Watertight Is the Legal Seal against Access for Foreign Fishing Vessels?' (2016b) 31(3) *International Journal of Marine and Coastal Law* 422.

Shelton D, 'Hierarchy of Norms and Human Rights: Of Trumps and Winners' (2002) 65(2) *Saskatchewan Law Review* 301.

Shelton D, 'Righting Wrongs: Reparations in the Articles on State Responsibility' (2002) 96 *American Journal of International Law* 833.

Shigeta Y, 'Obligation to Protect the Environment in the icj's Practice: To What Extent Erga Omnes?' (2012) 55 *Japanese Yearbook of International Law* 1.

Simma B, 'From Bilateralism to Community Interest in International Law' (1994) *VI Recueil des Cours* 221.

Simma B, 'Universality of International Law from the Perspective of a Practitioner' (2009) 20 *European Journal of International Law* 265.

Sinclair A, 'The Chameleon of Accountability: Forms and Discourses' (1995) 20(2–3) *Accounting, Organizations and Society* 219.

Slaughter AM and Snidal D, 'The Concept of Legalization' (2000) 54 *International Organization* 401.

Sodik DM, 'Non-Legally Binding International Fisheries Instruments and Measures to Combat illegal, Unreported and Unregulated Fishing' (2008) 15(1) *Australian International Law Journal* 129.

Somek A, 'The Concept of 'Law' in Global Administrative Law: a Reply to Benedict Kingsbury' (2009) 20(4) *European Journal of International Law* 985.

Song YH, 'The Efforts of ICCAT to Combat IUU Fishing: The Roles of Japan and Taiwan in Conserving and Managing Tuna Resources' (2009) 24(1) *International Journal of Marine and Coastal Law* 101.

Sreejith SG, 'Public International Law and the wto: A Reckoning of Legal Positivism and Neoliberalism' (2007) 9 *San Diego international Law Journal* 5.

Steffek J, 'Public Accountability and the Public Sphere of International Governance' (2010) 24(1) *Ethics and International Affairs* 45.

Stephens T, 'The Limits of International Adjudication in International Environmental Law: Another Perspective on the Southern Bluefin Tuna Case' (2004) 19(2) *International Journal of Marine and Coastal Law* 177.

Strøm K, 'Delegation and Accountability in Parliamentary Democracies' (2000) 37(3) *European Journal of Political Research* 261.

Subedi SP, 'The Doctrine of Objective Regimes in International Law and the Competence of the United Nations to Impose Territorial or Peace Settlements on States' (1994) 37 *German Yearbook of International Law* 162.

Sumaila UR et al, 'Fuel Subsidies to Global Fisheries: Magnitude and Impacts on Resource Sustainability' (2006) 14(6) *Fisheries Centre Research Reports* 38.

Sumaila UR et al, 'Global Fisheries Subsidies: An Updated Estimate' (2016) (69) *Marine Policy* 189.

Sumaila UR et al, 'Subsidies to High Seas Bottom Trawl Fleets and the Sustainability of Deep-Sea Demersal Fish Stocks' (2010) 34(3) *Marine Policy* 495.

Sundström A, 'Corruption and Regulatory Compliance: Experimental Findings from South African Small Scale Fisheries' (2012) 36(6) *Marine Policy* 12.

Swan J, 'Port State Measures: From Residual Port State Jurisdiction to Global Standards' (2016) 31 *International Journal of Marine and Coastal Law* 395.

Swan J, 'Port State Measures to Combat iuu Fishing: International and Regional Developments' (2006) 7 *Sustainable Development Law and Policy* 38.

Tahindro A, 'Conservation and Management of Transboundary Fish Stocks: Comments in Light of the Adoption of the 1995 Agreement for the Conservation and Management of Straddling fish Stocks and Highly Migratory Fish Stocks' (1997) 28 *Ocean Development & International Law* 1.

Takei Y, 'Assessing Flag State Performance in Legal Terms: Clarifications of the Margin of Discretion' (2013) 28(1) *International Journal of Marine and Coastal Law* 97.

Tanaka Y, 'Protection of Community Interests in International Law: The Case of the Law of the Sea' (2011) 15 *Max Plack Yearbook of United Nations Law* 329.

Tanaka Y, 'The South China Sea Arbitration: Environmental Obligations Under the Law of the Sea Convention' (2018) *Review of European, Comparative & International Environmental Law* 1.

Tanaka Y, 'Reflections on the Implications of Environmental Norms for Fishing: The Link between the Regulation of Fishing and the Protection of Marine Biological Diversity' (2020) 22 *International Community Law Review* 389–409.

Telesetsky A, 'Fishing Moratoria and Securing TURFs: Creating Opportunities for Future Marine Resource Abundance in the Face of Scarcity in Western Africa' (2013) 42(1) *Georgia Journal of International and Comparative Law* 35.

Teubner G, 'Substantive and Reflexive Elements in Modern Law' (1983) 17(2) *Law & Society Review* 239.

Theilen JT, 'What's in a Name? The Illegality of Illegal, Unreported and Unregulated Fishing' (2013) 28(3) *International Journal of Marine and Coastal Law* 533.

Thirlway H, 'Reflections on Lex Ferenda' (2001) 32 *Netherlands Yearbook of International Law* 3.

Thompson DF, 'Moral Responsibility of Public Officials: The Problem of Many Hands' (1980) 74 *American Political Science Review* 905.

Tiewul SA, 'International Law and Nuclear Test Explosions on the High Seas' (1974) 8(1) *Cornell International Law Journal* 45.

Tomuschat C, 'Obligations Arising for States Without or Against their Will' (1993) *Recueil des Cours* 209.

Torfing J and Triantafillou P, 'What's in a Name? Grasping New Public Governance as a Political-Administrative System' (2013) 18(2) *International Review of Public Administration* 9.

Treves T, 'The FAO Code of Conduct for Responsible Fisheries: Between Soft and Hard Law' (2014) *Peaceful Order in the World's Oceans* 301.

Tsamenyi M et al, 'The European Council Regulation on Illegal, Unreported and Unregulated Fishing: An International Fisheries Law Perspective' (2010) 25(1) *International Journal of Marine and Coastal Law* 5.

Tsamenyi M, 'Satellite-Based Vessel Monitoring Systems for Fisheries Management: International Legal Aspects' (2000) 15(1) *International Journal of Marine and Coastal Law* 65.

Ventura V, 'Tackling Illegal, Unregulated and Unreported Fishing: The ITLOS Advisory Opinion on Flag State Responsibility for IUU Fishing and the Principle of Due Diligence' (2015) 12(1) *Brazilian Journal of International Law* 50.

Verschuuren J, 'Public Participation regarding the Elaboration and Approval of Projects in the EU after the Aarhus Convention' (2005) 4 *Yearbook of European Environmental Law* 29.

Villalpando S, 'The Legal Dimension of the International Community: How Community Interests are Protected in International Law' (2010) 21 *European Journal of International Law* 387.

Vincent N, 'Review: The Holy Bureaucrat: Eudes Rigaud and Religious Reform in Thirteenth-Century Normandy' (2007) 30 *Biography* 389.

Von Bogdandy A, 'Globalization and Europe: How to Square Democracy, Globalization, and International Law' (2004) 15(5) *European Journal of International Law* 885.

Von Bogdandy A, 'Constitutionalism in International Law: Comment on a Proposal from Germany' (2006) 47(1) *Harvard Internationl Law Journal* 223.

Von Dornum DD, 'The Straight and the Crooked: Legal Accountability in Ancient Greece' (1997) *Columbia Law Review* 1483.

Van der Vyver JD, 'State Sovereignty and the Environment in International Law" (1992) 109(3) *South African Law Journal* 472.

Waldron J, 'Why Law: Efficacy, Freedom or Fidelity?' (1994) 13 *Law and Philosophy* 259.

Warner-Kramer D, and K Canty, 'Stateless Fishing Vessels: the Current International Regime and New Approach' (2000) 5(2) *Ocean and Coastal Law Journal* 227.

Warner-Kramer D, 'Control Begins at Home: Tackling Flags of Convenience and iuu Fishing' (2004) 34 *Golden Gate University Law Review* 497.

Weber EP, 'The Question of Accountability in Historical Perspective: from Jackson to Contemporary Grassroots Ecosystem Management' (1999) 31(4) *Administration and Society* 451.

Weil P, 'Towards Relative Normativity in International Law?' (1983) 77 *American Journal of International Law* 413.

Wendt A, 'Anarchy is What States Make of It: The Social Construction of Power Politics' (1992) 46 *International Organization* 391.

Wendt A, 'Collective Identity Formation and the International State' (1994) 88(2) *American Political Science Review* 384.

Wendt A, 'The Agent-Structure Problem in International Relations Theory' (1987) 41 *International Organization* 335.

Wennerberg H, 'The Concept of Family Resemblance in Wittgenstein's Later Philosophy' (1967) 33(2) *Theoria* 108.

Williamson ED, 'Realism Versus Legalism in International Relations' (2002) 96 *American Journal of International Law Proceedings* 262.

Wiser GM, 'Transparency in 21st Century Fisheries Management: Options for Public Participation to Enhance Conservation and Management of International Fish Stocks' (2001) 4(2) *Journal of International Wildlife Law and Policy* 95.

Witbooi E, 'Illegal, Unreported and Unregulated Fishing on the High Seas: The Port State Measures Agreement in Context' (2014) 29 *International Journal of Marine and Coastal Law* 290.

Wolfrum R, 'Means of Ensuring Compliance with and Enforcement of International Environmental Law' (1999) 272 *Recueil des Cours* 9.

Wright R, 'The Grounds and Extent of Legal Responsibility', (2003) 41 *San Diego Law Review* 1.

Xue JG, 'China's Distant Water Fisheries and its Response to Flag State Responsibilities' (2006) *Marine Policy* 30(6) 651.

Yang K, 'Further Understanding Accountability in Public Organizations: Actionable Knowledge and the Structure-Agency Duality' (2012) 44(3) *Administration and Society* 272.

Young M, 'Then and Now: Reappraising Freedom of the Seas in Modern Law of the Sea' (2016) 47(2) *Ocean Development & International Law* 165.

Young MA, and Rioseco SS, 'Evolution through the Duty to Cooperate: Implications of the Whaling Case at the International Court of Justice' (2015) 16(2) *Melbourne Journal of International Law* 311.

Yusuf M, Muhadar AR, and Karim MS, 'Legal Effectiveness in Combating Illegal Fishing' (2018) 72 *Journal of Law, Policy and Globalization* 66.

Reports Made or Endorsed by International Organisations

ILC

Crawford J, 'The ILC's Articles on Responsibility of States for Internationally Wrongful Acts' in *Report of the International law Commission on the Work of Its Fifty-third Session No 10* (2001) UN A/56/10.

Crawford J, *'Third Report on State Responsibility'* (2000) UN Doc A/CN.4/507/Add.4.

ILC, *'Identification of Customary International Law'* (2016) UNGA A/CN.4/L.872.

ILC, *Third Report of the Special Rapporteur on State Responsibility* (2000), para 06(b) A/CN.4/507/Add.3.

Wood M, 'Third Report of the Special Rapporteur on the Identification of Customary International Law' (2015) UNGA A/CN.4/682.

FAO

Swan J, 'Regional Fishery Bodies and Governance: Issues, Actions and Future Directions' (2000) FAO Circular No 959 (2000).

Ceo M et al, 'Performance Reviews by Regional Fishery Bodies: introduction, Summaries, Synthesis and Best practices' (2002) FAO Circular No 1071.

Swan J, 'Decision-Making in Regional Fishery Bodies or Arrangements: The Evolving Role of RFBs and International Agreement on Decision-Making Processes' (2004) FAO Circular No 995.

Rayfuse R, 'Regional Allocation Issues Or Zen And The Art Of Pie Cutting' in 'FAO Sharing the Fish: Allocation Issues in Fisheries Management' (FAO, 2006).

FAO, '*The State of the World Fisheries and Aquaculture*' (FAO, 2008).

FAO, 'Report of the fao/unep Expert Meeting on Impacts of Destructive fishing Practices, Unsustainable Fishing, and Illegal, Unreported and Unregulated (IUU) Fishing on Marine Biodiversity and Habitats' (2009) FIRF/R932.

Doulman J and Swan J, '*A Guide to the Background and Implementation of the 2009 fao Agreement on Port State Measures to Prevent, Deter and Eliminate Illegal, Unreported and Unregulated Fishing*' (2012) FAO Circular No 1074.

FAO, '*The State of the World Fisheries and Aquaculture*' (FAO, 2016).

FAO, 'Expert Workshop to Estimate the Magnitude of illegal, Unreported and Unregulated Fishing Globally' (2015) FIRO/R1106.

Poseidon Aquatic Resource Management, 'Review of Studies Estimating IUU Fishing and the Methodologies Utilized' (2016).

FAO, 'Global Record of Fishing Vessels, Refrigerated Transport Vessels and Supply Vessels' (2017) C-2017/23.

Hosch G and Blaha F, 'Seafood Traceability for Fisheries Compliance: Country-Level Support for Catch Documentation Schemes' (2017) FAO Technical Paper 619.

OECD

Restrepo V, 'Estimation of unreported catches by ICCAT' in *Fish Piracy: Combating Illegal, Unreported and Unregulated Fishing* (OECD, 2004).

OECD, 'Fishing for Development: The Role of Regional Fisheries Management Organisations' (2014) TAD/FI.

Miscellanea

UNCTAD, 'Action on the Question of Open Registries' (1981) TD/B/C.4/220.

Milazzo M, 'Subsidies in World Fisheries: a Re-Examination' (1998) World Bank Technical Paper No 406.

Tsamenyi M et al, *Fairer Fishing? Trade and Fisheries Policy Implications for Developing Countries of the European Community Regulation on Illegal Fishing* (Commonwealth Secretariat, 2009).

UNODC, *Transnational Organised Crime in the Fishing Industry* (2011).

World Bank Group, '*The Sunken Billions Revisited: Progress and Challenges in Global Marine Fisheries*' (2017).

Online Academic Materials

Agnew DJ et al, 'Estimating the Worldwide Extent of Illegal Fishing' (2009) 4(2) *PloS One* e4570.

Bovens M, 'Analysing and Assessing Public Accountability: A Conceptual Framework' (2006) European Governance Paper No. C-06-01, 20 [https://dspace.library.uu.nl/bitstream/handle/1874/35005/Analyzing%20and%20assessing%20accountability.pdf;sequence=3].

Schillemans T, 'The Public Accountability Review: A Meta-Analysis of Public Accountability Research in Six Academic Disciplines' (2013) Working Paper,

Utrecht University School of Governance [https://dspace.library.uu.nl/handle/1874/275784].

Kagiaros, and Tzevelekos VP, 'The Importance of State Practice in the Shaping of International Standards Pertaining to the Clash between Free Speech and the Banning of Negationism' (2020) *Open Research Exeter* [https://ore.exeter.ac.uk/repository/handle/10871/39737].

Koehler HR, '*Promoting Compliance in Tuna RFMOs: A Comprehensive Baseline Survey of the Current Mechanics of Reviewing, Assessing and Addressing Compliance with rfmo Obligations and Measures*' (ISSF, 2013) [https://pdfs.semanticscholar.org/2e87/20cd0d9fecbb0765146a0763451e662d112a.pdf].

Lutchman I, Newman S, and Monsanto M, 'An Independent Review of the EU Illegal, Unreported and Unregulated Regulation' (IEEP, Undated) [http://minisites.ieep.eu/assets/858/IEEP_Independent_Review_of_the_EU_IUU_Regulations.pdf].

Pagano M, 'The Mellifera Case and Access to Environmental Justice under the Aarhus Regulation: New Findings, Old Story' (2018) *EU Law Analysis Blog* [http://eulawanalysis.blogspot.com/2018/10/the-mellifera-case-and-access-to.html].

Pramod G et al, '*Sources of Information Supporting Estimates of Unreported Fishery Catches (IUU) for 59 Countries and the High Seas*' (University of British Columbia, 2008) [https://open.library.ubc.ca/cIRcle/collections/facultyresearchandpublications/52383/items/1.0058180].

Sand PH, '*The Right to Know: Environmental Information Disclosure by Government and Industry*' (2005) [http://citeseerx.ist.psu.edu/viewdoc/download?doi=10.1.1.507.2590&rep=rep1&type=pdf].

NGO Reports

Environmental Justice Foundation (EJF), 'Keeping Illegal Fish Out of Europe: Ensuring Success for the IUU Regulation' (2013) 10 [https://ejfoundation.org/reports/keeping-illegal-fish-out-of-europe-ensuring-success-for-the-iuu-regulation].

EJF, 'The EU IUU Regulation: Building on Success EU Progress in the Global Fight Against Illegal Fishing' (EJF, 2016) [https://ejfoundation.org/reports/the-eu-iuu-regulation-building-on-success-eu-progress-in-the-global-fight-against-illegal-fishing].

EJF, Oceana, Pew and WWF, 'Ensuring better control of the EU's external fishing fleet: One number, one boat – The need for mandatory IMO numbers for EU vessels fishing outside of European Union waters' (EJF, 2016) [http://www.whofishesfar.org/files/Case_Studies/Case_Study_FAR_ENG.pdf].

ISSF, Position Statement for WCPFC12 (2015) [https://www.wcpfc.int/system/files/WCPFC12-2015-OP01%20ISSF%20Position%20Statement%20WCPFC12.pdf].

ISSF, 'Tuna RFMO Authorised Vessel Lists: A Comparative Analysis to Identify Best Practices' (2018) [https://iss-foundation.org/download-monitor-demo/download-info/issf-2019-05-tuna-rfmo-authorised-vessel-lists-a-comparative-analysis-to-identify-best-practices/].

EJF, Oceana, The Nature Conservancy, Pew, and WWF, 'Achieving Transparency and Combating IUU Fishing in RFMOs: Reinforcing the EU's Multilateral Actions to Promote Best Practices' (2019) [http://www.iuuwatch.eu/wp-content/uploads/2020/07/RFMO-2019-Paper-2020-Annexes-EN.pdf].

International Organisation Website Resources

FAO, Fish Code Review No 21 (2009) [http://www.fao.org/tempref/docrep/fao/010/a1449e/a1449e00.pdf].

FAO, List of Countries with National Plans of Action [http://www.fao.org/fishery/ipoa-iuu/npoa/en].

FAO, Parties to the Port State Measures Agreement [http://www.fao.org/fishery/psm/agreement/parties/en].

FAO, Regional Fishery Bodies [www.fao.org/fishery/RFMO/en].

FAO, The Marking and Identification of Fishing Vessels [http://www.fao.org/3/a-i7783e.pdf].

IHS, IMO Identification Numbers for Ships, Companies and Registered Owners [http://www.imonumbers.lrfairplay.com/help.aspx].

Interpol, Purple Notices Public Versions (2015) [http://www.interpol.int/INTERPOL-expertise/Notices/Purple-notices-%E2%80%93-public-versions/2015 on 28 July 2016].

OECD, Evading the Net: Tax Crime in the Fisheries Sector (2013) [http://www.oecd.org/tax/crime/evading-the-net-tax-crime-fisheries-sector.pdf].

OECD and FAO, International Regulatory Co-operation and International Organisations: The Case of the Food and Agriculture Organization of the United Nations (2016) [https://www.oecd.org/gov/regulatory-policy/FAO_Full-Report.pdf].

Tuna RFMOs Consolidated IUU List [http://www.tuna-org.org/vesselpos.htm [accessed on 17 February 2017].

UNODC, Fisheries Crime Factsheet (2017) [http://www.unodc.org/documents/about-unodc/Campaigns/Fisheries/focus_sheet_PRINT.pdf].

National State Agency Website Resources

MAGRAMA, IUU fishing activities in the Southern Ocean, Expediente Sancionador 1/2015/SGP, [http://www.magrama.gob.es/es/prensa/160317resolucionexpediente operacionsparrow_tcm7-415228_noticia.pdf].

National Oceanic and Atmospheric Administration of the United States of America (NOAA), 'Improving International Fisheries Management Report to Congress Pursuant to Section 403(a) of the Magnuson-Stevens Fishery Conservation and Management Reauthorization Act of 2006' (2015) 23–30 [http://www.cofemersimir.gob.mx/expediente/17096/mir/34790/anexo/951234].

Index